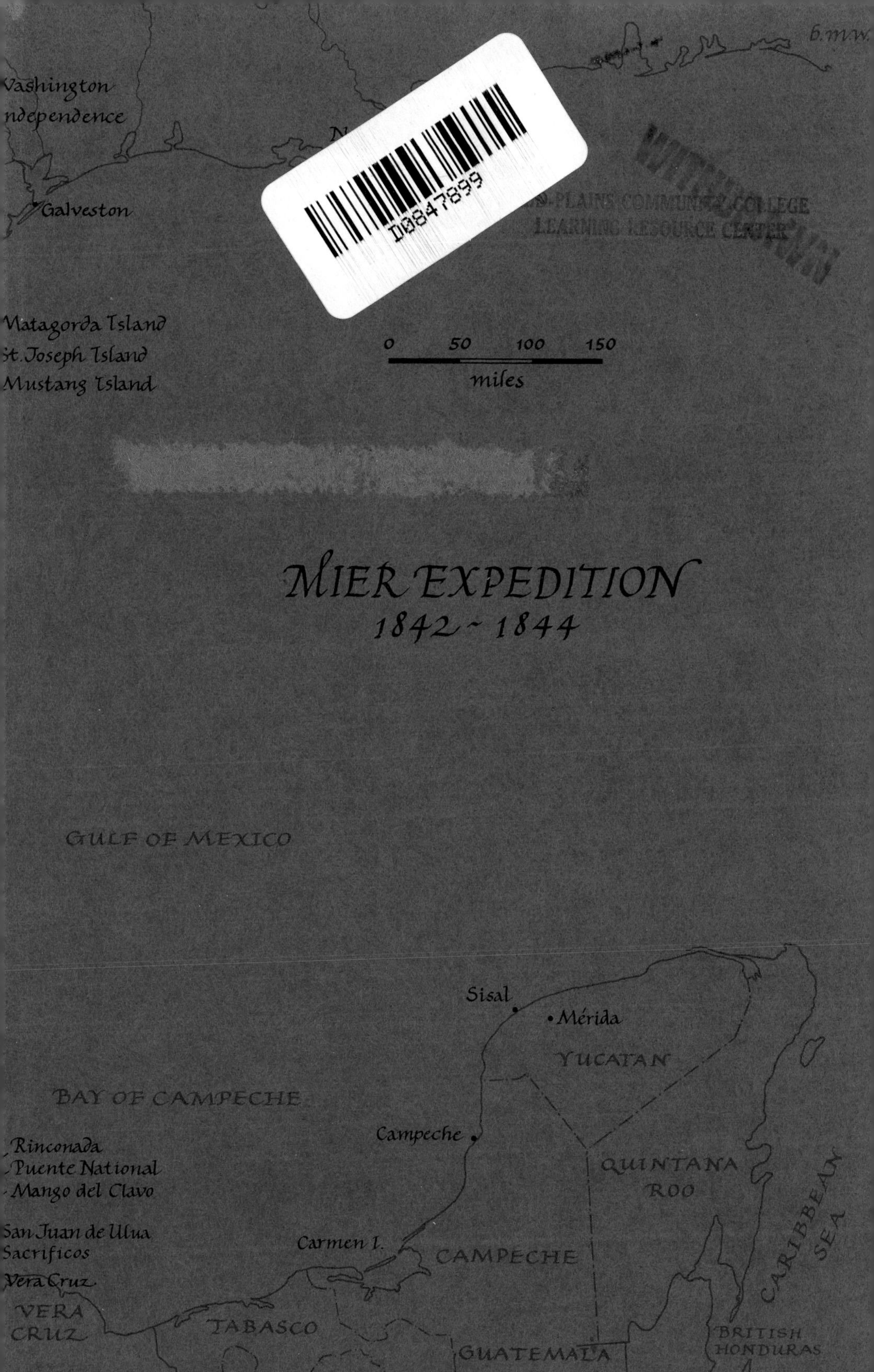

b.m.w.
Vashington
ndependence
Galveston
Matagorda Island
t.Joseph Island
Mustang Island
0 50 100 150
miles
MIER EXPEDITION
1842 – 1844
GULF OF MEXICO
Sisal
Mérida
YUCATAN
BAY OF CAMPECHE
Campeche
Rinconada
Puente National
Mango del Clavo
QUINTANA
ROO
CARIBBEAN
SEA
San Juan de Ulua
Sacrificos
Carmen I.
CAMPECHE
Vera Cruz
VERA
CRUZ
TABASCO
GUATEMALA
BRITISH
HONDURAS

Mier Expedition Diary

A Texan Prisoner's Account

NUMBER EIGHT

The Elma Dill Russell Spencer Foundation Series

Mier Expedition Diary

A Texan Prisoner's Account

by Joseph D. McCutchan

Edited by Joseph Milton Nance

Foreword by Jane A. Kenamore

University of Texas Press, Austin & London

Publication made possible through the cooperation of the Rosenberg Library, Galveston, Texas

Library of Congress Cataloging in Publication Data

McCutchan, Joseph D 1823–1853.
Mier Expedition diary.

(The Elma Dill Russell Spencer Foundation series; no. 8)
Bibliography: p.
Includes index.
1. Mier Expedition, 1842. 2. McCutchan, Joseph D., 1823–1853. 3. Soldiers—Texas—Biography. I. Nance, Joseph Milton. II. Title. III. Series.
F390.M123 976.4'04 78-17611
ISBN 0-292-74006-9

Printed in the United States of America

To

JEREMIAH MILTON NANCE II

and

MARY LOUISE (HUTCHISON) NANCE

Whose Love and Devotion Instilled in Their Children a Desire for Knowledge and the Truth

Contents

Foreword

Joseph D. McCutchan's journal of the Mier Expedition became part of the Rosenberg Library manuscript collection as a result of the donation of the holdings of the Texas Historical Society of Galveston to the library in 1931. Before that time the manuscript rested in numerous unlikely places; indeed, from an archivist's point of view it encountered nearly as much trauma and uncertainty as did the men who took part in the expedition.

The odyssey began when attorney Christopher Columbus Garrett of Brenham, Texas, donated the manuscript to the Galveston Historical Society in 1875. A dozen men had formed this organization four years earlier in order to help preserve the unique history of Texas, which in their words "was filled with shining examples of human activity and notable records of virtue and of crime." For almost ten years the society actively collected manuscripts, printed material, and other items related to Texas history. This material, which would later form the nucleus of the Rosenberg Library archives, included the papers of James Morgan, commandant of Galveston island from 1836 to 1837; early newspapers of the area; Freedmen's Bureau circulars; and the McCutchan diary; as well as other material that did not survive.

The society, which became inactive during the 1880s, elected one of its own members to be custodian of the historical collection. Unfortunately, he suffered a mental breakdown shortly thereafter and entered a hospital outside the city. Unknown to the rest of the members their custodian's legal trustee placed the collection in storage. Members Philip C. Tucker and Andrew Benner discovered that the historical documents were being sold for storage charges in 1885. Skirting formalities, they elected themselves president and secretary-treasurer of the inactive organization and proceeded to buy back the items they deemed valuable—including the McCutchan manuscript. Wary of granting responsibility for the collection to any single individual, Tucker and Benner arranged to store the documents in the library of Galveston's Ball High School.

In 1894 Tucker led the reorganization of the society, which voted to change its name to the Texas Historical Society of Galveston. It renewed an active collecting policy and within three years was forced to move the holdings to larger quarters in the Galveston Public Library, which was located on the top floor of the Masonic Building. The disastrous hurricane of 1900 blew the roof off the building, and many of the documents, including the McCutchan Diary, suffered water damage.

As a result of the disaster, the members transferred their holdings to the safer quarters of the new Rosenberg Library, which opened in 1904. Though the membership became inactive once again, the historical collection continued to grow. The society eventually named the library custodian for the collection, and in 1931 it donated its entire holdings to the institution.

The McCutchan manuscript has long interested scholars and others attracted by the intrigue of the Mier Expedition. To read it, however, required a special trip to Galveston and the perseverance to decipher the faded handwriting on water-stained paper. The Rosenberg Library is pleased that the journal is at last available to the public in printed form.

Jane A. Kenamore, Archivist
Rosenberg Library
Galveston, Texas

Preface

> *I am obliged to keep calm and shy with this journal, for if it should be found, and its contents ascertained by any of this yellow race, they would* journalize *and* poste me up *in eternity, giving five ounce balls, as a credit to my account and that would not set well, to a hungry man.*[1]

For more than a hundred years Joseph D. McCutchan's diary of the Mier Expedition has rested in a public library and was known only to a few individuals. The author has recorded in considerable detail and in an interesting manner his experiences and sometimes those of others as members of that ill-fated expedition into Mexico, resulting in their captivity for twenty months and twenty-one days. Ever mindful of the great risk he ran if his diary should be discovered, McCutchan, who at age nineteen embarked upon a campaign that was to be filled with excitement and pathos, commenced his diary "about the Latter part of April 1844" after he was transferred to Perote Castle. In his diary he attempted to summarize his experiences up to that time by relying not only upon his own memory, but also upon the notes and memory of other members of the expedition. Regular day-by-day entries in the diary were not begun until June 1, 1844, and these were continued until his arrival at Galveston, Texas, on Sunday, November 10, 1844. The diary was concluded at Galveston (or possibly elsewhere) shortly after his arrival in Texas at a time when the annexation issue was at its height following the United States presidential election of November 1844. McCutchan's account and that of Thomas W. Bell, *A Narrative of the Capture and Subsequent Sufferings of the Mier Prisoners in Mexico*, constitute the most complete story of the Mier Expedition by participants therein from the march of Somervell from the Medina River on November 25, 1842, to the release and return of the main body of prisoners to Texas on November 10, 1844. Owing to illness, McCutchan was not with the main body of Texan prisoners in the march from Matamoros to Tacubaya and was, therefore, not present at the "escape" and the "decimation." For what occurred during this interval with the main body of prisoners he had to rely upon the memory of others. Nevertheless, the diary makes a valuable contribu-

1. McCutchan's diary, June 8, 1844.

tion to the literature of the Mier Expedition, even if tainted at times by its author's hatred of Sam Houston.

The McCutchan diary was donated to the Texas Historical Society of Galveston early in 1875 by Christopher Columbus Garrett of Brenham, Texas, lawyer and later distinguished chief justice of the Court of Civil Appeals of the First Supreme Judicial District of the State of Texas.[2] The collections of the Texas Historical Society later became a part of the holdings of the Rosenberg Library of Galveston.

The diary consists of two manuscript books (described by the library as two "volumes" with a total of 388 pages by library numbering in pencil)—one large (size 8″ x 13″) and the other small (size 6¼″ x 7⅞″). The author broke the small book internally into three parts: Book No. 1, Book Second, and Book Three. The small book, because its size afforded greater security from being discovered by his captors, seems to be the original diary; but, apparently some time after his release from imprisonment, McCutchan began to rewrite his narrative in greater detail in the larger book, which shows no evidence of having been folded and, therefore, would not have been easy to hide while in prison. Evidence of the effort to rewrite the story, at least in part, is shown by the fact that the first twenty-two pages of the small diary are missing, and the top half of page 23 has a large *X* drawn across it.

The title page of Book No. 1 (in the small book) is "Narrative of / The Mier Expedition / By / Jos. D. McCutchan." McCutchan's numbering of the pages begins with page number 23 and runs to 96 for Book No. 1; the Rosenberg Library's numbering is pages 1 to 74. For Book Second, McCutchan's page numbering runs from 1 to 188, whereas the library's numbering is pages 75 to 264. For Book Three, McCutchan's paging is 1 to 121, whereas the library's begins with page 265 and carries through 388, with page 388 being the back and blank. When recopying his original manuscript into the larger booklet and elaborating upon his story, the author broke his manuscript into "Introduction," "Preface," and chapters. The larger manuscript book begins: "No. 1 / Introductory Chapter / I have not now at my command . . ."[3] In this book McCutchan's page numbering is 1 to 73; but on the first thirty pages the upper-right-hand corners have crumbled away owing to deterioration of the right margin of this badly water-

2. E. G. Littlejohn, comp., "Texas Scrap Book," II:160; *Galveston News*, Feb. 7, 1875.

3. See Chapter III, footnote 25.

stained manuscript. The library's paging of this same material is 1 to 77. There are thirteen blank pages at the end of the book.

The clarity of the handwriting and the condition of the larger manuscript, except for the right-hand margin, along with the fact that the document had not been folded, seem to indicate that the author began to revise his diary after his arrival at Galveston or at some later date. An overlap and slight change in wording of some pages seem to bear out this conclusion. I have followed the later version but, in order that nothing the author has written may be omitted, I have reproduced in the appendices those sections having any significant deviation in wording.

In editing the diary I have preserved the sentence structure, capitalization, and spelling of the author but have used some discretion in interpreting the punctuation in order to improve the readability of the document. I have not attempted to correct all of McCutchan's errors of fact or to elaborate upon his statements or to write a history of the Mier Expedition.

For their assistance and encouragement in preparing the diary for publication, I wish to express thanks to Miss Harriet Smither, former state archivist; to Miss Winnie Allen, retired archivist, the University of Texas Library; to Dr. Llerena Friend, former librarian, Eugene C. Barker Texas History Center, the University of Texas Library; to Miss Amelia Williams, distinguished co-editor of the *Writings of Sam Houston*; to Charles O'Halloran, former librarian of the Rosenberg Library, Galveston, for extending to me the privilege to edit and publish the Joseph D. McCutchan Diary; to Robert Dalehite, former custodian of the Manuscript Collection of the Rosenberg Library for his valuable assistance in the throes of the final editing; to Miss Pamela A. Puryear for her valuable assistance on Washington County history; to John D. Hyatt, librarian of the Rosenberg Library, for his cooperation, assistance in numerous ways, and kindly encouragement; and to the Mini-Grant Fund of Texas A&M University for assistance in the final draft of the edited manuscript. Finally, I wish to recognize my wife, Eleanor Hanover Nance, who took valuable time from research on her "roots" to draft the map for this book.

Joseph Milton Nance
College Station, Texas
December 26, 1977,
the One Hundred and
Thirty-Fifth Anniversary
of the Battle of Mier

Biographical Sketch of Joseph D. McCutchan

Joseph D. McCutchan,[1] adventurer, soldier, amateur poet, merchant, lawyer, and judge, was born July 18, 1823, in Wilson County, Tennessee,[2] later moving to Carroll County, Mississippi, where in 1839 he joined the Presbyterian church and, thereafter, was known to be a faithful member of that religious organization and a devoted Christian.

From Mississippi, in company with his brother William H. McCutchan, some eight years his senior, he emigrated to Texas by way of New Orleans, passing out of the mouth of the Mississippi River at night late in December 1840,[3] and arriving at Galveston early in January 1841. The two brothers soon settled in Washington County.

When the Mexican raids upon San Antonio began in 1842, Joseph D. McCutchan affiliated with the local militia organization. On October 17, 1842, at the age of nineteen, he was enrolled as a second lieutenant in Captain William P. Rutledge's company and went with that company to San Antonio. Upon the organization of the troops in the vicinity of San Antonio on November 7, 1842, into the First Regiment of the South Western Army, Captain Jerome B. Robertson was elected to command the company; however, McCutchan continued to serve as second lieutenant of the company and was mustered into the South Western Army of Operations under the command of Brigadier General Alexander Somervell on November 21, 1842, by Robert H. Dunham, brigade inspector.[4]

All of the effective units of militiamen of the counties of Matagorda, Fayette, Victoria, Brazoria, Fort Bend, Austin, Colorado, Gonzales, Bastrop, Montgomery, and Washington had been ordered to San An-

1. The name McCutchan has been spelled variously—McCutcheon, McCutchings, and McCutchan—but all evidence seems to indicate that the man himself wrote it as McCutchan. In reporting the donation of the diary to the Texas Historical Society of Galveston, the *Galveston News*, Feb. 7, 1875, p. 2, gave the name as James D. McCutchings.

2. M. Yell to editor of the *Texas Ranger and Lone Star*, June 9, 1853, p. 2; McCutchan's diary, July 18, 1844.

3. McCutchan's diary, Nov. 4, 1844.

4. Copy of Muster Roll of Jerome B. Robertson's company, First Regiment of South Western Army, in Sam S. Smith Collection, Archives, University of Texas; Joseph Milton Nance, *Attack and Counterattack*, pp. 445, 478, 643–644.

tonio to repel the Mexican invader. Before the arrival of these forces, however, Texas volunteers rallying under the leadership of Colonel Mathew Caldwell had repulsed the Mexican invading force under General Adrián Woll and forced its retirement from Texas.

President Sam Houston on October 3 named Brigadier General Alexander Somervell, who commanded the militia forces west of the Trinity River, to take command of the troops concentrating in the San Antonio area. If upon reaching the southwestern frontier Somervell should conclude that he could advance with success into the enemy's territory, he was to do so immediately. But, also, it was emphasized that the troops must be well disciplined, subordinate and obedient to his orders, and willing to cross the Rio Grande if ordered to do so. The full story of the Somervell Expedition to the Rio Grande in November and December, 1842, resulting in the Texan capture of Laredo and Guerrero, has been told.[5]

Following the capture of Guerrero, as the Texan army lay on the east side of the Rio Grande opposite the town, those of the Somervell Expedition who did not wish to return home without having both chastized the enemy and obtained suitable mounts and provisions for the return journey urged Somervell to prosecute the campaign further. When he refused to do so, they sought permission to separate from the command with the idea of continuing the march down the river. Again, Somervell refused to accede to their request; whereupon, 305 dissatisfied officers and men withdrew from the command on December 19, 1842, to carry on a private war of their own.[6] McCutchan had earlier withdrawn from Robertson's company on December 11 to join that of Captain William S. Fisher as a private. When Fisher was elected on the nineteenth to command what came to be known as the Mier Expedition, Claudius Buster was chosen to command the company. Fisher was accorded the rank of "colonel."

McCutchan was among those who surrendered at Mier on the afternoon of December 26, 1842, to the forces under General Pedro de Ampudia. In his report of the battle of Mier, General Ampudia listed McCutchan's occupation as printer.[7]

From Mier the Texan prisoners were taken to Matamoros and

5. Nance, *Attack and Counterattack*, pp. 427–578.
6. Memucan Hunt to Francis Moore, Jr., editor of the *Telegraph*, [dated] Bexar, Jan. 8, 1843, in *Morning Star*, Jan. 17, 1843; McCutchan's diary, p. 32; Thomas Jefferson Green, *Journal of the Texian Expedition against Mier*, p. 66. Green says 304 men separated from Somervell's command.
7. Pedro de Ampudia to Ministro de Guerra, José María Tornel, [dated] Mier, Dec. 29, 1842, in *El Cosmopolita*, Jan. 25, 1843, pp. 2–3.

from there were ordered to Mexico City. As the prisoners prepared to leave Matamoros on January 14, 1843, the complaint was made that several of the men were too ill to travel. The Mexican surgeon general of the post was sent to examine them, and he reported that six of the prisoners, including McCutchan, were unable to travel. These men and three boys of the expedition were retained at Matamoros, and at the end of nine weeks were joined by several of their comrades who had been left wounded at Mier. About March 1 ten of the Texan prisoners at Matamoros were sent on the route via Monterey toward Mexico City, and on March 11 McCutchan and four others were dispatched along the route via Tampico and Real del Monte to Mexico City. McCutchan and his companions arrived at Mexico City on May 27 and three days later joined the main body of prisoners at Tacubaya, where their comrades were working to improve the road that ran from the town of Tacubaya to the Archbishop's Palace, the residence of President Antonio López de Santa Anna, which was situated at a distance of several hundred yards from the city.

On September 5, 1843, Santa Anna's secretary announced that the road had been completed, and the prisoners were returned to the Convent Santiago, where they had earlier been imprisoned, preparatory to being transferred to the Castle of San Carlos de Perote, on the road between Mexico City and Vera Cruz.

The prisoners reached Perote Castle on September 21. Four days later an epidemic of typhus (thought at first to have been jail fever) struck the prisoners, and eventually all but three of the Mier men suffered from its attack. More than a few died and were buried in the moat that surrounded the castle. McCutchan was one of the first to fall victim to the epidemic, which caused him to be hospitalized for thirty days, and "for fourteen of that time [he was] entirely insensible to all earthly things, even to suffering itself."

After undergoing many unbelievable hardships, experiencing cruel treatment, and suffering woefully inadequate food and clothing, the last of the Mier prisoners were released on September 16, 1844, after an imprisonment of twenty months and twenty-one days. Most of them headed home to Texas as quickly as transportation could be obtained. They reached New Orleans on November 4 and from there went to Galveston aboard the *New York*.

As McCutchan landed at Galveston on November 10, he was, like most of his companions, destitute and downhearted because there was no royal welcome or spread of a red carpet for the returning "heroes" from the dungeons of Mexico. Then all of a sudden he saw approaching his brother William H., who had heard of the arrival of the prisoners and had hastened to the wharf. It was a heart-warming greeting, and Joseph recalled the experience in his diary: "Then I was *at Home* in the complete sense of the word."[8] Finally, on October 31, 1850, he received compensation from the state of Texas in the amount of $685.43 for his services as a lieutenant (October 17 to December 11, 1842) and as a private (December 12, 1842 to October 16, 1844) and for losses (one horse) on the Mier Expedition. His pay as a lieutenant was at the rate of $67.33 per month and as a private at $22.00 per month.[9]

Soon after his return to Texas, McCutchan became involved with his brother and others in a variety of trade activities. By the fall of 1845 he had returned to Washington, and by December 1845 the McCutchan brothers and J. Montgomery had established a partnership to engage in business as "*cotton factors*, *commission merchants*, and *General Dealers* in dry goods and groceries," and to "offer for sale in Houston, Harris County, and Brenham, Washington County, a full assortment of dry goods," ready-made clothing, and other articles of trade, including "first quality Kentucky bagging and rope."[10] Joseph D. was to manage the Brenham store, while his brother managed the one in Houston. Among other activities, Joseph D. McCutchan in 1848 was the agent for the *Galveston Weekly News* in Washington County. In the 1850s William H. McCutchan owned a steam sawmill at Longpoint, but whether his brother was involved in this particular operation is not known.

On October 25, 1845, Joseph McCutchan acquired from Jesse Farral and James Hunt, of Washington County, for $100 two and one-eighth acres of land on New Year's Creek in the Arabella Harrington League about two and one-eighth miles from Brenham.[11] In 1851 Joseph McCutchan and McNight were engaged in the Santa Fe trade, with an agency at Santa Fe, New Mexico,[12] but apparently McCutchan remained in Texas.

In August 1847 both of the McCutchan brothers married. On August 9 marriage licenses were issued to J[oseph] D. McCutchan and Miss E[lizabeth] Hutchinson, daughter of Captain Burrel B. Hutchinson, and to William H. McCutchan and Miss Elizabeth Farquhar,

8. McCutchan's diary, Nov. 10, 1844.
9. Joseph D. McCutcheon, Public Debt Papers (Texas), Texas State Archives.
10. *Telegraph and Texas Register*, Dec. 10, 1845–Feb. 4, 1846.
11. Deed Records, Washington County, Brenham, Texas, vol. G, pp. 35–37. Transaction was dated Oct. 25, 1845, and deed filed Oct. 27, 1845.
12. *San Antonio Texan*, quoted in *Northern Standard*, June 14, 1851.

daughter of James L. Farquhar. Joseph D. was married August 18 and his brother, the next day. The Rev. John Lember was the minister who performed the ceremony of marriage for Joseph, and the Rev. B. B. Baxter did the same for William.[13]

On November 18, 1847, Joseph D. McCutchan was received into the Presbyterian church in Washington, when the church was officially enrolled in the Brazos Presbytery. His wife, Elizabeth, was received into the same church by letter from the Methodist Episcopal Church South of Washington on May 23, 1848.[14]

By 1849 McCutchan had moved to Springfield, Limestone County, where he was an attorney-at-law.[15] A public meeting was held on June 2, 1849, at Springfield to promote the selection of a site east of the Brazos River for the state capital. The Constitution of 1845 had called for a special election to be held in 1850 to locate the state capital for twenty years. Joseph D. McCutchan was called to the chair and James M. Davis was appointed secretary of the meeting. The meeting at Springfield had been prompted by a call of the citizens of Palestine for a meeting of representatives from the eastern counties of the state at Palestine on July 4, 1849. The June 2 meeting requested the citizens of Limestone County to meet in a county convention at Springfield on June 14 to choose delegates to the Palestine convention.[16] Upon meeting, the convention recommended Springfield as the site for the state capital because of its climate, water, and other considerations, including the fact that it was near the geographic center of the inhabited area of the state. Three weeks later, the convention at Palestine recommended Springfield as the site for the seat of government.

In January 1850 while living in Limestone County, McCutchan sold his small tract of land on New Year's Creek, on which he had built a home and made other improvements, for $1,050 to Patrick H. Lusk, who had been a member of the Mier expedition and was then living in Washington County.[17] The year 1850 marks the first United States census taken in Texas. It shows that McCutchan's wife, Elizabeth, had

13. W. Broadus Smith, *Marriage Records, Washington County, Texas*, pp. 24–25.

14. Washington Presbyterian Church Minutes, 1846–1888, pp. 2 and 6, Archives, University of Texas.

15. Ray A. Walter, *A History of Limestone County*, p. 30; V. K. Carpenter, (transcriber), *The State of Texas Federal Population Schedules, Seventh Census of the United States, 1850*, item no. 222.

16. *Northern Standard*, July 14, 1849.

17. Deed Records, Washington County, vol. IJ, p. 192; transaction dated Jan. 14, 1850, and deed filed Feb. 22, 1850.

been born in Alabama and was in 1850 nineteen years of age, that Joseph D. was twenty-seven years old, and that they were the parents of one child, a son (Joseph D.), age one month.[18] The census also lists McCutchan's occupation as attorney-at-law.

In the elections in Limestone County for county and district officers on August 5, 1850, McCutchan was a successful candidate for the office of chief justice of the county.[19] A year later, he was chosen to represent the Twenty-seventh Representative District of Limestone and Navarro to the House of Representatives of the Fourth Legislature of the State of Texas over General Edward H. Tarrant by a majority of twelve votes.[20] When the legislature met on November 3, 1851, and organized, however, Tarrant contested the election, and the House of Representatives ordered its Committee on Privileges and Elections to investigate the matter. The committee made its report on November 6.[21] It found that Tarrant had actually received 476 votes to 423 for McCutchan, making, it said, a majority of forty-seven votes in favor of Tarrant;[22] and the committee, therefore, declared that General Tarrant had been elected, although the chief justice of Limestone County (McCutchan) had given the certificate of election to McCutchan. It found that the vote of Tarrant County, which was attached to the District of Limestone and Navarro, had not been submitted to the judge by the required date for submission and therefore had not been counted in the returns from the district. The committee's report read:

> *Your committee cannot believe that it was the intention of the law, to deprive the free people of this county of their right of suffrage, or to exclude the Representative of their choice, from the rights and privileges conferred upon him by their votes, by a mere technicality, and such would be the case if Mr. Tarrant were not permitted to take his seat in this body. Had the vote of Tarrant County been received by the Chief Justice of Limestone before the certificate was given to Mr. McCutchan, no one can*

18. Carpenter (transcriber), *State of Texas Federal Population Schedules, 1850*, item no. 222.
19. Hampton Steele, *A History of Limestone County, 1833–1860*, p. 25.
20. *Texas State Gazette*, Sept. 13, 1851.
21. Texas Legislature, *Journals of the House of Representatives of the State of Texas, Fourth Legislature*, pp. 19–20, 23; *Northern Standard*, Nov. 29, 1851.
22. The figures do not jibe. It is possible that the typesetter misread 470 to be 476 for Tarrant.

> *imagine for a moment that the certificate would have been given, but on the contrary, the certificate of election would have been given to Mr. Tarrant. Should, then, the will of the people clearly expressed, as it has been on this occasion, be defeated by an irregularity of the mails, or by any other course over which they had no control! Your committee think not.*[23]

Thus General Tarrant was declared elected, although a portion of the votes had not been returned by the deadline set for reporting.

During the early 1850s there was a strong influx of new settlers into Limestone County, and Springfield itself felt a significant growth in population. On August 2, 1852, when the next election for county and district officers took place, McCutchan was a candidate for re-election to the office of chief justice and was successful in winning a second term.[24]

In March 1853 McCutchan was again a candidate for public office. This time he sought the office of district attorney for the new Thirteenth Judicial District created by the last legislature, consisting of the counties of Limestone, Robertson, Leon, Falls, and Navarro. The election took place on Monday, March 14.[25] Opposing McCutchan of Springfield were Robert Simonton Gould of Centerville, Glover W. Barton of Wheelock, and Roger Q. Mills of Corsicana. Initial published returns on April 2 from Leon County (incomplete) showed Gould, 133 votes; McCutchan, 22 votes; Barton, 18 votes; and Mills, 10 votes.[26] A week later the *Texas State Gazette* reported, that, although all returns were not yet in, there was little doubt but that Gould had been elected.[27] Finally, on May 21, the *Texas State Gazette* reported the official vote, as given in the *Leon Pioneer*, to show the election of Robert S. Gould with McCutchan coming in a poor fourth in a field of four candidates.[28]

Less than six weeks after the election for district attorney Joseph D.

23. Texas Legislature, *Journals, House of Representatives*, Fourth Legislature, pp. 19–20.
24. Steele, *A History of Limestone County*, pp. 25, 76.
25. *Texas State Gazette*, Mar. 19, 1853.
26. Ibid., Apr. 2, 1853.
27. Ibid., Apr. 9, 1853, citing *Leon Pioneer*.
28. The final vote stood as follows: Robert S. Gould, 290; Roger Q. Mills, 287; Glover W. Barton, 277; and Joseph McCutchan, 198. The vote at Whitaker's box, Falls County, was not received in time to be counted. It stood as follows: Gould, 4; McCutchan, 10; Barton, 10. *Texas State Gazette*, May 21, 1853.

McCutchan, following an illness of about four weeks, died on Sunday, April 24, 1853 while yet in his twenty-ninth year. The editor of the *Leon Pioneer* described him as an "honest man, a good citizen and respected by all who knew him."[29] Although he suffered much in his last illness from severe pain, he endured all "with Christian fortitude and frequently spoke of the goodness of God."[30] He, and later his brother, were buried in "the old cemetery" two or three miles east of Burton.[31]

Of the many diaries and extensive accounts of the Mier Expedition written by the participants, Joseph D. McCutchan's diary adds much to the literature and to the portrayal of the feelings of the men involved in that episode in the history of the Republic of Texas. For one who had been in Texas less than two years before embarking upon a campaign against the country's remorseless enemy, a campaign that ended so disastrously, McCutchan's love, dedication, and devotion to Texas remained unchanged throughout his life.

29. Quoted in *Texas State Gazette*, May 21, 1853.
30. M. Yell to editor of the *Texas Ranger and Lone Star*, June 9, 1853.
31. Worth S. Ray, *Austin Colony Pioneers*, p. 159.

Joseph D. McCutchan's Narrative of the Campaign in 1842—Which Was Begun under Brgd Genl Summerville, and Ended under Col. Wm. S. Fisher. Battle of Mier, and the Subsequent Imprisonment of That Band, Known as the "Mier Men," with an Account of the Sufferings, While Confined in Mexico during the Space of Twenty Months and Twenty One Days. Also Their Release; Journey towards, and Arrival at, Galveston, Texas:—Commenced in the Castle of San Carlos de Perote, Thence Onward—Written as Things Transpired, and Concluded in Galveston, Texas, Shortly after the Writer's Arrival.

What May Not Man Endure!

Narrative of the Mier Expedition

By Jos[eph] D. McCutchan

[Book] No. 1

Introductory Chapter

I have not now at my command the exact date, but what matters it? Is it important to me who perhaps will lay my bones in the moat of Perote Castle[1]—that I should be particular about dates when pening items that the public will never examine, and which will most probably fall into the hands of my captors? I say is it requisite that in the begining I should note the date, when thus surrounded by mysterious circumstances which may end, I cannot say *how* or *when*? If my body sinks to rest here, the narrative closes with my life! if I reach my home and bear it with me, it will rest in my possession to recall the freeing of my soul, when trampled and abused.

Suffice it then, to say that I begin about the Latter part of April 1844; and as a reason for thus employing a portion of my time, I will only give that I desire to give my mind some line of thought that will occasionally lead me from the contemplation of these miseries, by

1. The Castle of San Carlos de Perote, in the state of Vera Cruz, lay to the left of the road that one traveled from Vera Cruz to Mexico City and approximately a mile to the northwest of the town of Perote, upon the site of an ancient Mexican village called by the natives Pinahuizapan. The fort, or castle as it was called, was situated in a narrow valley at the foot of the north side of the Cofre de Perote, whose inactive volcanic peak towered 13,552 feet above the sea. Farther to the north were higher mountains along the main road from the port of Vera Cruz to Mexico City, "but it [the fort] had long served as a state prison, a refuge for troops, an arsenal and a depot for the rich convoys that went this way," according to Justin H. Smith, *The War With Mexico*, II:61. Following an order issued Nov. 20, 1769, by the Marques de Gurillas, forty-fourth viceroy of New Spain, construction of the fortress was begun under Don Manuel Santiesta on June 25, 1770, in the reign (1759 to 1788) of Charles III of Spain and completed in 1773 at a cost of 659,886 pesos, and the structure was named in honor of the king. Later the inscription "Ferdinand VII" was added over each door in large letters and was still visible in the period 1842 to 1844, although the ruthless hand of revolution had run a paint brush over the name of a king who had trod upon the liberal Spanish Constitution of 1812. Reuben Ross Papers, Archives, University of Texas; Thomas Jefferson Green, *Journal of the Texian Expedition against Mier*, pp. 238–240; J. J. McGrath and Walace Hawkins, "Perote Prison—Where Texians Were Imprisoned," *Southwestern Historical Quarterly* XLVIII (1944–1945):340–345.

which I find myself surrounded; and thus, if possible avoid predicting evil, ere it comes.

> "Misfortune brings
> Sorrow enough; 'tis envy to ourselves,
> To augment it by prediction."

Those men with whom I am associated are of such a character, generally speaking, that their country may well be proud of them; and it should much lament their fall. The time that I have kept *close* company with them has been long enough to give me a good idea of their respective Dispositions. Many of them I know to be courageous and from those nations of chivalrous and honest people which are [three words obliterated by a tear and water stain] the self-styled refined position in society; they are all men of noble spirits—brave, generous and true to their country and friends ready to sacrifice life for the interest of the land of their adoption. And were I capacitated for the effort, and called upon to storm the gates of perdition with such men would I undertake it; and be assured that, if the Monarch of Hell could be captured by man, with that band of such men would I lead his Satanic Majesty in chains the world around!

They are men too, of generosity; and men who will aid each other with their last medio[2] (Peso[3]) in support to say the least. I have learned that

> "Misfortune does not always wait on vice;
> Nor is success the constant guest of virtue."

In taking up and persuing the narrative of events which have already occured, I shall have to depend somewhat upon the notes of others; a little upon the memory of the men of our [b]and; and principally upon my own recollection of matters and things as they transpired, under my own observation. I shall aim to be as accurate as possible; I also will treat with great brevity, those circumstances, for the correctness of which I only take assertions of others. But for those which occured in my own view and knowledge, I will answer for, and shall per-

2. *Medio*: a Mexican coin valued at one-half dollar, but worth six and one-fourth cents in United States money in 1844. Emilio M. Martínez Amador, *Diccionario inglés-español y español-inglés*, s.v.; Arturo Cuyás, *Nuevo diccionario: Cuyás inglés-español y español-inglés de Appleton*, s.v.; George W. Kendall, *Narrative of the Texas Santa Fe Expedition* II:xii, 239; and Green, *Journal of the Texian Expedition against Mier*, p. 203, reported in 1845 that a *medio* was one-sixteenth of an American dollar.
3. *Peso*: a Mexican dollar.

haps dwell longer upon. Those that I have from others I could well agree to answer for also, except (as may be the case) where they have passed through Mexican authority. Where the latter occurs, I shall speak of it and give my opinions, with regard to its validity.

I look forward to many comparatively happy [hours?[4]]

How oft is the understanding moulded by the unrelenting whisper as it passes from mouth to mouth, He is dead! He is no more! We, in the midst of Life, we are in the midst of death. I remember once to have stood in the chains of Death, on a Christmas night, for hours, watching by the side of cold and lifeless clay. I was beside the dead, while from a neighboring house came the merry sound of the violin, accompanied by the smothered sound of moving feet and the hum of the Ball-room. Plain and distinct came this sound while mingling with it came from an adjoining room to that of Death the heartstricken groans of a widowed husband and the cries of motherless children. Ball-rooms may be harmless places of amusement, but had the votaries of that scene of fashion and vanity, the reflecting part of them, been present with me in that chamber of death, by the side of that cold clay, on that memorable night me thinks never again would they have entred the Ball-room's portals. The very sounds seemed to leave a spirit of mockery for the dead and scorn for the grief of the living. Had the gates of Hell been opened, that the howls of the damned could reach the earth and vibrate upon the sense of human hearing, the discord would not have been more dysmal, or the horror creating din more terrible.

We are startled by the report of a death, but the impression made upon our minds is but momentary. Scarcely is the voice hushed, that brings us the news, ere we forget the warning—shut our eyes to the truth that we too must die. We attend the funeral of a friend, see him laid in the cold dark toomb, while contemplating the sad solemnity of that last [sacrifice[5]] our minds are [forced to[6]] think of death and we shudder to think that wisdom must [cas]t his cold terrors; but ere the grass has grown upon the grave, aye, ere the new earth has dried by heaven's noonday sun, we forget the warning and persue the even tenor of our old way as though life had no end or death no terrors.

Meanwhile, through the understanding of this moral, I will be enabled to pass, while struggling through my darkened existence. That sun, which at one time shone with such brillancy upon us, except [it]

4. Water stain. The illegible portion appears to be a short four- or five-letter word.

5. Portion of manuscript missing.

6. Portion of manuscript missing.

has been darkening for two or three years untill now, its light has been entirely shadowed by the gloomy walls of Mexic[an] Dungeons! My destiny seems a dark one! But hold, begone such reflections! Let me not murmur, when I behold those around me who if at liberty would serve their country to advantage. I am of no service at home, and less here! Then why live out a useless life—live the life of a slave! Live to die the crinimal's death? Yet fate can yet change the darkness that over hangs me with light, and the day may come—though it be in the future —when surrounded by friends, *I may lead a useful life*. But Ah! When fancy would lead me off upon the downy wings of a visionary bliss; and when soaring aloft amid rich fields of future anticipations, one move of my foot causes the clank of iron to ring through my brain, hurling hope to Earth, dashing the cup of bliss from fancy, and impressing upon my mind the stern reality of my imprisonment, among a people dead to valor, honor, truth, and generosity! And that call from the overseer, now resounding throughout our room reminds me that I must join the Noble band of "Street Sweeping Texians," and *broom* in hand make an assault upon the *dirt* and *trash*, now filling the streets of the Castle.

"Life! 'tis but a dream at the best
And when 'tis shortest, soonest O'er."

Castle San Carlos de Perote, Mexico — Joseph D. McCutchan
April, 1844

Chapter of Preface

In the Spring, previous to the concentrating of those who entered upon the Mier Expedition, a body of Seven or Eight hundred men under the command of *Genl. Vasques*[1] entered San Antonio, and took up their quarteres, driving all who were hostile to the interest of the Mexican Government from their homes, and committing other depredations upon the peace and good order of the citizens of the country and laws of the land. This band of Mexicans conducted themselves in such a manner as to encourage the belief that they were merely the advance of a large invading army. Texas was unprepared & poorly suited to the fatigues and hardships of such an event as a powerful invasion would have brought upon her; her citizens were then in the midst of the labours of their crops; upon which many of them were wholely dependent for sustainance; yet this troop of Mexicans brought Texians to their arms, caused them to leave their homes, and half finished crops and enter the field for the protection of our western frontier.

Soon *Genl. Vasques* found San Antonio untenable for his diminutive force; and hence prudence led him to evacuate the town ere the Texians could gain an opportunity of bringing him to an engagement. The only damage he was able to effect was that sustained by the farmers, in thus leaving their crops at that season when their labour can least be dispensed with. This, however, was great; and had it been repeated, that this was the principle aim held in view by the Mexican Commandant;

1. Rafael Vasquez commenced his military career as a captain of patriots of the Hacienda de Ciénega de Mata, Feb. 20, 1827; served in the Trigarante army; and was promoted through the various ranks to general of brigade. He commanded a brigade of cavalry in 1834 against Chilapa and was in the Texas campaign of 1835. During the Federalist uprising of 1838 to 1840, he fought on the side of the Centralists and in the battle of Saltillo in 1840 sought to draw the Texans under Colonel Samuel W. Jordan into an ambush. He later served as commandant general of Jalisco from 1851 to 1852. Alberto M. Carreño (ed.), *Jefes del ejército mexicano en 1847*, pp. 219–220; *Telegraph and Texas Register*, Mar. 16, 1842; *Civilian and Galveston Gazette*, Mar. 12, 1842.

With a force of approximately seven hundred artillerymen, infantrymen, *rancheros*, and Indian warriors Vasquez seized San Antonio, Texas, on Mar. 5 and occupied it two days before retreating unopposed to the Rio Grande. Joseph Milton Nance, *Attack and Counterattack*, pp. 26–38.

for, Mexico had seen that she need not hope to reduce Texas in the field alone; and was led to believe that good might result to her, by preventing the cultivation of their crops. And this belief was carefully founded, for had she been permitted thus to act for a few successive years, without retaliation, it is very probable that the major part of the citizens of Texas would have been reduced to a state bordering upon starvation. And we may conclude that had not some cause intervened the same course would have been persued by her in the ensuing spring, and thus in each succeeding one, untill her object had been attained. As to what this cause may have been, I can give no better one, than the spirit of retaliation evinced by the people of Texas in the alacrity with which they entered upon the Mier Expedition. For this gave proof to Mexico of the fact that Texas had the will to annoy, rather than be annoyed; and that people, though but three hundred in number, could do unparalleled execution, by their valor, abroad as well as at home. She had no disposition to aggrivate the Texians to another invasion of her soil, least they might come in greater force.

Again, in the ensuing fall of 1842 *Genl. Woll*[2] entered San Antonio with about *Thirteen hundred men*, no doubt, with the design of capturing the Court, then in session in that place, in which he succeed[ed] with but slight resistance, taking into his custody Judges, Jurors, Lawyers, and clients, amounting to something over Fifty in number, all of whom he sent forthwith towards the confines of Mexico. It is probable that Woll was, in some extent, influenced by the advice of Col. Seguin[3] who had been heard to declare that "*Another Court should never set in the town of San Antonio.*"

2. Brigadier General Adrián Woll, a Frenchman, was born on Dec. 2, 1795, in St. Germain-en-Laye near Paris; served in Napoleon's army; fled France after the fall of Napoleon; joined General Francisco Xavier Mina's filibustering expedition from the United States in behalf of Mexican independence; and soon became a staunch follower of Antonio López de Santa Anna. Woll captured San Antonio, Texas, on Sept. 11, 1842, and evacuated the place on Sept. 20, 1842, following the battle of Salado Creek on the eighteenth. Joseph Milton Nance, (trans. and ed.), "Brigadier General Adrián Woll's Report of His Expedition into Texas in 1842," *Southwestern Historical Quarterly* LVIII (April 1955):523–552; idem, "Adrián Woll: Frenchman in the Mexican Military Service," *New Mexico Historical Review* XXXIII (July 1958): 177–186; idem, *Attack and Counterattack*, pp. 308–408.

3. Juan Nepomuceno Seguín, son of Erasmo Seguín, served as captain of a company of Mexican soldiers under General Sam Houston in the battle of San Jacinto; represented Bexar County in the Senate of the Third and Fourth Congresses of Texas; was mayor of the city of San Antonio, Jan. 4, 1841, to

Seguin, a native Mexican, descended from the Spaniards, had participated in the struggles of Texas, represented one of the western counties (Bexar, I think) two or three times in the Texian Congress. He was the owner of Texas lands, and [was] regarded as true to Texas, untill from some cause unknown to me, he quit Texas and united with Mexico. This led to fear upon his part that he would loose his title to lands; and if I mistake not, I have been informed that he had suits pending in the San Antonio Courts, at the time of his departure. Of the balance in relation to him we must judge from conjecture; and therefore I will say no more relating to him, his prospects, or his acts.

Genl. Woll advanced from San Antonio, to meet Col. Caldwell,[4] to whom he gave battle, in his position, on the *Salado* five miles East of the town. The Texians under Caldwell numbering from two to three hundred, and the Mexicans under Woll, from eleven to thirteen hundred, supported by artillery.[5] Texas was victorious, driving her enemy from the field, and forcing him to a precipitant retreat from San Antonio, in which he was hotly persued by the Texians, and his rear once brought to action near *El Rio Hondo.*

Previous to leaving the battle field of the Salado, Woll surrounded and cut to pieces one company from La Grange, under Capt. Dawson[6]

Apr. 18, 1842, until forced to resign, after which he sought asylum in Mexico. For the case against Seguín, see Nance, *Attack and Counterattack*, pp. 52–54.

4. Mathew Caldwell, signer of the Texas Declaration of Independence and frontier miltary leader, was born in Kentucky about 1798. He came to Texas in 1831 from Missouri and eventually settled at Gonzales. President Mirabeau B. Lamar appointed him to the command of a company of rangers for the defense of Goliad from Mexican raiders, and two months later he became a captain in the First Regiment of Infantry in the regular army of Texas. He was wounded in the Council House Fight in March 1840 with the Comanches but recovered sufficiently to participate in the battle of Plum Creek later that year (Aug. 12) against the Comanches. He served as captain of Company D of the scouting force on the ill-fated Santa Fe Expedition of 1841 and spent many months in a Mexican prison. He arrived home from confinement in Mexico just in time to help drive General Adrián Woll's force out of San Antonio. Walter P. Webb and H. Bailey Carroll (eds.), *Handbook of Texas* I:268; Nance, *Attack and Counterattack*, p. 293.

5. The Texan force under Colonel Caldwell numbered 225 "strong." Mathew Caldwell to the citizens of Gonzales, [dated] Salado, two miles above the Old San Antonio Crossing, Sept. 17, 1842, in *Telegraph and Texas Register*, Oct. 5, 1842. Woll's force at the Salado numbered about 1,210. Nance, *Attack and Counterattack*, pp. 355–358.

6. Captain Nicholas Mosby Dawson, a veteran of San Jacinto, with a small

—killing forty or upwards, and capturing about ten, while two made their escape; one uninjured, and the other severely, though not mortally, wounded.

The people of Texas becoming over anxious, perhaps, for war, made clamor to that effect; and *Genl. Houston*[7] wishing to appease them, issued his proclamation to the intent, that "The first and second classes of millitia should take up arms, and pursue the Enemy even into his own country, and chastize him there, for his insolence."[8] This

---

party of men from Fayette County started for San Antonio immediately upon learning of the call for assistance in driving out the Mexican force under General Woll. His company consisted of fifty-three men, of whom thirty-six were killed, fifteen captured, and two (Alsey S. Miller and Henry Gonzalvo Woods) escaped. A full account of the Dawson fight may be found in Nance, *Attack and Counterattack*, pp. 364–381.

7. Samuel Houston, president of Texas from 1836 to 1838 and from 1841 to 1844, was opposed to offensive operations against Mexico; yet, he believed that Texas should be ready at all times to repel any Mexican invasion of her soil. In the spring and summer of 1842, no longer feeling that he could resist the pressure from the inhabitants of western Texas for a campaign against Mexico, he sought to organize an expedition, knowing that such an expedition would be doomed before it could ever get off. The same situation again followed Woll's seizure of San Antonio, Sept. 11 to 20, 1842. President Houston caved in to western demands and those who were in favor of aggressive action against Mexico were, at least temporarily, appeased. He ordered Brigadier General Alexander Somervell on Oct. 3, 1842, to "proceed to the most eligible point on the southwestern frontier of Texas" and to unite under his command not only the militiamen of Montgomery and Washington Counties who had been ordered to San Antonio, but also all volunteer troops who might be willing to submit to his orders. If Somervell believed that he could advance with success into the enemy's country, he was to do so immediately. "You will . . . receive no troops into service," said the president, "but such as will be subordinate to your orders and the rules of war. You will receive no troops, but such as will march across the Rio Grande under your orders if required to do so." Sam Houston to Brigadier General A. Somervell, [dated] Washington, Oct. 3, 1842 (copy), in Domestic Correspondence (Texas), Texas State Archives; Texas Congress, *Journals of the House of Representatives of the Seventh Congress*, Appendix, pp. 3–4.

8. This is not a direct quotation from any known proclamation or military order. General Somervell was designated to command the troops being concentrated in the west since he was the senior militia commander west of the Trinity River, and he was accorded permission to invade Mexico under certain conditions as noted above and to do so forthwith. What so many of the men of the Mier Expedition later overlooked in their efforts to exculpate themselves from disobedience of orders were the facts that Somervell held

order was accordingly acted upon; and San Antonio made the place of general rendesvous. At which place we assembled from different parts of the country about the First of November 1842; encountering many and various obstacles for that purpose, as well from the disagreeableness of the weather, as the highness of the waters. The Washington County troops, about three hundred in number, had much swimming to do—as well as bad fording, being upon the road near three weeks, from Fullers[9]—the place of our county rendesvous, above Independence, to San Antonio.

We lay about San Antonio untill many of our men becoming discouraged quit the Camp, and returned to their homes. For this they merit no blame indeed; those who did remain, must have been gifted with an uncommon degree of perseverance. Many of them had been in the field some time previous to the arrival of the Washington troops,[10] and I know that we came near to lying there long enough to wear out the patience of a Job.

"Patience in cowards is tame helpless fear;
But in brave minds, a scorn of what they bear."

And worst of all—what was most trying to our forbearance, and blasting to our hopes—we were reduced to the necessity, for the sake of order, and through obedience to the laws and authorities of our country, of submitting ourselves to the Command of *Brigadier General A. Summerville*,[11] in whom not one of us could place any confidence. We

---

his authority from the Texas government, and that the president had admonished the commanding general that the troops must be "willing to submit to your orders" and to be "subordinate" to those orders and to the rules of war.

9. Captain [Samuel?] Fuller lived in Washington County a short distance above Independence. In 1840 he was listed as a member and patron of the group promoting the founding of Rutersville College. The deed records of Washington County show that a Samuel Fuller was issued a license on Jan. 4, 1840, to marry Dedamia Watson. Walter P. Freytag (ed.), *Chronicles of Fayette*, pp. 79–81, 99.

10. The Washington County militiamen began to arrive at San Antonio on Nov. 3, 1842; others came in on the fourth and fifth. Henry Alexander Adams, "[Journal of an] Expedition against the Southwest, in 1842 and 1843," Nov. 3–5, and 10, 1842, Archives, University of Texas.

11. Alexander Somervell was born in Maryland on June 11, 1796, and in 1817 moved to Louisiana to engage in business. From there he came to Texas in 1832, received a grant of land in Austin's second colony, and in 1833 entered into a partnership with James F. Perry in a mercantile business at San Felipe de Austin. In November 1835 he was at San Antonio where he parti-

believed that he might be brave, but his very looks and deportment combined to prove him no General. I say that we lacked confidence in the commander placed over us; and whether we were justified in entertaining this contemptable opinion of his military abilities, his after conduct, and the sequel to the campaign will prove.

During our stay at San Antonio, nothing occurred worthy of note. An occasional rumer would come to our eares, but all were alike disbelieved.

Previous to taking our final leave of Texian settlements, we moved out to the Rio Medina and encamped at the crossing of the Presidio road, where we lay for several days, during which time many of us freaquently visited San Antonio.

We moved out this road for the purpose of giving the Bexar Mexicans to believe that the Town of *Presidio Grande*,[12] was the destined

---

cipated in the Grass Fight. He was elected lieutenant colonel of the First Regiment of Texas Volunteers in March 1836 and fought in the battle of San Jacinto, after which he served as secretary of war in President David G. Burnet's cabinet from May 30 to Aug. 8, 1836. Later he was elected senator to the First and Second Congresses of Texas to represent the district composed of the counties of Colorado and Austin. Soon after the adjournment of the Second Congress, Somervell moved to Fort Bend County and there on Nov. 12, 1839, was elected brigadier general of the First Brigade, Texas Militia. In 1842 he was appointed by Houston to command the Texan troops in the Vasquez and Woll campaigns. Sam Houston Dixon and Louis Wiltz Kemp, *The Heroes of San Jacinto*, p. 126; Amelia Williams and Eugene C. Barker (eds.), *Writings of Sam Houston*, II: 493n.; *National Cyclopaedia of American Biography*, V:244.

12. Presidio del Río Grande, as it came to be commonly known, was founded in the summer of 1701 as the Real Presidio de San Juan Bautista del Río Grande at the site of the mission San Francisco Solano, which had been founded on Mar. 1, 1700, at La Ciénega de Río Grande. Close by was the mission of San Juan Bautista, recently removed from the Río Sabinas to the Valle de la Circuncisión at La Ciénega de Río Grande, five miles northwest of Paso de Francia of the Rio Grande. The presidio was located a quarter of a league east of mission San Francisco Solano for the protection of both missions in the area from hostile Indians. Finally, in 1702, a third mission was established in the area. This was the San Bernardo mission, to the northeast of mission San Juan Bautista. In time it became the bastion of Spanish, and later Mexican, defense of the northern frontier against Indians and foreign intruders. Presidio del Río Grande became the principal gateway to Texas until the founding of Laredo in 1755. For a while the missions in its vicinity were the most prosperous in all northern New Spain. Ben E. Pingenot, "San

place of attack, knowing that they would inform the Rio Grande Mexicans of the course we had taken.

Juan Bautista," in *Handbook of Texas*, ed. Eldon Stephen Branda, III:848–849; Robert S. Weddle, *San Juan Bautista*; and Sarah S. McKeller, "Old Presidio Site at Guerrero," *News Guide*, Centennial Edition, 1949.

Chapter 1

Departure for the Rio Grande. Leave the Presidio & enter the bogg. Arrival at the Loredo road, the Crossing of the Nueces, and arrival in the vicinity of Loredo.

Upon the western bank of the Rio Medina, on a bright and beautiful morning of the latter part of November 1842,[1] "The Mier Expedition," or, as it was then termed, the "South Western Army of Operations"—Eight hundred or upwards strong[2]—under the Command of Brigd. Genl. Summerville, took up the line of march for the "Far West."

Our intention being placed upon Loredo,[3] a small Mexican town

1. The date of departure from the Medina River was Nov. 25, 1842. Joseph Milton Nance, *Attack and Counterattack*, pp. 480, 483.

2. At the time of departure from the Medina River, Somervell's army numbered slightly more than 750 men, rank and file. Ibid., p. 484.

3. La Villa de San Augustín de Laredo, commonly known as Laredo, had been founded by Don Tomás Sánchez de la Barrera y Gallardo on May 15, 1755, and was one of the oldest towns on the lower Rio Grande. Its location was favored by two fordable crossings of the river in its vicinity. A short distance to the north was El Paso de Jacinto and a few leagues to the south was El Paso de Miguel de la Garza, which, after its founding, caused Laredo to become the popular preference as the gateway to Texas rather than the Presidio crossing of the Rio Grande farther to the north. El Camino Real in the late eighteenth and early nineteenth centuries shifted southward to make Laredo the gateway between northern Mexico and San Antonio, Texas.

In recent years Laredo had fallen on hard times, owing to repeated attacks of Comanches and Apaches and the thieving Lipans, the last being allies of the Texans. In the spring of 1842 the Rio Grande had flooded, causing much damage. The town's population had been on the decline since 1828 and in 1842 numbered scarcely two thousand inhabitants. The houses were in ruins and an air of desolation pervaded the whole city. The surrounding ranches in 1842 were in a deplorable condition, and trade with San Antonio and other places had suffered greatly from freebooters during the last few years. I. J. Cox, "The Southwest Boundary of Texas," *Quarterly of the Texas State Historical Association* VI (1902–1903):91; Harold Schoen (comp.), *Monuments Erected by the State of Texas to Commemorate the Centenary of Texas Independence*, p. 90; Thomas W. Bell, *A Narrative of the Capture and Subsequent Sufferings of the Mier Prisoners in Mexico*, p. 15; Carlos E. Cas-

situated upon the eastern bank of *El Rio Bravo del Norte*—the bold river of the north. We struck a little out from the Medina, and took our course for the Loredo road, in near a Southwest by South direction. We hoped to baffle the observation of the Bexar Mexicans by this manouver, and leave with them the impression that the Presidio crossing was the place destined for our first attack. But I am disposed to admit a doubt whether it succeeded, for those fellows *are sharp of sight*, and swift of foot, where treason is concocting, or treachery their aim. We were convinced that, if they did, or had discovered the point for which we aimed, they would not be long in communicating the intelligence to their breatheren of the copper colour on the Rio Grande —or rio Bravo—as it is indiscriminately and alternately called. At the lower end of the imprudent Medina is a subject for a separate chapter.[4]

We moved in high spirits, and bright anticipations, proudly looking forward to the time when, face to face we should meet our country's foe, and hurl his haughty insolence back, to his teeth! Never once dreaming of the trials that were awaiting our approach, we did not notice circumstances or we could have formed more correct ideas of that fate which was awaiting us. It would, to an observer, appear clear that we were doomed to disappointments, trials, and sufferings; but being not easily detered from the prosecution of an expedition, which we had good reason to expect would result in honor to ourselves, and glory and advantage to our country, in which we were willing to endure anything in *life*, and even *Death* itself were it necessary to Texian interests. I say, under these impressions, the thought was not at any time entertained, that we, by our conduct, would gain the censure of our countrymen, whom we had left in the enjoyment of peace and plenty! But, nevertheless, it seems that we have been censured; but, whether diservedly or not, I leave the world to judge. We have been pained by learning that some have even dared to brand us with the epithets—so disgraceful in themselves—of "Coward, Traitors, and Robbers!" What! Can such be the fact? Nay, let our *actions* speak. Though the world should thus brand us while living, posterity will deal in justice with us. He who impeaches the honesty of *my motives shall* estab-

---

tañeda, "A Trip to Texas in 1828 by José María Sánchez," *Southwestern Historical Quarterly* XXIX (1925–1926):251; Florence Johnson Scott, *Historical Heritage of the Lower Rio Grande*, pp. 42–43; Seb S. Wilcox, "Laredo during the Texas Republic," *Southwestern Historical Quarterly* XLII (1938–1939):83–107. For a further description of Laredo, see Nance, *Attack and Counterattack*, pp. 512–513.

4. This contemplated chapter seems never to have been written.

lish the truth of such impeachment, by proof drawn from my course of conduct, or answer the injured for the falsehood, and attone with his life!

We have been disowned by our government it is said! Can this be true? What? disowned and thrown upon the mercy of our enemies—a mercy that would, or will, result in the death of all who are in the power of Santa Anna. For he is a man to whose bosom the sentiment of mercy is an entire stranger; in whose heart justice can never dwell. But I digress from the course of my narrative; for which, however, I deem myself excusable in as much as our eares are ever saluted by abuses of the harsher kind.

On the morning of the third day from our encampment on the Medina, we resumed our line of march in every high spirits, considering the thorough drenching which we had received on the previous evening, and night from a rain as heavy as we are in the habit of seeing in the western country. Before proceeding far, we were forced to dismount, leave the lines, and every man shift for himself. Our guides had lead us into a boggy post oak woods, where our horses went to the girth [with] ever[y] step, while their riders often came near going down to the knee.[5] Often, when holding my horse by the bit, in order to give him my assistance, I came near bogging myself. Never had I witnessed such a scene, and hope never to be an actor in the like circumstances. We were scattered over the woods as far as the eye could reach in utter confusion. Thus circumstanced, we held on our course untill near nightfall, when we camped on a little eminence horror stricken at our anticipations for the next day. In this day's hard march we had gained about seven miles, and had [lost] some portion of our order, but none of resolution. Here, upon a spot of porus ground not exceeding a mile in circumference, we passed the night, both men and horses rendered uneasy by the scantiness of our accomodations. The surrounding country gave the appearance of a vast morass, and our little eminence we found to be, in reality, but little better, for many horses broke through the solid crust of earth covering the hill, which, being only from ten to twelve inches through, was easily done. Early on the following morning we set to work constructing a bridge of trees and brush across a morass of some fifty feet bredth, upon which we safely crossed dur-

5. Here the author refers to what the men called the "Atascosa Bogs." The Spanish word *atascosa* means *boggy*. The fall of 1842 had been a wet one, and it was raining heavily during the time the expedition crossed the sandy post-oak country in the vicinity of the Navarro ranch. See Nance, *Attack and Counterattack*, pp. 487–490, for further details of the men's experiences with the bogs.

ing that and the following day. On the morning of the third day after our arrival at this encampment, above mentioned, we bid adieu to this vicinity and fronted our columns towards the Loredo Road, at which we arrived that evening with our horses much worsted by the fatigues of the bogg—many of them unfit for use. Thence forward, our march was uninterrupted by any circumstance or accident worthy of note, untill our course brought us to a good camping ground within four miles of the *Nueces*, where we pitched our tents for the night; that is, those who had them; those who had not, "*spread their blankets.*"

Having been on the road and in camp together for some time, and living upon beef, with an occasional meal of bread, anything that appeared eatable was ceased [seized] with rapacious avidity by the mass, or at least by a goodly number of the army. Hence when there had been a root (resembling in flavor somewhat the irish potatoe) found by these men at this encampment, many of them roasted and consumed a considerable quantity of it. The majority of those who partook of it were punished by a few hours of torturing sickness, some even with thoughts of death. I presume, however, that it had a good result in rendering them more cautious for the future.

On the following morning, Capts. J. B. Robertson[6] and Mitchel[7]

6. Captain Jerome Bonaparte Robertson, son of the empresario Sterling C. Robertson, was born in Woodford County, Kentucky, Mar. 14, 1815, and died in Waco, Texas, Jan. 7, 1891. In his youth he was apprenticed to a hatter and worked for ten years in Kentucky and Missouri until the age of seventeen. At seventeen he began the study of medicine at Owensboro, Kentucky, and later continued his studies at Transylvania University from which he graduated in 1835. In February 1836 he raised a company of Kentucky volunteers for the Texas Revolution but arrived in Texas after the battle of San Jacinto. He returned to Kentucky to settle his affairs with the intention of settling permanently in Texas. In 1837 he settled at Washington-on-the-Brazos, and in the following year married Mary Elizabeth Cummins. He practiced medicine for three years at Washington-on-the-Brazos and served as the town's mayor (1839 to 1840) and postmaster (1841 to 1843). In 1841, because of poor health, he moved to a farm near Washington. On the Somervell Expedition he served briefly as brigade inspector and as captain of the largest company in the First Regiment. Walter P. Webb and H. Bailey Carroll, eds., *Handbook of Texas*, II:487; Pat Ireland Nixon, *The Medical Story of Early Texas, 1528–1853*, p. 355; Nance, *Attack and Counterattack*, pp. 478, 495, 643–644.

7. Captain Isaac N. Mitchell, of Lavaca, served on scouting duty around San Antonio early in March 1842 and in the Somervell Expedition to the Rio Grande and was elected one of the eleven captains in the First Regiment of the Second Brigade. His company contained forty men enlisted on the Lavaca

were dispatched with their companies to examine the Nueces, find a suitable crossing and construct a bridge, if necessary, for the transportation of the army to the western bank. Upon nearing the stream, we discovered a vast sheet of water spread out before us; and had it not been for the timber rising from it, we might well have believed that we had struck an arm of the Gulf of Mexico. Instead of the narrow stream confined within perpendicular banks, we found a broad Ocean like body of water extending from hill to hill. Col. Cook,[8] who had advanced with us, with that "go ahead" disposition that characterized all of his actions, striped to his underclothes, and struck out alone across the water, leaving us to awate his return. In about two hours he returned, reporting that a bridge of brush had been constructed across the main channel by Capts. Hays[9] and Bogart,[10] commanders of the advance, and that he had found a way practicable for us on foot with-

---

and at Washington. During the Somervell campaign the companies of Mitchell and Jerome B. Robertson constructed a temporary bridge across the flooded Nueces River. Twenty-five of the men in Mitchell's company returned home from the vicinity of Guerrero with General Somervell in late December 1842. Mitchell was among those returning home. He later married Mary K. Kerr, a cousin of John Henry Brown, the historian of Texas. Nance, *Attack and Counterattack*, pp. 25, 33, 445, 478, 495, 565, 637; John D. Morris to Dear Brother [Richard Morris? Galveston], [dated] Seguin, March 8, 1842, *Telegraph and Texas Register*, Mar. 16, 1842; John Henry Brown, "Autobiography," Archives, University of Texas; John Henry Brown, *History of Texas*, II:236, says that William S. Fisher's and Mitchell's companies were sent to bridge the Nueces; also see, "Abstract of the Muster Rolls of the Companies Comprising the Army on the South-Western Frontier, commanded by Brigadier [General] Somervell, that marched from Guerrero in obedience to Order No. 64," in Texas Congress, *Journals of the House of Representatives of the Ninth Congress of the Republic of Texas*, Appendix, p. 75.

8. Colonel James R. Cook of Washington County was acting inspector general and general mustering officer of the South Western Army of Operations (i.e., the Somervell Expedition) by appointment of President Sam Houston. On Nov. 11, 1842, he was elected commander of the First Regiment of the Second Brigade of that army. He returned home from the vicinity of Guerrero with Brigadier General Alexander Somervell. Nance, *Attack and Counterattack*, pp. 291, 407, 441, 478, 532, and 545.

9. Mayor John Coffee Hays, son of Harmon A. and Elizabeth (Cage) Hays, was born at Little Cedar Lick, Wilson County, Tennessee, Jan. 28, 1817. He was one of eight children and was from the same section of Tennessee as the McCullochs, Sam Houston, and Andrew Jackson. It is said that Jackson purchased the property later known as the Hermitage from Hays' grandfather, John Hays, who served with Jackson on several Indian campaigns

and built Fort Haysboro. John C. Hays' father also fought with Jackson and named his son for General John Coffee, one of Jackson's trusted officers. Orphaned at age twelve Hays was forced to leave school at fifteen. He went to Mississippi where he learned to be a surveyor. Shortly after the battle of San Jacinto he arrived in Texas bearing a letter of introduction from President Andrew Jackson addressed to Sam Houston. He found employment for a while as a surveyor and became noted as a gentleman of much ability and energy and of "the purest character." On Nov. 7, 1837, he was appointed by President Houston to be chief justice of the frontier county of Victoria, but by 1840 he had come to devote most of his time to the duties of a frontier ranger. In the battle of Plum Creek in 1840 against the Comanches he exhibited great courage and was soon thereafter placed by President Mirabeau B. Lamar, and later by Houston, in charge of the ranger force at San Antonio, where he was commander during the Vasquez and Woll campaigns. John S. Ford, "Memoirs," Archives, University of Texas. See also *Jack Hays*, pp. 1–63; Walter Prescott Webb, *The Texas Rangers*, pp. 32–34, 67–123; Elizabeth H. West, "John Coffee Hays," *Dictionary of American Biography*, VIII:463; J. D. Affleck, "History of John C. Hays," Archives, University of Texas; James Kimmins Greer, *Colonel Jack Hays*.

10. Captain Samuel A. Bogart of Washington County was born in Carter County, Tennessee, Apr. 2, 1797, and fought in the battle of New Orleans in 1815 and in the Black Hawk War in 1832. In 1839 he settled in Washington County, Texas. Harvey Alexander Adams says (in Nance, *Attack and Counterattack*, p. 447) that "he was one of the first to appear in the rescue of *Old Paint* [Caldwell]" and had stayed on at San Antonio after many of the volunteers had returned home. On Nov. 7, 1842, his company was accorded the privilege of acting as an independent spy company. On Nov. 13 seventeen of his men were ordered to go into the regiment, presumably because the company was too large for a spy company and because some of the mounts could not pass a rigorous inspection; and Bogart and the men remaining in the company were ordered by General Somervell to fall in under Major John C. Hays. Bogart refused to do so. Finally, an agreement was made between Hays, Bogart, and Somervell, whereby Hays, senior in rank to Bogart, would command the spy company, that reconnaissance parties would consist of men drawn equally from both companies and the spoils would be shared equally by all members of the two companies. When the commanding officer of one company was out with the spies, the other would command the remnants of the two companies left behind. A. Somervell, General Order No. 14, Nov. 12, 1842, in "A Record Book of the General & Special Orders and Letters of the South Western Army," p. 13, New York Public Library, New York City; A. Somervell, General Order No. 18, Head Quarters, Camp Leon, near San Antonio, Nov. 13, 1842, in ibid., pp. 14–16; Nance, *Attack and Counterattack*, pp. 63, 431, 447–448, 464, 478, 490–491; Webb and Carroll (eds.), *Handbook of Texas*, II:181; E. W. Winkler (ed.), "Sterling Brown Hendricks' Narrative of the Somervell Expedition to the Rio Grande, 1842," *Southwestern Historical Quarterly* XXIII (1919–1920):117.

out swimming. He led us forward, each man for himself, leading his horse. Often, we were to our middles in mud and water, then to the knee, and again, with a sudden plunge, to our shoulders; but as far as I am aware, none were compeled to swim, untill he had reached the bank of the main stream. Here finding at one or two trials that our horses could not cross on the bridge, we unpacked, unsaddled, carried our baggage over on the miniature construction, and consigned our horses to the flood. The[y] all reached the opposite bank in safety; and we moved a short distance up the river to the encampment of Hays and Bogart, there to awate the arrival of the main body, the last of whom did not arrive untill the next morning. The crossing of this stream required exertion and labour; but combatting toil, without abatement of ardor, we found ourselves on the western bank of the Nueces, in as high spirit as men could possibly possess under such circumstances. Neither labour, nor hardships of any kind, seemed capable of cooling our ardor, or thwarting that resolute determination that had animated the breast of each one from the beginning. We had endured the maraudings of Mexico without retaliation, untill forbearance had ceased to be a virtue; it was, therefore, a natural consequence that we should be firm and resolute in our undertaking.

We passed two nights at this encampment, on the last of which our horses took it into their heads to "leave!" and most unanimously did they act it out. Of the whole command, there were but few that did not join the *stampede*; but on the following morning—the *sixth* of December—we managed to gether all with very little trouble in time to make a good long march before encamping for the night. Our encampment for the evening we reached about one hour after dark, and found water scarce and bad, and wood hard to procure.

We ascertained that Capt. Hays, who with his company had left the Nueces more than a day before us, had captured two Mexicans in the vicinity of Loredo, from whom he learned that there were Eighty Regular soldiers quartered in a small fort on the West Bank of the Rio Grande. Therefore, on the morning of the Seventh December, Genl. Summerville ordered Col. James Cook, a bold and valuable officer, to take three Companies of the best mounted men, with them to make a forced march, cross the river, either above or below town, as circumstances might dictate to his judgement, and cut off the retreat of the Enemy; while he, in person, would move on with the main body, more at leasure, and arrive, at least in time to give him assistance, if any were necessary. This plan was well and propperly concocted, and with good reason we looked forward in anticipation of its complete success. If these soldiers could be thus cut off, they would inevitably surrender, sooner than be cut to pieces; and thus would we, at one blow, have accomplished our main object, that being to procure a sufficient number of prisoners from the enemy, to give in exchange for our countrymen, who were then enduring the severeities of an incarceration in Mexican Dungeons, or making long and fagiguing marches, perhaps, in chains!

After the usual ceremonies of leaving camp, generally performed by Texians; such as breakfasting, packing, and mounting, the main body moved on; and after two miles marching, we came upon the encampment of Hays & Bogart, from whom we gained the intelligence that one of the prisoners had escaped; and as a matter of course had made his way to Loredo. This Prisoner, being wounded, was not as strictly guarded as he should have been, and thus the opportunity offering, he effected his escape.

About noon, the main body came up with Cook's division, where they had halted, knowing that this Mexican had undoubtedly fled to the town, and that on learning our vicinity to the place, the soldiers would perform a precipitate retreat. They had halted here, within twelve miles of the town, that they might receive the further orders of the General, in as much as their first design had been frustrated, in a manner, and at a time, so unfortunate to our prospects.

Near sunset, we took up the line of march, in a body, and moved forward towards the Town, which we wished to reach about daylight, on the following morning. Our march was rendered slow, by the number of ravines that crossed our way and by the number of halts we made from time to time. During the night we lost a man, whose name I forget, and since that time we have heard nothing of him.

The country we had passed over from San Antonio to the Nueces was often of good soil, but scarcely any timber, and apparently very dry. After crossing the Nueces, the face of the country changed materially, and for the worse. From the Valley of that stream to the Valley of the Rio Grande, the land is not worth owning, being poor, without timber of any considerable size, and almost destitute of water. I can see no use to which it can be applied, without probability of advantage. However, some portions of it would produce pretty well.

Chapter II

Capture of Loredo by the Texians. Their conduct at Loredo. Division of the Texians, a portion return home under Col. Bennett, the remainder under Genl. Summerville, proceed down the river. Arrival at the river near Guererro. Crossing of the Texians before a force of Mexican Cavalry. The Texians lay Guererro under contribution; and recross the River. Genl. Summerville orders the army back to the settlements of Texas. The officers hold a consultation, and obtain permission for those to remain on the river who wish to do so. Summerville takes his departure for the Settlements of Texas, followed by the majority of the army.

After a night passed in the saddle with an occasional respite, during which the men were permitted to slumber, under arms with the rein in hand, the Texians were drawn up in the form of a "Half moon," surrounding the Town of Loredo, from the River above to the bank below Town, at break of Day on the morning of the Eighth of December, 1842. They were weary of the fatiguing, perplexing march of the previous night, and longed anxiously for a "Side of Beef ribs," a cup of coffee, and a good long nap on the natural couch formed of "Mother Earth"—so luxurious to the toil worn Campaigner. But still, they had a relish for a little skirmish, by way of earning their breakfast, could it be obtained. This was not to be hoped for here. Well they knew that the inhabitants were apprised of their advance, and yet here they were, within gunshot of the town, their banner floating to the breeze, their arms clashing in the hum of preparation for coming events, but no hostile movement was indicated by their neighbours of the town. One or two women, passing perhaps for water, approached near the line, when on a sudden, discovering the bristling ranks of armed men by dim light of the morning extending from right to left, they uttered a short shrill scream and gave fine play to their propelling powers, making a streight line for the town. Soon a deputation from Town paid their respects to the *Renouned* Summerville, and made a formal surrender of the Place.

Entering the town, thereupon, the Army passed through, leaving the

Plaza on the left, and encamped one mile above on the River bank.[1]

Here was *glory*! a town, without *protection*, without *soldiers*, without *arms*, and of *no importance*, either to the *Texians* or the *Mexicans*, had *surrendered* without loss of *blood*—without the *fire* of a *gun*—to the *Redoubtable* commander of the Texian "*South Western army of opperations!*"

About *Two* o'clock, in the evening of the same day, the army moved down the River, passing through the town, and encamped two miles below in a place naturally well entrenched being almost surrounded by a deep ravine, from which it would have required no inconsiderable force to have dislodged them.[2]

On the 9th, notwithstanding the sentinels had strict orders to the contrary, many men were permitted to pass out, without orders from the Commanders, or permission of any kind. Some of these, entering the town, behaved in a manner most disgraceful to that expedition, while there were but few engaged in—I might say—the act of pillage. I forbear, through shame for my countrymen, to enlarge upon what I have said. Many were thoughtless in the act, but still the crime is the same. I was thankful that I had not gone to town on that day; for all who went, though many took no part in it, were considered as partially culpable. I do not accuse all. Oh, no! There were some whom I know—whom I had seen at home—whom I felt must be innocent, but I knew not who the guilty were. Sooner than I would have had that act to rest upon me, I would have laid my bones on the Enemies Soil, if it were but single handed, I had sought death. Here was a Town, on the soil claimed by Texas; its inhabitants, claiming to be Texians, had opened their doors to us, as to friends—had received the soldiers of Texas as deliverers; and yet, those inhabitants were not safe in the possession of their private property. Suffice it to say, Texas must wear a stain for the conduct of a few disorderly volunteers, who might have

1. General Somervell pitched his camp about a mile or a mile and a half above Laredo upon a sand bar to await the arrival of the supplies that had been requisitioned. John Henry Brown, *History of Texas*, II:238; Joseph Milton Nance, *Attack and Counterattack*, pp. 514–515.

2. The Texan army took up its position at Camp Chacón, a campsite named after the adjacent stream. E. W. Winkler (ed.), "Sterling Brown Hendricks' Narrative of the Somervell Expedition to the Rio Grande," *Southwestern Historical Quarterly* XXIII (1919–1920):126–127. See also J. D. Affleck, "History of John C. Hays," I:40, Archives, University of Texas. Affleck says the Chacón was a small stream emptying into the Rio Grande five miles below Laredo.

been restrained had the officers have taken the propper course. The greater portion of the property, however, was returned to the Alcalde.[3]

On the Evening of the 10th the army took up the line of march—none knew whither; but it was evidently a retreat, although no enemy had appeared. Their course lay through a dense chaperal, or thicket of musquete and other thorny shrubs and bushes, in which, upon a small open space they encamped without water;[4] and for some unknown and foolish reason very few fires were permitted. Provision was quite scarce, having nothing but half-dried beef.

On the morning of the 11th, they moved a few miles farther to water and encamped for breakfast.[5] The water was bad in taste, and quite muddy, but still it was thankfully received. The Texians seem to be, of all people in the world, save the Arabs, the most satisfied in camp. They are discontented with neither the quantity nor the quality of provisions, provided the[y] see that the best is done for them under the circumstances. The mornings repast, though light and illy prepared, was enjoyed with as great relish, in as high spirits, as if they had been seated around the festal board of an Emperor. Jokes were passed, anecdotes related, and merriment produced as usual, but it cannot be denied that owing to the misterious and unaccountable conduct of the General on the previous evening, had created considerable discontent and produced many loud murmurs. The men contended, with justice too, that they had not left their homes, their wives and children, and travelled over many miles of Prairie at the most unfavorable season, swimming many streams, to skulk about in the Chaparal—a despicable hoard of cowards—when the enemy's country lay before them, and a meeting with the foe was practicable. They were becoming awake to the merits of their General; and many of

3. The alcalde of Laredo was Don Florencio Villareal. Seb S. Wilcox, "Laredo during the Texas Republic," *Southwestern Historical Quarterly* XLII (1938–1939):101; Kathleen DaCamara, *Laredo on the Rio Grande*, p. 17. A full account of the plunder of Laredo may be found in Nance, *Attack and Counterattack*, pp. 514–515, 519–526.

4. McCutchan's timing of events is off by a day. The encampment on the night of Dec. 9, 1842, was made about ten o'clock in the evening in a small mesquite flat about seven miles below Laredo in the direction of the San Antonio Road.

5. Early in the morning of Dec. 10, the army resumed its march and, after pursuing a circuitous route, two miles on the back track, located a scanty supply of water in the Cañon de San Andres and halted for breakfast. Harvey Alexander Adams, "[Journal of an] Expedition Against the Southwest in 1842 and 1843," Dec. 10, 1842, Archives, University of Texas.

them had boldly expressed their contempt and derision of his movement.

These murmurs caught the general's attention; and fearing an outbreak, which in the truth was to be dreaded, [he] ordered a general perade, an order which was obeyed with the greatest alarcity. After arranging them to suit his notion, and delivering an address, with as little sense as patriotism in it, but still setting forth the object of the expedition, and permitting those to return home, who desired to go, he called for volunteers to follow him across the Rio Grande. This call was answered by about Five Hundred and fifty "stout hearts and ready hands," who stept out almost as a man, and took a position assigned to those who sought active service under the "Lone Star" of Texas; while those, who wished to return to the peace and quietude of home, stood fast in their position. After the division had been made, many persuasions were used on both sides; by those who contemplated returning, to induce their friends to return with them; by those who were bent upon active service, to induce their friends to go on with them and partake of the toils and glories of combat; but the persuasions of each were alike unsuccessful, every one seeming determined on persuing the inclinations of his own councils. The band of "the Homeward bound" were placed under command of Col. Bennett,[6] to

6. Colonel Joseph L. Bennett came to Texas in 1834 and settled in Montgomery County. During the Texas Revolution he served as lieutenant colonel of the Second Regiment of Texas Volunteers and fought in the battle of San Jacinto. In 1837 he was promoted to the rank of colonel and assigned a regiment to protect the frontier. He served from Montgomery County in the House of Representatives of the Third and Fourth Texas Congresses. He commanded the Montgomery County regiment of militia ordered to the defense of San Antonio by President Houston on Sept. 22, 1842. When mustered near Gonzales on Oct. 15, his regiment numbered some three hundred men but in the weeks of inactivity ahead came to be severely reduced by desertions.

The order to Bennett to command the troops on the return march home was countermanded shortly after it was issued, and Colonel Jesse L. McCrocklin of Washington County was assigned to command the returnees. A. Somervell, General Order No. 60, Head Quarters, Camp near Laredo, Dec. 10, 1842, and A. Somervell, General Order No. 61, Head Quarters, Camp La Ratama, Dec. 10, 1842, in "A Record Book of the General & Special Orders and Letters of the South Western Army," p. 9, New York Public Library, New York City; Amelia W. Williams and Eugene C. Barker, eds., *Writings of Sam Houston*, III:131 [Elizabeth LeNoir Jennett, ed.], *Biographical Directory of the Texan Conventions and Congresses*, p. 51; Nance, *Attack and Counterattack*, pp. 412, 436, 472, 530–531, and 535–536.

whom orders were given to proceed, by the most direct and practicable rout[e], to Gonzales, where he should discharge his command; the command of the remainder was still vested in Brigadier General Summerville. On the evening of the same day we marched down the valley in which the division had taken place to a more convenient encampment, where both divisions passed the night—the last that they were to pass together.

On the morning of the 12th[7] of December 1842, the two divisions departed, Col. Bennett's directing their course homeward, and Genl. Summerville's setting their faces towards the soil of their country's foe. Of Col. Bennett's command we here bid a final farewell, hoping, in the meantime, that they may have reached their homes in safety,[8] and that they found their Fathers, Mothers, Wives, Children, and Sweethearts in fine health and joyous spirits. Many of them were noble hearted, whole souled men worthy of Heaven's choicest blessings; but some few, I fear, were not true and good men. Many of them were men of the highest standing—but I forbear, for it is not my province, nor do I wish, to enter into an investigation of characters either to the condemnation or the exculpation of any of those who then returned. Pick a body of two hundred and fifty men, be they ever so nicely chosen, and you will hardly fail to discover a few germs of dishonor! I make no imputation or insinuation, either for or against any one; this is not necessary, for the innocent will perceive the[i]r exculpation, and the guilty will feel the sting. Farewell, then, to that band, farewell! and may peace and plenty hover over, and the smiles of prosperity attend them and their children to the latest posterity, is the earnest wish of one who though he could not participate with them in their homeward journey, felt at the time of their departure, and still feels, an abiding interest in their welfare.

After the reduction of his forces, General Summerville determined upon the capture of Guererro,[9] a small town situated thirty miles be-

7. The separation occurred Sunday morning, Dec. 11, 1842. Those returning home under Colonel Joseph L. Bennett and Lieutenant Colonel Jesse L. McCrocklin numbered 187 and were largely portions of the Montgomery and Washington County militia that had been ordered to the frontier. Nance, *Attack and Counterattack*, p. 535.

8. Colonel Bennett proceeded by the most direct route to Gonzales and disbanded his command. About the middle of January 1843 Colonel Bennett's men, numbering about 150 of the Montgomery County drafted militiamen, arrived in Montgomery. *Telegraph and Texas Register*, Jan. 18, 1843.

9. Guerrero (formerly Reveilla), renamed in 1828 in honor of Vicente Guerra, a ranchman of the province of Coahuila who had recommended to José

low Loredo on the Western side of the river; accordingly, thither he bent his course, followed by a small army full of spirit and fire and ready for action under any circumstances. But their march being circuitous, several days were consumed in its accomplishment, [. . . reducing[10]] some portion of the ardour of the army. On the night of the 12th a beautiful encampment was secured, but provisions were alarmingly scarce. Many of the messes were totally destitute of meat, nor did they procure any untill the night of 13th, when hunters who had been dispatched for the purpose returned to camp with a good supply. Grass was also scarce, and water bad, at this encampment. On the Night of the 14th, fortunately for both men and horses, the army encamped in a beautiful valley, where any quantity of grass of the best quality could be had, with plenty of meat and tolerable water; but they were annoyed during the night by the fears of some, who presumed that an enemy was in their vicinity; but still, however, the enemy made not his appearance, and morning dawned without molestation to our army.

The march of the troops on the 15th led through quite a handsome valley, occasionally though rendered valueless by the number of gullies, fizures, and ravines into which it had in many places been cut and carved by long drouths and suden rains. At noo[n]day, we halted on the bank of the Rio Grande, opposite the Town of Guererro, which is situated about three miles from the River on a smal stream, called the Salado, above the mouth of which, and immediately in its vicinity, we determined upon crossing. Captains Hays and Bogart, commanders of the advance, commenced crossing in lighters, made something after the fasion of a common Ferry boat, carrying over their baggage and swimming their horses. Scouts were sent out to reconnoiter, who returned ere Hays and Bogart had completed their crossing, announcing the approach of about Three hundred Mexican Cavalry, then within less than two miles. Those fearless soldiers, nothing daunted by such intelligence but rather rejoicing at the prospect for an action, sent an express over to Summerville to push on reenforcements, that the enemy were on the march to attack them, and that, be their force what it might, they would remain and receive the shock, so as to sustain, if

---

Escandón the settling of families in that area, was founded in October 1750 upon the northern bank of Río Salado, at six miles from the Rio Grande and some fifty-four miles below Laredo. Guerrero in 1842 was approximately the size of Bexar (San Antonio). Nance, *Attack and Counterattack*, pp. 536, 540, 554.

10. Word obliterated by water stain. Evidence from other sources indicates that the word was probably "reducing."

possible, the position they had acquired on the western bank. Summerville busied himself, but before he could throw them much assistance, the enemy hove in sight, and took a position on an eminence, at the distance of near a half mile from the little band of Texians. The Texians were between the second bank of the river and the margin of the watter, where they could manouver at discression, entirely screened from the enemy's view. Fearful that the Mexican force might be too great for that of their own band, Hays or Bogart, I know not which, disposed their forces in such a manner and with such orders that they could present themselves, their heads above the bank, peering at the foe as thoug mere curiosity, and then disappearing, show themselves at other places, far distant from the former. This was to create a belief that their force was greater than it really was, and proved successful; for, after reenforcements enough had arrived, the Texians made their appearance boldly, passed up the bank, and took a position nearer the enemy, and [at] some distance from the river, but still the enemy moved not from their position, untill they finally saw from the movements of the Texians that a longer tenancy of their position could only be held at the hazard of an engagement; they then moved off, more rapidly than they had advanced, leaving the Texians masters of the field, without the discharge of a single shot. Here was one bloodless conquest that Texas had made; a conquest which secured for them a peaceable crossing of the river. Had the Mexicans have discovered the smallest advantage, I have no doubt but that leaden messengers would have carried an exchange of civillities between them and the invaders of their soil. But this advantage, only in numbers, was not perceptable, and they, therefore, deemed it prudent to retire. The whole of the army could not well cross before night, and therefore Summerville madly determined to divide his forces for the night, notwithstanding information had reached him conveying the intelligence that there was a force of ner three thousand Mexicans fifteen miles above. This measure was foolish because his army being week at most, with [when?] all together, he could not expect with one half to withstand the onset of three thousand of the enemy. His reasons I do not know, but they proved good at the time because the report was not true. But he had no right, reasonably, to disbelieve it; and therefore, it was his duty to prepare for it with as much alacrity, and as great caution, as though he had known it by actual observation.

On the morning of the 16th, one portion of the army being over, the remainder crossed; and towards evening the whole force advanced on the town of Guererro; but from some cause or other, the General changed his mind ere he had reached it, and ordered a halt, near one mile off, where he permitted a Mexican to pick his encampment. This was chosen on the bank of the Salado, and [on] the side of a bleak, barren, rocky hill, where we were exposed to great disadvantages should an enemy appear, and wood sufficient to make fires could not be procured. The night was very cold; the rain continued to fall; we had no shelter, no fires, and but little to eat; our arms were wet; not one gun of the army perhaps would have fired clear; and one twelve Pounder, on the opposite side of the river, well managed, would have created dreadful execution among the men ere they could have retired! Indeed, our position was miserable, dreadful, and perrilous! In that situation, the Texian army passed the night within one mile of town, where good, safe, and comfortable quarters could have been secured. Early on the following morning a contribution was laid upon the town for sugar, coffee, shoes, blankets, *Etectra*; under which the *Alcalde* sent out abot *ten pounds of sugar, as much coffee, eight* or *ten pars of shoes, six or eight hats*—well worn, *very aged* in fact, and a *few old blankets*! Nothing was fit for one but the sugar, coffee, and shoes, and they were so small in quantity that the army would have done equally as well, perhaps better, without them. The very act of the filling a requisition in this manner was an insult sufficient to have justified Summerville in an act of punishment on the town; but no, this he could not think of.

On the 17th, the memorable day upon which the town of Guererro was laid under contribution by the *renouned* Summerville, the army made a retrograde movement towards the river; at which they arrived in time for some few to cross [from] that country, but the majority were compelled [to] encamp on the western bank. Here they remained through a wet, cold, and miserable night, without outposts or sentries, and but little wood.

The 18th was principally occupied in recrossing the River.

On the 19th Genl. Summerville came out with general orders,[11] *commanding the forces under him to take up the line of march on that evening for Gonzales via the junctions of the Rio Frio and Nueces.* This was a death blow to prospects of the Texian army; but Summerville was consulting his own feelings and considering the danger that he would likely encounter by remaining longer on the river, he thought that he had gained glory enough. A council was held among the offi-

11. Order No. 64, Head Quarters, Camp opposite the mouth of the Salado, East Bank of the Rio Grande, Dec. 19, 1842, in "A Record Book of the General & Special Orders and Letters of the South Western Army," p. [50]; see also, A. Somervell to G. W. Hill, [dated] Washington, Feb. 1, 1843, in *Morning Star*, Feb. 18, 1843.

cers; and it was agreed among them that permission should be asked of the *Commander in Chief* for a part, or as many as wished, to go down the river, in as much as many were badly mounted, and some on foot. This permission was asked and granted.[12] About three hundred, it was thought, would avail themselves of it; and perhaps, as many as *Three hundred and five*, *rank and file* (I think that was the exact number), were ready and anxious to go on and meet the foe. The Idea of encountering the fatigues of a five hundred miles march, to no purpose, was one that did not set well with their belligerent spirits and dauntless hearts. At *one* o'clock, General Summerville took up the line of march "with all the pomp and circumstances of glorious war," for the home of his Joys in the far distant settlements of Texas, followed by the remainder of the army—that portion who had become wearied of camp life. This force amounted, perhaps, to near three hundred men,[13] to whom, with their *redoubtable* General, we must here bid adieu. We may, perhaps, find occasion to allude to them hereafter, but we are done with their history. The most of them, perhaps all, were good men at home, peaceable citizens, and valuable in their vocations, and good soldiers when under a good commander. Upon them I bestow no censure, but rather, I would praise their endurance, for had they have seen any chance to do good service, I verily believe that they would have remained to a man. Farewell, then, to that band, Farewell! and may Heaven bestow upon them all that heart can wish or man desire. May their posterity, to the latest period of Time, ever be animated by the "Patriotism of their Fathers."

12. McCutchan holds that the request for permission by 305 of the men and officers to go down the Rio Grande for the purpose, they said, of obtaining badly needed supplies of food, clothing, and horses had been granted. This contention, however, is incorrect. Somervell refused the request, and those who refused to march home under his command violated orders. The contention of the more vociferous of those who marched to Mier that their separation from the command and descent against the Mexican frontier was "authorized" is not borne out by the facts. This editor, and student of the Mier expedition for more than thirty years, has found no evidence to support their claim.

13. The size of Somervell's returning force was 189, rank and file, being mostly the remainder of the drafted militiamen of Montgomery and Washington counties, the staff officers, and a part of the Houston volunteers. Nance, *Attack and Counterattack*, p. 565.

Chapter III

The Texians reorganize under Col. Wm. S. Fisher. Green placed in command of the lighters, and sent down by water, with instructions to keep pace with the army, and destroy all boats he might find on the river. Crossing of the Rio Grande on the 23d; entree into Mier; and the disposition of the Texians while in Town. Col. Fisher places the town under contribution. The Alcalde of Mier is taken as a hostage for the safe and punctual delivery of the articles required. Death of Jesse Yokehun. The Texians recross the river. The army descends the river, capture of two of their number, and their arrival at the point designated for the delivery of the Contribution. Appearances prognasticate a skirmish. The articles fail to arrive. Capture of a Mexican by the Scouts. The Captured Mexican gives considerable information in relation to a Mexican force. Col. Fisher determines on crossing to give battle. The Texians cross the river; Fisher addresses them; they receive the news of the capture of two of their scouts, and advance on the town of Mier. Crossing of the Alcantro and Battle of Mier. Surrender of the Texians. The loss in killed and wounded on both sides. The forces of the two armies; and a few general remarks.

On the Evening of the 19th the Texians moved down the river a short distance to a more convenient encampment, where they chose, by a voice unanimous, *Capt.* William S. Fisher[1] as their commander. On

1. Born in Virginia, William S. Fisher emigrated to Texas in 1834 and settled in the municipality of Gonzales in Green DeWitt's Colony. John Henry Brown says, in *Indian Wars and Pioneers of Texas*, pp. 16, 140–141, that Fisher was "a man of finished education and remarkable intelligence and one of the tallest men in the country. As a conversationalist he was captivating, ever governed by a sense of propriety and respect for others—hence a man of commanding esteem wherever he appeared." He represented Gonzales in the General Consultation in November 1835, served as a volunteer in the battle of Gonzales in October 1835, and assisted in the expulsion of General Martín Perfecto de Cos from San Antonio the following December. He was captain of Company I, First Regiment of Texas Volunteers, in

Fisher departing from his company, his First Lieutenant, Claudius Buster,[2] was chosen its Captain.

Fisher settled his plans at once, acting with energy, decision, and alacrity he sent General Green,[3] then a private in the command, with

---

the battle of San Jacinto; represented Gonzales in the House of Representatives of the First Congress of the Republic of Texas; served as secretary of war from Dec. 21, 1836, to Nov. 13, 1837; served for a brief period as chief recruiting officer for the regular army of Texas under the law of Dec. 21, 1838. In addition, Fisher participated in the Cherokee campaign during the summer of 1839; commanded the Texan troops in March 1840 in the Council House Fight with the Comanches who had come to negotiate at San Antonio; and in 1840 participated in the Federalist Wars in northern Mexico in support of Colonel Antonio Canales. Upon the organization of the troops in the vicinity of San Antonio on Nov. 21, 1842, Fisher was chosen to command a company of sixty-seven men in the First Regiment under Colonel James R. Cook on the Somervell Expedition. Brown, *Indian Wars and Pioneers of Texas*, pp. 16, 140–141; William C. Binkley (ed.), *Official Correspondence of the Texas Revolution*, I:467, 500n.; Joseph Milton Nance, *After San Jacinto*, pp. 29, 54, 90, 243, 271–272, 329, 362.

2. Claudius Buster was born Jan. 21, 1816, in Somerset, Pulaski County, Kentucky, son of William Woods and Margaret (Vaughan) Buster. He came to Texas in October 1836 with his father and settled in Washington County. He received a second class certificate (no. 112) for 640 acres for immigrating to Texas after Mar. 2, 1836, and before Oct. 1, 1837. He later located his section of land in Robertson County. From Mar. 25 to June 4, 1841, Claudius Buster served as a volunteer under Captain Thomas Green of Colonel Mark B. Lewis's command in a campaign against the Indians in the San Saba area; and in March 1842 he served as a private under General Edward Burleson in the Vasquez campaign and later in the Woll campaign. In the Somervell Expedition he was a second lieutenant in Captain William S. Fisher's company, Oct. 17 to Dec. 18, 1842; and, when Fisher was elected to command the Mier Expedition, Buster became captain of his company from Dec. 18, 1842, to Oct. 16, 1844. Claudius Buster, Public Debt Papers (Texas), Texas State Archives; *Galveston Daily News*, Apr. 23, 1882; J. M. Carroll, *A History of Texas Baptists*, ed. J. B. Canfield, p. 63; Certificate of Service by Captain of Volunteers Thomas Green, June 4, 1841, in Public Debt Papers (Texas); "Sketch of the Life of Claudius Buster," Daughters of the Republic of Texas Library, Alamo, San Antonio, Texas; Joseph Milton Nance, *Attack and Counterattack*, pp. 561n., 632.

3. Brigadier General Thomas Jefferson Green was born in Warren County, North Carolina, Feb. 14, 1802. He was a student at the University of North Carolina in 1819, and in 1822 he received an appointment to the United States Military Academy at West Point but stayed only four months (July 1 to Oct. 30, 1822). In 1823 he represented Warren County in the House of

about forty men, to take charge of Four Lighters which had been found near the mouth of the Rio Salado. These Lighters, made after the fashion, somewhat, of a common Ferry Boat, and Copper bottomed, would transport, with ease forty or fifty men, across the river—perhaps more, and were therefore a great acquisition to the Texians. General Green—Thomas Jefferson Green—had been in Texas for several years, and though a brave man, he certainly possessed but few qualifications as a General—that is, to fit him for that station. He was possessed with that degree of vanity that prompted him rather to rashness than cool, determined valour. He might be termed, by some, a man of tallent, which he did to some degree possess, but they were of an order that I would believe quite ordinary. Vain, bombastic, fond of praise, and withall, ambitious of military glory, he could well be called darring, even fearless; but he was unfit to command an army, though he had, I believe, held the rank of General, at least, such was his title.

Representatives of the North Carolina Legislature. Four years later, on Jan. 8, 1830, he married Sarah A. Wharton of Nashville, Tennessee, and settled in Mississippi. From there he moved to a plantation near St. Marks, Florida, where his only child, Wharton J. Green, was born. Thomas Jefferson Green served two years (1834 to 1835) in the territorial legislature of Florida. Following the death of his wife in March 1835 the war in Texas attracted his attention. He organized the Texas Land Company in 1836 and moved to Texas; but he quickly abandoned his colonizing project and on Mar. 19, 1836, obtained a brigadier general's commission in the Texan army from President David G. Burnet and returned to the United States to recruit volunteers for the Texas cause. He reached Velasco on the steamer *Ocean* on June 3, 1836, with some two hundred-thirty volunteers from New Orleans. He flouted the Texas government and ordered President Antonio López de Santa Anna and his officers removed from the Texan schooner-of-war *Invincible* on which they had been placed preparatory to being sent to Vera Cruz in conformity with the treaties of Velasco of May 26, 1836. He insisted that Santa Anna stand trial by court-martial but was unable to carry through on this idea.

Green represented Bexar County in the House of Representatives of the First Congress of the Republic of Texas and in 1837 was elected to the Senate of the Second Congress; but his seat was declared vacant after twenty-five days. He was a private, but a troublemaker, in the Somervell Expedition. When Somervell ordered the men home, Green elected to continue the campaign against Mexico and was second in command of the Mier Expedition. Upon his escape from prison in Mexico he wrote a history of that expedition in which he made a vigorous attack upon President Sam Houston. Walter P. Webb and H. Bailey Carroll (eds.), *Handbook of Texas*, I:728; Nance, *At-*

He was instructed to keep pace with the army in its march so as to offer facillities for its crossing, if necessary; and to destroy every boat he found on the river. This was done to prevent the enemy from crossing so sudden as to supprize the Texian troops. This flotilla was Bombastically called the Texian Fleet, and from the Texians Green ironically received the title of Commodore.

On the morning of the 20th the little band took up the line of march in as high spirits as ever a bridegroom went to his wedding with, and with equal impatience; all were anxious to try their rifles on the foe of Texas. They were much pleased with the spirit of their commander. The army proceeded down the river slowly, nothing occurring, except the occasional burning of a few small boats found on the river by Green's party, and the gathering of a few horses by the land forces.

On the morning of the 23rd, finding his position near the town of Mier,[4] Fisher determined on crossing and entering the town. As the better plan, he put out a Camp Guard, about fifty in number, in the charge of whom was left the horses, baggage, etectra, of the army, which crossed early and took the road to town, then about six miles distant, on foot. On entering the town, Fisher was informed that General Canales[5] was in the vicinity with seven hundred rancherro cavalry,

---

tack and Counterattack, pp. 517–518; Thomas Jefferson Green, *Journal of the Texian Expedition against Mier.*

4. The Lugar de Mier was a quiet, desolate, rough, gloomy adobe town founded by José de Escandón on Mar. 6, 1752, in a bend of the east bank of the Alcantro (Alamo) at a point nearly four miles from its junction with the Rio Grande. Countless revolutions had passed over it. Its people were poor farmers and cattle raisers. By land Mier was about thirty miles below Guerrero and by water much farther.

5. General Antonio Canales, whose rank in the Mexican army was that of colonel, was accorded the rank of general during the Federalist uprisings of 1838 to 1840, in which he headed the military forces of the short-lived so-called Republic of the Rio Grande. Before 1839 he had practiced law at Mier and had been a member of the legislature of Tamaulipas in 1832, where he had been president of the Chamber of Deputies.

Antonio Canales was not a military man by profession, but a lawyer with considerable education and culture. As Hobart Huson expressed it in "Iron Men," a manuscript found in the Archives, University of Texas, he was "the most persistent and unconquerable leader of Federalism in Northern Mexico," and it might be added that he pursued his political ideal with everything but talent. Canales was a small man of brown complexion, whose eyes, reported Gustave Dresel who met him in Houston in 1840, were "as false as those of a mustang." See p. 101 of Max Freud (trans. and ed.), *Gustave*

to which, however, no farther regard was paid than to keep the troops under arms while remaining in town to prevent a surprize. Capt. John R. Baker,[6] formerly Capt. Cameron's[7] first Lieutenant, but now the

---

Dresel's Houston Journal. Another person described him in the *Colorado Gazette and Advertiser*, May 23, 1840, as being approximately thirty-five years of age, "with a mild and intelligent expression of countenance and a high forehead denoting intellect." Although he possessed a rather magnetic personality, his skill in military leadership, upon which Mexican politics too often depended, was very limited. He had been one of the dominating forces in the closing days of the Federalist Wars, 1838 to 1840 and had been accorded the rank of general; but in Mexican military circles and among many Texans he still carried the title of colonel. His doublecross of the Texans who aided the Federalists in their cause was never forgotten or forgiven. In the battle of Mier he commanded the local *rancheros* (militiamen) or auxiliaries from the Villas del Norte of Camargo, Reinosa, Mier, and Guerrero. For a more comprehensive treatment of Canales's activities the reader is referred to Nance, *After San Jacinto*; and idem, *Attack and Counterattack.*

6. John Reagan Baker was born near Blue Springs, Green County, Tennessee, Aug. 6, 1809. He visited Texas in 1836 and returned in 1839 to participate in the Federalist Wars in northern Mexico, where he fought with Captain Ewen Cameron and Colonel Samuel W. Jordan in the battle of the *hacienda* Ojo de Agua, near Saltillo, Oct. 23, 1840. Afterwards, he settled at Aransas City and was elected sheriff of Refugio County on Feb. 1, 1841. In March 1842 he served under Ewen Cameron during the Vasquez disturbances and during the battle of Lipantitlán on the Nueces frontier in July 1842. He fought at Salado Creek as a lieutenant in Ewen Cameron's company on Sept. 18, 1842, against General Adrian Woll. On Nov. 3, 1842, he reached San Antonio as captain of a company of fifty men bent on carrying the war into Mexico. Webb and Carroll, (eds.), *Handbook of Texas*, I:99–100; Nance, *After San Jacinto*, p. 152; idem, *Attack and Counterattack*, pp. 348, 361n., 436, 561, 561n., 597, and 629.

7. Ewen Cameron was born in Scotland about 1807. He came to the United States before 1836. In 1836 he enrolled in the Kentucky Volunteers for the Texas Revolution. After San Jacinto he lived on the frontier around Victoria and Goliad, where he belonged to a group of "Cow Boys" who raided Mexican ranches below the Nueces River and drove out cattle. From Apr. 29, 1836, to Jan. 10, 1839, he served in the Texas army almost continuously, with the exception of a few months, as a "Permanent Volunteer" for varying periods of enlistment. He saw service under Clark L. Owen, Captain G. C. Briscoe, and Major George W. Bonnell, who lost his life on the Rio Grande as a member of the Mier Expedition. Cameron fought in the Federalist Wars, 1838 to 1840, in northern Mexico, where he gained the enmity of General Antonio Canales; he commanded a company in the battle of Lipantitlán,

Captain of the Spy Company, had accompanied the command with ten or fifteen mounted men. They reconoitered in the vicinity of the town, but made no discovery of any armed forces.

Fisher's demand on the town was an eight days' supply of sugar and coffee for Twelve hundred men, with some few other necessaries;[8] all of which the Alcalde promised to deliver at a designated point on the river on or before the next evening.

The behaviour of the men was unexceptionable in every respect during their stay in town.

Towards the close of the afternoon the army moved out of town in the same order in which they had entered it, taking the Alcalde with them as a hostage for the fulfillment of the stipulated requisition. The men becoming careless, and believing no danger near, paid little or no attention to order after they had passed out of sight of the town on their march to camp. About sundown, before we reached the river, Jesse Yokeham,[9] a lad of fourteen years old, was shot by the accidental discharge of Mr. Hill's[10] gun. The Ball passed through the small of his

---

July 1842 and in the battle of Salado Creek against General Adrián Woll in September 1842. Travis Bounty No. 136; Musters Rolls-Bounty File, Peter Goss; Robertson 2-651; Bounty Certificate No. 4241, Survey No. 32, San Patricio County; Bexar Bounty No. 1068; all in Land Office Records (Texas) in General Land Office. See also, Huson, "Iron Men," p. 77; Nance, *After San Jacinto*, pp. 64, 152, 213, 226, 326, 424, 475, 554–556; idem, *Attack and Counterattack*, pp. 253n., 348, 361, 399, 478–479.

8. Terms of the requisition are given in Green, *Journal of the Texian Expedition Against Mier*, pp. 75–76, and in a letter by Memucan Hunt to Francis Moore, Jr., editor of the *Telegraph*, [dated] Bexar, Jan. 8, 1843, in *Morning Star*, Jan. 17, 1843.

9. Jesse Yocum was one of the few survivors of the Yocum families of Liberty and Jefferson counties of east Texas who were accused of various crimes by their neighbors and were attacked, murdered, and virtually driven from the area during the Regulator-Moderator War in east Texas from 1839 to 1844. *Galveston Daily News*, Aug. 4, 1901; Maude Wallis Traylor, "Those Men of the Mier Expedition," *Frontier Times* XVI (April 1939):299–309; George Louis Crocket, *Two Centuries in East Texas*, pp. 193–203; Warren Wildwood, *Thrilling Adventures among the Early Settlers*, pp. 107–113.

10. John Christopher Columbus Hill was fifteen years of age at the time of the Mier Expedition and was born in Columbus, Georgia, Nov. 15, 1827. He came to Texas in the spring of 1835, settling with his father and other members of his family at Fayetteville, near La Grange. Following the death of Jesse Yocum, Hill may have had some second thoughts about coming back to Texas. His display of valor at Mier was no doubt an inducement for Santa

back, producing almost instant death. The Lad was borne to camp, and buried on the following morning will [with] all the honors attending military burial.

The command was late in crossing, and some did not reach camp untill long after dark. Col. Fisher, with two or three others and myself, were the last crossing. We had reached the river after dark and found no boat there fore our transportation. This had something alarming in it, for we presumed that they would not return for us without our hallowing for a boat, as they would not be likely to miss us for some time, at least; if we attempted to call, that call might bring down Canales's force upon us, as it was presumable he had been hanging on our rear! But, at length, having taken shelter in a thicket, on[e] of the men left us, and having gon[e] some distance above, called for a boat, which was immediately dispatched to our relief. I know not what may have been the feelings of the others of the party, but I was greatly relieved in mind when I found myself beyound gun shot from the enemy's shore and rapidly approaching the encampment of the Texian army.

The burial of young Yokehum, a noble boy, on the morning of the 24th, was a sad duty of the army, among whom he was a favorite. We gave him a soldier's burial, brushed away the falling tear, and discharged a farewell volley over his grave. That was all we could do. The poor youth had left without the consent of his friends who reside in Liberty County. He was a brave boy, possessed of great merit; had endured the hardships of the march with manly firmness, and at last, ere he could face the foe, was cut down in the bloom of youth by an unfortunate accident. But far more enviable was his fate than that which his unfortunate companions in arms were doomed ere long to encounter. Low lays his head; no useless coffin confines his breast; no gaudy shrod encumbers him; no funeral pile [pyre] marks the spot; but he rest in the grave of a soldier, where soldiers have laid him. May his rest be according to the deserts of the brave, the good, and the free.

Shortly after leaving the encampment on the morning of the 24th

---

Anna to adopt him in 1843. He lived the rest of his life in Mexico where he became a distinguished engineer. He died at Monterey, Mexico, Feb. 16, 1904, at the age of seventy-six. *Dallas Morning News*, Mar. 25, 1880; *Dallas Daily Herald*, Mar. 25, 1880; *Galveston Daily News*, Aug. 4, 1901; Webb and Carroll (eds.), *Handbook of Texas*, I:813. A photostatic copy of the death notice of Dr. John C. C. Hill, dated Monterey, Mexico, Feb. 16, 1904, is in the San Jacinto Museum of History.

A. S. Holderman[11] and Alexander Mathews[12] crossed the river in search of horses. Shortly after they had left the bank of the river, Mathews returned under full speed an[d] with the greatest tripirtation called for the boats, which were fortunately just passing. They rowed up to the bank, and taking him on board, enquired what could be the cause of his alarm? He replied that six or eight Mexicans had attacked himself and Holderman with such suddenness and skill that Holderman was captured and he had barely escaped with life and limb. I was with the boats in their descent and well remember the fear stricken features of Mathews, as, standing upon the bank, he called to us, "For God Sake! to bring over a boat and take him on board." His alarmed appearance induced us to believe that he might have been frightened, and thus sepperated from Holderman, and that the latter might yet come in; but our hopes were vain; he was indeed taken!

On this day, we moved but a short distance and encamped in a handsome place; Baker's Spy company on one side—that of the enemy, and the main army on the other—that of Texas. At dusk Gideon K. Lewis,[13] one of Baker's men, was captured within two hundred yards of Baker's encampment. This daring act was achieved by *Agatóne*,[14]

11. The Public Debt Papers (Texas) show this name as Allen K. Holderman. He appears as Allen S. Holderman on both the Muster Roll of James H. Gillespie's Company of Volunteers, Vasquez Campaign, 1842 in the Army Papers (Republic), Texas State Archives, and the Muster Roll of Captain Bartlett Sim's company, Nov. 21, 1842, South Western Army, Col. Ja[me]s R. Cook, in the Sam S. Smith Collection, Archives, University of Texas. He was a member of Captain William M. Eastland's company and died at San Luis Potosí, Mexico, in 1843 while a prisoner.

12. Alexander Matthews was a member of Captain Ewen Cameron's company of the Mier Expedition, later known as Captain Israel Canfield's company. Israel Canfield's diary, muster rolls, Texas State Archives.

13. Gideon K. Lewis gave up his job as cub reporter on the New Orleans *Daily Picayune* to enlist in the service of Texas as a member of Captain H. W. Allen's Mississippi Guards after the Vasquez invasion of 1842. Harbert Davenport to J. M. Nance, [dated] Brownsville, Texas, June 28, 1948, signed letter in possession of editor; Muster Roll of Captain H. W. Allen's Company [of] Mississippi Volunteer Guards in Service of the Republic of Texas, in Militia Rolls (Texas), Texas State Archives.

14. Agatón Quiñones, a celebrated Rio Grande robber and guerrilla leader, commanded the First Company of Explorers, numbering fifty men, in Lieutenant Colonel Ramón Valera's advance upon Goliad in March 1842 and was captain of a group of "explorers" in the Woll campaign of August and September 1842. Nance, *Attack and Counterattack*, pp. 15, 39, 223, 392; *Telegraph and Texas Register*, Apr. 3, 1844.

the celebrated Rio Grande Robber. Lewis said, after we had joined him in prison, that ere he was aware of the vicinity of an enemy, he was gaged, bound, and almost suffocated. He was then taken to Mier and sent before Ampudia.[15]

On the morning of the 25th, the Army moved down the river, and at 10 o'clock A. M. they encamped at the point designated as the place at which the articles of the requisition should be delivered according to promise.

Shortly after the army came to a halt, the scouts who had been sent down the river on the western bank returned, bring[ing] with them a Mexican, whom they had captured but a short distance from the Texian Camp. He was one armed, and apparently harmless in every respect; but the scout who discovered him thought it best to bring him into camp and present him to the Texian Commander. George Lord,[16] one of the spy company, who came in about this time—perhaps he brought in the prisoner, I do not remember—reported that he had discovered the trail of about six or eight hundred cavalry; stating that there were at least *six hundred*; but as his own opinion, from the breadth of the trail, he would say *not less than one thousand*. The prisoner, on being interrogated, stated that Genl. Ampudia, the com-

15. Pedro de Ampudia was born in Cuba in 1803 and began his military career in the Spanish army as a cadet of infantry. In August 1821 he landed at Vera Cruz with General Juan O'Donoju's forces and fought on the side of Mexican independence. After serving in various capacities in the Mexican army, he was named in 1839 commandant general of Tamaulipas and in 1840 for a short period served as provisional commander of the Army of the North. In 1842 he was again named commandant general of Tamaulipas and changed his headquarters from Tampico to Matamoros to be nearer to Texas. In December 1842 he hurried north from Matamoros to counter the Texan invasion. He commanded the defense of Mier. Alberto M. Carreño (ed.), *Jefes del ejército mexicano en 1847*, pp. 141–154.

16. George Lord was born in Essex County, England, on Apr. 21, 1816. In June 1834 he went to Canada, and two years later he was in New Orleans, where he worked on Mississippi steamers. He landed at Galveston, Texas, in February 1837 and soon joined the Texas army at Camp Independence on the Lavaca River. In 1838 he participated in a fight against the Indians on the Cibola River, and in March 1839 fought in Colonel Edward Burleson's company against Vicente Córdova near present-day Seguin. In 1839 he participated in the Federalist Wars in northern Mexico, after which he returned to Texas and settled at Victoria. In 1842 Lord joined the Somervell Expedition as a member of Captain Ewen Cameron's company. Traylor, "Those Men of the Mier Expedition," *Frontier Times* XVI (April 1939):299–309; idem, "Benjamin Franklin Highsmith," *Frontier Times* XV (April 1938):309–317.

mander in chief of the military post at Matamoros, was at Mier, with three hundred and fifty men and two pieces of artillery. Upon receiving this information. Col. Fisher turned to those about him, remarking, "Well, boys, as the enemy have made the necessary preparations to give us *powder* and *lead*, instead of *sugar* and *coffee*, we will attend the summons and draw our rations." This would seem a poor substitute in the eyes of hungry men, but one, nevertheless, which the Texian army was glad to anticipate. A Camp Guard was detailed forthwith, consisting principally of old men and the sick, numbering about forty-five, to whom was committed the care of the camp, horses, and baggage. It is my impression that a few of those who remained in camp would have been glad to be privileged to accompany the army in its attack on the town; but their day for duty had arrived, they had been detailed for the purpose, and no remedy could be had. After the disposition of the Camp Guards Capt. John R. Baker was sent forward, with ten or twelve mounted men, to reconoiter; and the army was ordered to begin their crossing. From twelve to two P. M. was occupied in crossing; and by half past two, it was ready for farther orders. The force consisted of two hundred and sixty one men—some say two hundred sixty two—all were armed, in high spirits, and generally good marksmen. The crossing was barely accomplished when the report of firearms came booming on the breeze. Many were the conjectures of the probable cause of these reports, and what their result, for they lasted but momentary. Fisher addressed the army in few but applicable words, setting forth the intention of the attack and using means to fire the valor and patriotism of his band, but he had not concluded ere the clatter of horse's hoofs on the smooth hard ground caught his ear, and suspended his harangue; and in a moment after, one of Baker's men galloped up and informed him that three of the advance under Capt. Baker had been led into an ambushcade, and two, Patrick H. Lusk[17] and Sam. H. Walker,[18] Captured! Fisher turned

17. Patrick H. Lusk participated in the Vasquez and Woll campaigns and joined the Somervell Expedition at the age of nineteen as a member of Captain Jerome B. Robertson's company, later changing to Ewen Cameron's company. He was captured at Mier and imprisoned in Mexico until released on Apr. 23, 1844, at the age of twenty-one. His mother was a sister of General John Coffee, one of General Andrew Jackson's favorite officers. Patrick H. Lusk, Public Debt Papers (Texas); Jonnie Lockhart Wallis and Laurance L. Hill, *Sixty Years on the Brazos*, p. 186; Nance, *Attack and Counterattack*, p. 644.

18. Samuel Hamilton Walker was born in Prince George County, Maryland, on Feb. 24, 1817, and at age nineteen enlisted for service from June 1836 to

to his men—shouting "Column! Forward! March!" Like magic, and with rapid strides, that little band moved off towards the foe. Then, for the first time during the Campaign, they saw and hailed with joy the prospect of joining in Battle with their swarthy antagonists. At dusk they came in sight of a retreating column of Cavalry, but were not able to come within rifle shot. In a short time the Scouts and pickets of the enemy began to fire and retreat untill their outposts were driven in; but still no execution done on either side.

About seven o'clock, P. M., the Texians came to a halt in the vicinity of Mier, separated from the town by the River *Alcantro*.[19] From this position men were dispatched to find the most suitable ford, one of whom, Joseph Berry,[20] fell from a precipice, or bluff, breaking his thigh about the middle. Berry was sent to a neighbouring hut, which had been vacated by its inhabitants, where he was left in charge of Doctor Sinixon[21] and nine of his company—or mostly of his company—as a guard, among whom was his brother, Bate[s] Berry.[22]

The ford was at length found, and ten men dispatched to take up a

---

May 1837 in the Indian Wars. In 1842 he came to Texas, where he became a member of Captain Jesse Billingsley's command in the Woll campaign and performed the duties of a scout. Later in the year he served in the Somervell and Mier expeditions. He soon became one of the most distinguished of Texas rangers. He was one of the leaders in the overthrow of the Mexican guard by the Mier men at the *hacienda* Salado but was among those recaptured and imprisoned in Perote Castle. During the Mexican War he was killed while leading a charge into Humantla, Tlaxcala, on Oct. 9, 1847. Eldon Stephen Branda (ed.), *Handbook of Texas*, III:1076; Nance, *Attack and Counterattack*, pp. 368, 382.

19. Río Alcantro (sometimes called the Alamo or El Cantaro) flowed eastward into the Rio Grande. In a bend of its bank nearly four miles from its junction with the Rio Grande (Río Bravo) was the town of Mier.

20. Joseph Berry was the son of John Berry and brother of Andrew Jackson Berry and John Bates Berry. He came to Texas in 1826 and settled at Bastrop in 1834. Webb and Carroll (eds.), *Handbook of Texas*, I:151; *Galveston Daily News*, Apr. 23, 1882.

21. John J. Sinnickson settled in Brazoria County, Texas, as early as 1836. In the spring of 1842 he served as a private in Captain John P. Gill's company in the Vasquez campaign and in the same capacity in Captain John S. McNeill's company in the Woll campaign, subsequently transferring to Captain Charles K. Reese's company. He was a physician and served as assistant surgeon on the Mier Expedition. In September 1870 he was a resident of Philadelphia, Penn. Nance, *Attack and Counterattack*, pp. 593, 635; *Daily Picayune*, Aug. 8 and 9, 1843; J. J. Sinnickson, Public Debt Papers (Texas).

22. For John Bates Berry see note 20 above.

position above and open a fire on the town in order to draw their attention and to permit of the crossing of the main force. This stratagem succeeded far enough to admit of one company reaching the opposite bank. As soon as the enemy was apprized of the error they had committed, they whealed and charged the position of the foremost company, which repelled the charge with such great slaughter that the squadrons, eleven hundred strong, all cavalry, left the contest and "retired for the night"; nothing more was seen or heard of them untill the following morning. During the time of crossing, however, the infantry, posted in the center of the town, kept up a heavy fire upon the Texians, which, being at a great distance, did no damage, with the exception of wounding one man, and that was but slight in its effect. Pursuing their march after crossing the Alcantro, the little band arrived upon the street below the square, where they were compeled to halt, while the head of the column should force an entrance into a house. They chose one which they supposed was in immediate connection with the main position of the enemy, but when too late to repair the error, they discovered their mistake. Their aim was to undermine the main position of the enemy, who occupied the tops of the houses, by working through the partition walls under cover of the outer walls, and thus bring on a conflict hand-to-hand, which they were confident would be decided in their favor. While resting in this position, awaiting the movement of the advanced body, the enemy began a heavy fire of musquetry upon that position more immediately exposed; to which the Washington County Company, commanded by Capt. Buster, was most exposed. As the fire commenced, Buster coolly ordered his men to kneel; and well it was that he gave this order, for although the night was dark, their balls were so well directed that they fell like hail against a wall immediately in the rear of Buster's Company, which was not over five feet high. Well do I remember the roar of that continuing peal of musquetry, the clatter and whistle of balls, and the bright blaze of their firearms, which displayed to our view the long line of Mexican soldiery upon [the] top of a house about eighty yards from us. Their fire made such light that we could distinguish almost their faces. Buster received this fire for several minutes without returning it, hoping that Fisher would either lead them on, or order them to return the fire; but neither one, nor the other being done, Buster, assuming the responsibility, order his men to "rise and fire!" In the execution of this order, one man, John C. Jones,[23] of Houston,

23. The name is John E. Jones, a member of Captain Claudius Buster's company.

fell dead; but the enemy's fire was, for the time, silenced; nor were the Texians further molested by it till after they had entered a house. While resting in this position, the first Cannon boomed through the air.

After having gained possession of a house, the Texians discovered that they had no cover leading to the square, but it was now too late to change their position. But, to make amends, as near as possible, for their misfortune, they possessed themselves of another house on the opposite side of the street, to which Maj[or] Murry[24] was sent with about one hundred men. When safely sheltered from the heavy fire of the enemy, which had now recommenced with redoubled vigor, a part of the men quitely laid themselves down to sleep, and others engaged in conversation, while about forty amused themselves by picking their chance to fire upon the enemy's artillery, which was planted within one hundred yards of the position of the Texian army.

The enemy's fire was incessant throughout the night, both musquetry and artillery. There is no sight more grand or sublime than the flash of opposing firearms at the hour of midnight, during one of those times when nature has put on her blackest mantle; and no sound is calculated to produce such an idea of grandure, and engender such intense excitement as the ringing report of rifles, the hoarse roar of musquetry, the awful thunder of artillery, and encouraging shouts of man, opposed to man, all mingled in[25] dinn an[d] confusion.

This night was by far the most exciting Christmas scene that ever I had witnessed! Never shall I witness another such! and there was more powder bursts, and a more oppressive shower of iron and lead than I desire to encounter again to as little purpose.

On the morning of the 26th the fire from the Texian force was poured in with greater and more distructive rapidity. Then it was, in fact, that the battle was begun in good earnest; then it was that the

24. Thomas W. Murray was adjutant-general of the Mier Expedition. Israel Canfield diary, muster rolls; Green, *Journal of the Texian Expedition Against Mier*, p. 441; and John Henry Brown, *History of Texas* II:250, give the name as "Thomas A. Murry" and "Thomas A. Murray." The Muster Roll of Capt. Ewen Cameron's company, First Regiment of South Western Army, Col. Ja[me]s R. Cook, in the Sam S. Smith Collection, gives the name as "T. Murray."

25. From this point to "On the morning of the 26th . . ." there is a slightly different version in a portion of a small-sized diary from which the diary here reproduced seems to have been copied with certain deletions and alterations made by its author. The original draft is reproduced in Appendix I of this book.

drowsy and inactive spirits of the Texians, rendered so by the dullness of a camp life, were roused to energetic activity; and then it was that the Mexicans learned that they delt with no tame or timorous foe. To one who has taste for the sublime this would have been a time of absorbing enjoyment, for though those instruments were deadly, and of terror engendering nature, there is a grandure—an awful sublimity in the mingled roar of rifles, musquetry, and artillery, when accompanied by the shouts of contending foes—cries of exaltation and imprecations of discomfiture, which would give animation to the dullest mind, and almost move to deeds of daring the heart of the Craven! After about two hours of hard fighting, the Mexicans were compelled to abandon for the time their cannon, the Texians having kill[ed] two entire artillery companies, with the exception of five men, three of whom were wounded, leaving only two fit for duty. The Mexican infantry fought principally from the tops of the houses, around the flat roves [roofs] of which there extends a rampart from two to three feet in highth, making an excellent defense; and at this time there were but few soldiers bold enough to raise their heads above their ramparts, and but few of those who did act so injudiciously, ever withdrew them in time to escape the unerring aim of more than one alert Texian rifleman. Ultimately, however, they withdrew their infantry from the tops of the houses in an order to charge the position of the Texians with the evident intention of dislodging them, and taking their position at the point of the bayonet. The fire was still kept up by the Texians whenever an object appeared worthy of their notice, and the enemy too kept up a constant fire with the exception of a short interval about the time of the disabling of their artillery; and even during that interval their fire was incessant from remote parts of the town too far off to take effect. During the manuvering of a large body of Infantry which appeared to have a design of coming to close quarters, an event which the Texians calmly and cooly awaited, with a momentary anticipation of it; during this time the Mexicans had gained possession of their artillery by roping it from behind a house and drawing it off. As soon as they had regained possession of it, the[y] planted it in a less exposed position, and maning it with Infantry, they let the Texians know that, though crippled, it was not disabled. At length the assaulting column of infantry began its advance. Their progress was rapid, and in most beautiful and impressive order; on, on they came, a dark frowning mass, with arms to a shoulder and bayonets set; in short, they presented a front that it would seem hard to break. About forty or fifty Texians, the only ones disengaged, led on by Col. Fisher, steped proudly and firmly into the street, formed in a single, or perhaps, double line across the street and calmly awaited the onset of that grim band of mustached soldiers. Not an eye quailed, not a muscle quivered, nor a hand trimbled of that little band, as quietly abiding their time, they carefully inspected their arms! it seemed, indeed, as if every one felt that his single arm alone would decide the coming struggle, which appearances justified them in believing would probably be hand to hand! At length, when within Eighty yards of the Texian Line the Mexican musquets came to a present, as if by the movement of a single hand—a momentary halt, and their whole front was involved in flame and smoke, a long contined roar burst forth, and the Leaden messengers of death speed on their way to the invaders of Mexican soil and redressers of the wrongs of Texas! Hark, that shout of exultation from Mexico, and wail from the Prairies of Texas, as another deadly, awful volley is poured in by the still advancing collumn, now spread into a mass of Platoons filling the street through which they advance as if the day were their own. A few of that band of Texians have fallen. Capt. William Ryon[26] is down, but up again as if by magic, while his eye is still fierce and his arm nerved for the contest! but few, perhaps two, remain on the earth, but the rest stand unmoved—unawed! The Mexicans have advanced to within forty yards, the smoke has cleared away, and now—mark nerved arms and steady eyes—the rifle is aimed, and hear the sharp clear ring of those rifles as they belch forth death to numbers of the advancing soldiery! Now pause and behold the scene; that fire was too well aimed, and the effect too deadly, for the objects of it to stand another. It has done its duty well; the enemy are broken—panic struck—and now that lastly "*Hurra for Texas*" coming from the Texian line is heard by a retreating foe. The Mexican[s] fled to shelter, leaving numbers on the ground to rise no more till the last trump[et] shall thunder in their ears a summons to judgment. The enemy made one or two other attempts to dislodge the Texians, with a like result

26. William M. Ryon was born in Winchester, Kentucky, and emigrated to Texas in 1837, landing at the mouth of the Brazos River. At Velasco he clerked, kept a hotel, and pursued various occupations. In 1839 he was a member of a surveying party that laid out the city of Austin. During the Ramón Valera-Vasquez invasion in the spring of 1842 he served as a private in Lafayette Ward's company from Jackson County from Mar. 6 to June 6. On Nov. 3, 1842, he reached San Antonio as a captain in charge of forty-six men, and on Nov. 21 his company went into the First Regiment of Somervell's army. William M. Ryon, Public Debt Papers (Texas); Brown, *History of Texas*, II:252; idem, *Indian Wars and Pioneers*, pp. 309–311; Nance, *Attack and Counterattack*, pp. 45, 436–437, 472, 597–598.

of the first. They had attempted the position of Capt. Cameron, but that brave Scotchman, backed by his "Western Boys," was as immovable as the rock of ages; and when pressed upon by a charge of the enemy, he quitly [quickly] set [down] his gun—his death dealing yager,[27] carring twelve balls to the Pound, and took to a convenient pile of stones from which he pelted them most soundly, and succeeded in repulsing the assault. About this time—between the hours of Nine and Twelve A. M.—the battle raged at its hottest contest. The Enemies cannon sent forth collumns of flame, their musquetry poured forth volley after volley in rapid succession, making an incessant roar; the Texian rifles answered promptly, belching forth death to the foe at every ring of their clear tones showers of iron, copper, and leaden hail fell thick and fast, and the Angel of distruction set clothed in blood-stained raiments of glory over the town of Mier.

Where firey distruction swept around,
Together were death and glory found!
Amid death shots, falling thick and fast,
Many great and brave men breathed their last.

During this wild rage of the contest, perhaps about Eleven o'clock, a man by the name of Davis[28]—known as *Walking Davis*, and Bate[s]

27. Yager was also spelled "jaeger" or "jager." The word "jaeger" means hunter, marksman, or gamekeeper in German but came to be applied to a specially designed rifle developed and used by hunters, marksmen, and trained marksmen in military units. It was a fine, short-barreled muzzle-loading rifle, usually European made, and used widely in Europe and America. It was considered by many to be the first really important rifle in history. Harold Leslie Peterson and Robert Elman, *The Great Guns*, pp. 80–89, with illustrations.

28. At this point in the diary McCutchan becomes a little confusing. What he means to say is that Thomas ("Walking") Davis and John Bates Berry escaped from the hut, when it was attacked, and made their way into the Texan position in town. Davis, of Washington County and previously from Ireland, was one of seven men left in a hut on the north bank of the Alcantro to protect Joseph Berry of Brazoria County, who had broken his thigh while descending the embankment of the river to go into Mier. McCutchan tells about nine rifles playing upon the Mexican cavalry, indicating that there must have been at least a total of ten or eleven men in the party of Texans in the hut. One can assume that Joseph Bates Berry was not able to fire a rifle at passing cavalry and that maybe even Dr. Sinnickson did not participate in the firing. McCutchan does not give the names of all of those in the hut. General Green says, *Journal of the Texian Expedition*, pp. 84 and 92, that with Joseph Berry and Dr. Sinnickson there was detailed a

Berry, two of the guard left with Joseph Berry, came upon the position when pursued by a band of Mexicans. This guard was left there under the general instructions to send for them as soon as the main body should acquire a place of shelter, but in the hurry, confusion and excitement of the evening they were forgotten and thus neglected, untill after daylight on the morning of the 26th, when it had become to late to bring them over, or even inform them of the locality of the Texian forces. We can better imagine than express their feelings when thus cruelly abandoned. The appearance of these two men created no little surprise. Their statement was to this effect: that about nine o'clock the enemy discovered their position, and immediately began an attack upon it by sending three hundred cavalry under Capt. *Elduret*[29] to dislodge them and ride them down. This body of cavalry was instantly repulsed by the nine rifles, which plaid upon them with distructive effect from holes hastily made in the old mud walls of the hut in which Berry's guard had been placed. Greatly incensed at this audacity on the part of so weak a garrison, and determined not to be by them foiled, the enemy planted a cannon—six pounder—a short distance from the little mud fortress, but out of the range of its rifles, and commenced a cannonade. The first few shot[s] from the cannon passed far above the mark, but Berry's guard knew that a few more discharges would give them the proper range; and being well assured that those thin mud walls would afford no protection against a six pounder, they, at Berry's earnest persuasion resolved upon leaving it, to try, at all hazards, to join the main body. To surrender, they could not think of. Bates Berry was not willing to leave his brother, but his brother told him to go—saying, "Your presence here cannot avail me; you would give me no protection; if the[y] kill me, they would also you; and I am crippled, and they may not hurt me; but if you remain, they may kill us both. Your presence might make against me, while it can do me no good. Go, then! and if I die, live to revenge my death!" It was arranged that Sinixson, being naturally a cripple, should remain with Berry, and that the others, nine in number, should sally from the

---

guard of seven and that David H. E. Beasley was one of the guard and was captured. Hubert Howe Bancroft, in his *History of Texas and the North Mexican States*, II:363, reports that Joseph Berry and three others were killed, three were captured, and two escaped into town.

29. Trinidad Aldrete had formerly lived in Texas on the Guadalupe River near Victoria, and it has been reported that after the Mexican War he was killed in Texas by the Berry boys. A. J. Sowell, *Early Settlers and Indian Fighters of Southwest Texas*, p. 49; idem, *History of Fort Bend County*, p. 187.

House, and make their way to their friends, or find an honorable death in struggling against the overwhelming numbers of the foe. One or two[30] of them fell directly after leaving the house and several others were brought down. Richard Keene[31] was so closely pursued that he took shelter in a house, where he was captured. Davis and Bates Berry had reached the middle of the Alcantro, when turning to discharge their rifles, which they had loaded as they ran, they discovered young Austin[32] halt a short distance from the stream, turn upon his rapidly advancing foe, and level his rifle, which missed fire; but the noble young man never again turned his back upon his foe. Seeing that they would be upon him he clubbed his rifle, and the next instant he was surrounded by the enemy's cavalry. He there, arms in hand, consecrated that spot to all who breathe the air of freedom by bedewing it with the uncowered blood of a youthful freeman. Davis and Berry fortunately crossed the river at the foot of the street upon which their friends were posted, and thus by apparent chance they reached the main position of the Texian Army. During this time the battle was raging fiercely; there was no time even to congratulate Davis and Berry upon their escape, or to surmise as to what might have been the fate of their companions. This mad rage continued, untill about one o'clock P. M. when the enemy ceased his fire and sent in a flag of truce. When the flag was seen advancing some few of the Texians wished to shoot it down; but Col. Fisher ordered the fire to cease, and the men

30. William Hopson and A. Jackson were shot down immediately outside the house. Both were members of Captain Claudius Buster's company; Hopson was a single man. Public Debt Papers (Texas); C. K. Reese, Miscellaneous Claims Papers (Texas), Texas State Archives.

31. Richard Y. Keene, of Washington County, had served in the Vasquez campaign under General Edward Burleson and was a member of Captain Claudius Buster's company in the Mier Expedition. He had lost property in Woll's invasion of September 1842. Muster Rolls (Republic), Texas State Archives; Memucan Hunt to Francis Moore, editor of the *Telegraph*, [dated] Bexar, Jan. 8, 1843, in *Morning Star*, Jan. 17, 1843.

32. James Austin, son of Captain Henry Austin of Brazoria County, was only eighteen years of age. He had begun to nag his father about joining the army when he was sixteen; but, commented Rebecca Smith Lee, in *Mary Austin Holley*, p. 311, "he showed," in the spring of 1841, "no inclination to become a soldier or a farmer or anything else that required him to assume responsibility. He liked to fish and hunt and go on expeditions in the new country, if someone else showed the way." See ibid., pp. 304, 311, 318–319; William R. Hogan, "Life of Henry Austin," *Southwestern Historical Quarterly* XXXVII (1933–1934):201.

not to molest the flag, saying, at the same time that "His name should not be sullied by an act of such barbarity." The flag arrived born by Doct. Sinixson, who had been left with Berry, and accompanied by Lieut. Elduret as interpreter, Col. Blanco,[33] and one or two[34] other Mexican officers. Col. Fisher demanded to know the occasion of the flag bein sent, and was informed that "*Genl. Ampudia*, commander-in-chief of the Post of Mattamoras, demanded the surrender of the Texian forces, and in case of a refusal *every Texian should be put to the sword*." Fisher requested an hour for consideration, which was readily and willingly granted, for Col. Blanco knew that he had the Texians then. During the truce, Fisher visited Ampudia at his quarters. What he thare said and done is not known sufficiently to be recorded. But it is known that a solemn treaty was entered into between them. This treaty was read to the Texians by Lieut. Elduret, who had formerly lived in Texas, and was perhaps educated in Kentucky. He read this treaty as setting forth that the Texians who would lay down their arms should receive the treatment due to prisoners of war according to the law of nations but the truth was, that by that treaty we were to be treated according to the magnanimous will of the magnanimous nation.[35] About three o'clock the Texians, by two or three and some times half a dozen at a time, marched into the square and laid down their arms in the presence of the Mexican forces; and found themselves cooped up in rooms—crowded together, at the will and mercy of the most barbarous people that are permitted to disgrace the name of civilization; and many of them for the first time beheld the glorious light of Heaven through prison gratings.

33. Santiago Blanco was a native of Yucatán who began his military career as a cadet of artillery, May 17, 1827, and graduated from the Colegio Militar on Mar. 12, 1830, as a second lieutenant of engineers. In 1834 he contributed to the restoration of order in Yucatán and in 1840 served as quartermaster of General Rivas' division in the battle of Santa Rosa. In 1842 he joined the Army of the North as adjutant to General Pedro de Ampudia. Carreño (ed.), *Jefes del ejército mexicano*, pp. 247–250.
34. Other Mexican officers entering the Texan position were Colonel José María Carrasco; General Rómulo Díaz de la Vega; Lieutenant Trinidad Aldrete, as interpreter; and Padre Rafael de Lira, the priest of Camargo—all of whom either had had previous contact with Texans during the Federalist Wars or had lived in Texas.
35. According to the terms of surrender, the prisoners were to be "treated with consideration which is in accordance with the magnanimous Mexican nation." *Telegraph and Texas Register*, Feb. 1, and May 3, 1843; *New Orleans Bulletin*, Jan. 26, 1843; *Morning Star*, Jan. 31, 1843.

Honor and Glory to every Texian who will lay down his life, rather than part with his arms. Let the Battle cry of Texas, henceforth be "*Victory or Death*!" and let her sons go forth with the determination to *Conquer* or *Die*, then Texas need fear no foe.

Would it be improper here to record again the name of Genl. Summerville in connection with the disaster just fallen upon the "Mier men?" It is to him, in part, that they owe their present imprisonment. Had he have conducted the expedition as he should—had he have crossed the river at Loredo immediately upon reaching it, the disgraceful robery of that town would not have occurred; the men, being engaged would not have become dishartened; and many of the evils which befell the army would never have been experienced. This force of near eight hundred men could have swept the valley of the Rio Grande by rapid movements, and returned home with honor and but little, if any, loss.

In this engagement, the enemy lost perhaps about six hundred or more killed and two hundred wounded, but the number, however, could not be correctly ascertained by the Texians. Ampudia, in a subsequent conversation with Fisher, stated that the engagement shortened his muster rool near one thousand men;[36] and that he suposed some of them had deserted. Ay, deserted, but most probably to enlist in the service of his Satanic Majesty.

The Texian losses in killed, eleven—six of whom belonged to Capt. C. Buster's Company from Washington County, and in wounded twenty-three. These poor fellows fell bravely, and by a noble death they escaped great suffering. It is not known that they were allowed a grave. But

> Their spirits are now with the glorious dead,
> While their bodies are among the enemy,
> And base and vilanious reptiles o'er them tread—
> Unwept, unmourned lie the sons of Liberty.

Unwept and unmourned, save by the remnant of their companions, who must ever remember them with animation and pride.

The Mexican forces consisted of about two thousand regular Infantry, one thousand or there abouts of Cavalry, and the citizens of the place, making a whole force of not less than three thousand men

36. No other account places the Mexican losses in killed and wounded this high. The Mexican losses, even according to their own admission, were far greater than the Texan losses.

at the lowest calculation.[37] Canales, a Mexican well known to many persons as the famous traitor of the Federation, commanded the rancherro[38] Cavalry. To oppose the Mexicans, there was a force of two hundred an[d] sixty one or two Texians—not more, at any rate.

The fight lasted about *Eighteen hours*. An account of this engagement justifies somewhat the great antipathy of Mexicans to anything like a contest with Texians.

After the engagement, it was ascertained that Joseph Berry was most barbarously murdered. One of [the] Texians—an old ship Captain[39] when out with a guard found the body of Berry's which was naked and pierced with fourteen lance holes. This act, as subsequently ascertained, was perpetrated by Capt. Elduret with the cold blooded ferocity of a coward and barbarian. Berry's thy [thigh] was broken by his fall on the previous evening, and when the enemy found him in the house, he was unable to raise himself up; and in this situation Elduret was dastardly enough to murder him. This act was boasted of by Elduret's friends as a feat of bravery! but the world will not call it thus.

Sinixson was reserved to bear the flag of truce, and it was surmised by many and believed by the majority that his liberty had been promised him. It seems that he was the only one who was placed upon parole, and that was done one or two days after the battle. It also seems that he was in momentary expectation of his liberation from the surrender untill it actually took place in the city of Mexico. He must have known something of the Mexican position, but nothing escaped his lips in relation to it when he came up with the flag of truce. It may have been that one word from him at that time would have saved his countrymen, and there could possibly have been no principle of honor that should have closed and sealed his lips.

Suspicions were, and are still, entertained of his faith by nearly all of the "Mier Men." It may be, however, that the Doctor was alarmed by the new relations which he had unwittingly contracted, and that being in the situation to which he was unused, he may not have been able to divine what really was his duty. It could seem, however, that

37. These figures are substantially correct.

38. See footnote 5 above.

39. Samuel C. Lyon, the old sailing master and Thomas Jefferson Green's next-door neighbor in Texas for six years, upon Green's recommendation was sent with the troops in search of the Texan camp on the east side of the Rio Grande. Lyons had guided the so-called "flagship" of the flotilla of six boats that had descended the Rio Grande from Guerrero under the overall command of General Green.

if he knew any thing, his duty was clearly marked out. Let others pass their judgment upon the facts.

In the succeeding chapter, other matters in relation to the Expedition, the men concerned therein, and incidents of the battle, will be more closely observed, as that will be devoted principally to general remarks.

Chapter IV

The disposition of the men as related to our engagement with the enemy; Col. Fisher's conduct, excused in part by the conduct of the men. An allusion to those who wished to make their escape by cutting their way out of the town through the Enemy's lines. Accounts of personal valor during the engagement. The cannon might have been taken—madness of such an attempt; with various other incidents connected with the battle. And A[m]pudia's desire to capture the Texian Camp Guard; his failure in that enterprise; Ampudia's disappointment at not getting a Texian flag; and his joy over the acquisition of a "Union Jack." An allusion to the services of Doct. Wm. F. McMath.

It would seem evident that a body of two hundred and sixty one men would rarely be found among whom fewer dastards would be gathered than there were among the Texians in their attack on the town of Mier. They entered the place without reluctance and nobly performed their duty while there. It may be, and it is said by some, that their composition was strongly impregnated with the genuine tincture of Cowardice; but that number must have been comparatively few, and as any discrimination in that respect might prove unjust, in at least a few instances, we will refrain from particularity.

Col. Fisher receives censure from many; but, though experience has taught, he may, in some particulars, have persued an ill course, let us by a plain and concise statement of facts and circumstances see whether all the censure is due him, or whether a portion should not rest upon the shoders of the majority of the army. Fisher is undoubtedly a brave and generous man; this none will doubt. He entered the town of Mier under the impression there were but few Mexican soldiers in the place, naturally supposing that had this overwhelming force have been present, with Ampudia at their head, the General would not have lain still to wate the attack of a mere handfull of men; but that, upon the contrary, he would have thrown his force between this small body and their homes, thus to cut them off from hope of retreat, and annihilate them at one stroke. Had the Mexicans only numbered four [hundred], six [hundred], or even one thousand men, the force of the Texians would have been none too small to combat them. The real force of the Mexicans was not ascertained untill the following morning, the 26th, and it was then too late to justify a retreat by the Texians. When the flag of truce came in, it was presumed that the Mexicans sought the capitulation in order to save private property in the town; but, this being the case, the confusion which the Texians presented was fully sufficient to induce the Mexican officer to demand a surrender. Now, this confusion was not the work of Fisher, but that of the men. Many of those who had fought gallantly were opposed to holding out, and some, it is confidently asserted, had laid down their arms before the hour of consideration had expired. No one who is acquainted with the general conduct of Texian volunteers will even ask why Fisher did not preserve better order, for it is known that they were generally men of their own heads. The truth is that Fisher acted unwisely when he requested an hour for consideration. When he heard Ampudia's proposal —when he heard that the Texians should surrender, or be put to the sword, he should have replied to this effect: "Return, doff your white flag, and say to Ampudia that he must take our lives, ere he gets our arms; and that if he feels disposed to put us to the sword, he must come on, and come at his peril," and in case he had given that reply Ampudia would have found his match. Even had Fisher have known that he must eventually surrender, this would have been a proper reply to a *Mexican* commander. But there are—besides the disorderly conduct of his men—many things which rise up to plead Fisher's excuse, to some of which it is seemed not improper to allude. The ammunition of the Texians was getting short, some were nearly destitute at the time of the surrender, and if the battle had gone on as it had for the three or four previous hours, nearly half of the Texians, if not more, would have been out of this essential requisite. They might, perhaps, have held the town till night and then have gone out; but this was opposed by perhaps a majority of the men; while others, who were willing to fight on till night and then effect their retreat, were opposed to an attempt at that purpose by daylight, which would have been madness in the extreme. What was a commander to do in this situation? What *could* he do with a set of men who obeyed but few, if any orders, save those which agreed with their own notions of Generalship? Fisher felt all the responsibility of his station, without the means of prosecuting any plan of his own; and hence, what could he do, more than to save, if possible, the lives of his men? True, *an honorable death* would have been far—far preferable to that life preserved at such costs; but let all the world remember that had Fisher have refused this flag and had the Texians been butchered—masacred—the town of

Mier would have been remembered and pointed out as the place of *Fisher's* consumate head strong folly, he would only have been remembered as the reckless adventurer who led to slaughter a small band of noble Texians! His name would have suffered alone. True it is, that from every circumstance afterwards ascertained, if the Texians had only ordered off the flag and held out one hour longer, Ampudia would have evacuated the town and performed a precipitate retreat upon Matamoras; but this was not known, nor even surmised by Fisher; nor had he any means, whatever, to ascertain what the situation of the Mexican army was at that time. The Texians had no idea that they had done half the execution among the Enemy that they afterwards ascertained had been done. They could see a few dead bodies, and could see that the Mexicans were, at times, somewhat disordered and confused by their well directed fire; but it was not untill after the surrender that they learned the awful greatness of the execution, that blood was dripping from the gutters of the house tops, and that they had struck terror to the heart of *Every* Mexican! Had they previously have known this much, or the half of it, they would not have given their arms into the hands of the Mexicans. Experience taught what wisdom could never have foretold. Then let not Fisher be exclusively blamed; but let the censure rest where it is properly due. When Fisher is called to stand before the bar of God, he will there be met by no accusation on account of his conduct at Mier! If any error he did commit, it was one into which others would have been as apt to fall.

However, according to the practice of Nations in civilized warfare, the Texians would have been justified in shooting down the flag of truce; or rather, in retaining its bearers; for, according to that practice when a flag is sent and received, both parties shall suspend all hostile movements and preparations; this was strictly adhered to by the Texians, but not so by the Mexicans for they took advantage of the truce to regain some of the positions from which they had been driven.

There were about sixty men who wished to cut their way out of town.[1] This mad attempt was to be headed by Maj. Murry. It is not probable that ten men of that number, had the attempt been made, would have got one mile from town. These men maddened by their situation were willing to undertake anything, but when reason admonished them of the madness of their project, they desisted and sullenly

1. This statement is probably accurate, but it was a forlorn hope to think that the men could have fought their way out of Mier, even had they been able to hold out until dark.

give up their arms. It is not necessary to mention any names of that party, other than that of its commander, which has already been given.

There were many deeds of valor performed, which, however, speak not so much in the deeds themselves, as the manner of their performance. An allusion to some, in particular, is not to be un[der]stood as detracting from those facts which may not be mention[ed]; nor must it be supposed that those persons mentioned were the only ones who possessed undauted hearts throughout the action. Upon the contrary, let it be understood, that if any distinction is really due, it is too difficult to tell upon whom it should fall among near two hundred and sixty men who acted almost invariable as valor dictated; there are however some few incidents that should be particularly mentioned; and many, too, which will not be noticed. Perhaps, among the bravest of the brave, the name of the lamented *Captain Ewing Cameron* should be recorded. The repulse which he gave the enemy with a shower of stones is perhaps among the best evidences of his cool contempt of the Mexican soldier's prowess, and his utter disregard of personal danger; but there were other feets performed by him upon that day which go equally far to prove his value as a soldier and citizen. He was particularly careful of the lives of others, but unmindful of his own, when good could be achieved by its exposure. And though by a foul murder he has passed from time to eternity—though his last battle is fought and his last blow struck, and though his body is mouldering in the dust of an enemy's country, his memory—the recollection of the man and of his deeds—is sustained in the hearts of his companions, who, perhaps less fortunate than himself, are yet doomed to clank their chains in the hole of Mexican power, with an uncertain fate—an unfixed destiny awating them in the revelations of future time.

Never did mortal man display greater contempt for danger than did the brave and regretted Doct. Brenham,[2] who has subsequently fallen in a struggle to regain that liberty so unfortunately lost.

Mr. Wicks (or Weeks[3]) displayed an energy and spirit that have

2. Richard Fox Brenham was born in Woodford County, Kentucky, about 1810; attended Transylvania University in Lexington, Kentucky, where he received a medical education. He migrated to Texas, where he served in the Texan army from June 15 to Sept. 15, 1836. He was one of the commissioners on the Santa Fe Expedition but had returned from imprisonment in Mexico in time to join the Somervell Expedition to the Rio Grande in violation of his Mexican parole and his own word of honor. Walter P. Webb and H. Bailey Carroll (eds.), *Handbook of Texas*, I:213.

3. Henry D. Weeks served as a member of the San Patricio Minute Men in 1841 under Captain A. T. Miles, until Miles' "odious," questionable charac-

never been excelled. He had been twice shot down, receiving wounds that seemingly would have disable[d] ordinary men at each of the two shots, and when brought to earth the third time, finding by repeated exertion that he was unable to rise—that the last ball had done its work too surely, in the hight and pride of his manly unconquerable soul he rested upon one arm, and where balls were flying thick and fast as hail, he drew a pistol, and waving it around his head shouting thrice in succession "*Hurra for Texas!*" and when his friends were bearing him to the house, he begged them to let him remain in the street to witness the glory of the arms of Texas. That man, after being three times badly wounded, made his escape from Mier within seven or eight weeks from the time of his capture, going off with seven others.

There were several small boys along[4] who behaved in a heroic manner.

At one time in the morning the Texians could have taken the cannon of the enemy; but such an attempt might probably have failed and at all events, they would have lost many men, which they had not to spare. From the time a party left the Texian position for that purpose they would have been exposed to a heavy cross fire from the enemy untill they had returned, which would have sacrificed many men in an object that was but poorly calculated to prove generally beneficial; for though the Texians might have gained something by the use of the cannon, it was but of little avail to the Mexicans, who performed no object worthy of note by its use during the whole engagement.

---

ter forced his removal from command in September 1841 and replacement by Captain W. J. Cairns to command the company. In Miles' company were such well-known men of the Mier Expedition of the following year as Thomas W. Murray, W. H. Van Horn, Patrick Maher, H. D. Weeks, L. F. Mills, Ewen Cameron, William Ripley, J. M. Simon, Henry Whalen, and George Anderson. L. S. Hagler to Saml. A. Roberts, Houston, Oct. 5, 1841, in Domestic Correspondence (Texas), Texas State Archives; Muster Roll of Captain A. T. Miles' company for May 14 to August 28, 1841, in Muster Rolls (Rangers), 1838–1860, Texas State Archives; Joseph Milton Nance, *After San Jacinto*, pp. 462–475, 554–556. Weeks also saw service in Captain John M. Smith's company of volunteers under Colonel Clark L. Owen from Mar. 6 to June 6, 1842, and in Ewen Cameron's company in the Somervell Expedition. See Militia Rolls (Texas), Texas State Archives, and Muster Roll of Capt. Ewen Cameron's company, South Western Army, Sam S. Smith Collection, Archives, University of Texas.

4. The boys of the Mier Expedition were John Christopher Columbus Hill, age 15; Gilbert R. Brush, age 17; and William Harvey Sellers, age 15.

Several Mexicans advanced so near to the Texian lines that we should be justified in thinking them brave. One or two were shot down within thirty or forty feet of the Texian line. One was shot down within twenty steps while trying to rob the dead body of a Texian; and when down, he still tryed to effect the same object, keeping his hands upon the body untill shot the third time and life became extinct.

"His ruling passion strong in death!"

Two men, Chalk[5] and St. Clare,[6] when they discovered that the Texians were going to surrender, conceived and successfully put into execution a bold plan for their escape. Without hinting to any one their intention, they entered a Bake Oven in the back yard of one of the houses then in possession of the Texians, and there lay concealed untill late at night, and then made good their escape, reaching the Texian camp about daylight on the following morning. It was not known by the Texians for some months after their capture what had become of these two men. A fortunate star guided their destiny.

Ampudia sent three hundred cavalry to take the Texian Camp Guard, supposing that there would be no difficulty in their accomplishing that object, as he had requested Col. Fisher to command them to surrender, who replied to him that if he wanted them he must go and take them. With this body of three hundred cavalry commanded by Capt. Pañia,[7] he sent one of the Texian prisoners, Capt. Lyons,[8] an old sailing master, with the instructions that he should tell his companions to surrender to Capt. Pañia. This body did not leave untill late on the evening of the 26th and consequently, when they arrived on the following morning upon the bank of the river opposite to the Texian encampment, there were but two Texians to be seen, Doct. Watson[9]

5. Whitfield Chalk was born in North Carolina on Apr. 4, 1811, and in 1823 he moved to Tennessee with his parents. After ordination as a minister in the Methodist Episcopal church, he came to Texas in 1839. He was a member of Captain John G. W. Pierson's company of the Somervell Expedition. Houston Wade, "The Story of Whitfield Chalk," *Frontier Times* XVIII (November 1940):77–78; *La Grange Journal*, Aug. 29, Sept. 5, 12, and 19, 1940.

6. Caleb St. Clair was from Gonzales. *Telegraph and Texas Register*, Jan. 25, 1843. Israel Canfield diary, Texas State Archives, shows the name as William St. Clair, which is incorrect.

7. The name is Miguel de la Peña; see *Almanaque Imperial para el año de 1866*, p. 224.

8. Samuel C. Lyon; see Chapter III, footnote 39.

9. Dr. Robert Watson was from Houston. In December 1837 President Houston nominated two persons for positions of surgeon in the army, one of these

and Maj. Bonnell,[10] and but small vestages of the encampment. Lyons informed these two fully of the situation of affairs and advised them to leave for the settlements of Texas with all possible despatch; and in return they informed Lyons that they had heard the firing in the town with great anxiety; that Vasques[11] (a Mexican who had been with the

---

was Robert H. Watson; but the president was requested by the Senate (for reasons not given) to withdraw Watson's name. This request was apparently granted, for there is no record of Watson having been approved by the Senate. Dr. Robert Watson was one of three persons who, on the eve of the Texan re-entry into Mier, had been assigned to scour the river below to secure or destroy all boats that might be useful to the enemy in effecting a crossing of the Rio Grande in the rear of the Texans. The men failed to rejoin the Texan force in its advance upon Mier. Watson was a member of Captain Buster's company. He succeeded in reaching San Antonio on Jan. 6, 1843. Sam Houston to the Senate of Texas, Houston, Dec. 5, 1837, in Amelia W. Williams and Eugene C. Barker (eds.), *Writings of Sam Houston*, II:164; Ernest William Winkler (ed.), *Secret Journals of the Senate*, p. 93; C. K. Reese, Miscellaneous Claims Papers (Texas) Texas State Archives; Memucan Hunt to Francis Moore, Jr., editor of the *Telegraph*, [dated] Bexar, Jan. 8, 1843, in *Morning Star*, Jan. 17, 1843.

10. George W. Bonnell, a native of New York, recruited and brought to Texas in 1836 a company of volunteers. He was living in Houston in 1837 when he became a charter member of the Philosophical Society of Texas. President Houston, in his first administration, appointed Bonnell commissioner of Indian affairs. Bonnell favored a firm policy in dealing with the Indians. In 1839 he moved to Austin and, with Jacob W. Cruger, was named government printer. On Jan. 15, 1840, Cruger and Bonnell began publishing the *Texas Sentinel* at Austin. In the same year Bonnell published his *Topographical Description of Texas to which is Added An Account of the Indian Tribes*. On Jan. 4, 1841, he became a charter member of the Austin Lyceum and in June of that year a member of the ill-fated Santa Fe Expedition. He was released from imprisonment in Mexico in time to join in the campaign against Woll and in the Somervell Expedition. John Henry Brown, *History of Texas*, II:249, 251; Thomas W. Streeter, *Bibliography of Texas, Part I, Texas Imprints*, II:508; Lucy Erath (ed.), "Memoirs of George B. Erath," *Southwestern Historical Quarterly* XXVII (1923–1924):46–49.

11. Vasquez (whose first name is unknown) fought with the Texans in the battle of Salado Creek, Sept. 18, 1842, and was one of several persons who identified Vicente Córdova, killed in battle. John Henry Brown, the historian, identified Vasquez as "old Vasquez, a New Madrid Spaniard in our command." At Mier, Vasquez was thought to be among the Texan prisoners; but, unknown to the Mexicans, he had deserted on the night of Dec. 25 when the Alcantro was crossed and had returned to the Texan camp east of the Rio Grande. Brown, *Indian Wars and Pioneers of Texas*, pp. 56–57, 66–69.

Texians, and accompanied them to the bank of the Alcantro, from whence he suddenly disappeared) had reached the camp late on the night of the twenty-fifth, but could give them no satisfactory information farther than that the Texians had entered the town and that when the firing ceased, their suspense was aweful, untill Chalk and St. Clare arrived between midnight and day, on the morning of the 27th, bringing intelligence confirmatory of their most fearful predictions. This communication passed across the river. The Texians had destroyed all the boats, save one or two, which were upon the opposite side of the river, and hence the Mexicans were brought to a stand. The last that Lyons saw of Watson and Bonnell, they were climbing up the second bank of the river, Watson being some distance in advance. Lyons was then conducted back to town by a few soldiers while Pañia set about preparing means to cross the river to pursue the retreating band of Texians. When Lyons and his guard returned and a report was made to Ampudia, he was angered to excess—foiled, as he conceived, and beaten. But there was still a hope; he thought that Capt. Pañia would likely succeed in capturing at least a few. In this hope he fondly indulged untill Pañia returned unsuccessful, and then his rage, for a time, knew no bounds. He accused Fisher of breaking the treaty, alledging that he had surrendered his whole force; to which Fisher replied that he had only surrendered those that could be taken by the Mexican troops. He ultimately became reconciled, and turned his attention to trophies of victory.

He demanded a stand of collors, and was told that there was none. The Texians had but one flag at the time of the Battle; this belonged to the La Grange Company and bore the inscription "*REVENGE OR DEATH*!" When its bearer found that a surrender was evident, he cut the flag into "mince pieces," and disposed of the fragments in some secure way, no one knew how. Finally, Ampudia was told that the flag had been cut up; whereupon, it is said, he offered one hundred Dollars for the pieces, but they were not produced. Upon one of the boats, however, Capt. Pañia found an *old English Union Jack*, which the Texians had taken from a party of Cronkawa Indians,[12] which served to allay to some extent the *mighty general's* displeasure, he not possessing sufficient discrimination to know that it was not a Texas flag.

It would be an act of palpable and base injustice to close this chap-

12. The name today is usually spelled Karankawa. A small band of these Indians had been surprised by the Texans at a rancho on the east bank of the Rio Grande and seven of its members captured on Dec. 20. By the end of the Republic of Texas the Karankawa Indians were considered to have become extinct.

ter and bid adieu to the incidents of the battle without mentioning with praise the name of *Doct. Wm. F. McMath*,[13] who, though perhaps he fired not a gun—or at any rate very few shots, performed other services of a more valuable nature which could not well have been dispensed with. There were other Doctors present, but they would pay no attention to the wounded. McMath was without surgical experience, or even practical experience as a physician, but he had read and knew something of the treatment due to broken limbs; and though he was anxious to make his rifle speak "*volumes*" to the enemy, yet as he saw men suffering around him, possessed with genuine feelings of bravery and humanity, he nobly smothered and conquered the feelings of ambition, set aside his rifle, and took up the hemp and splinters. He was often as much exposed as those who were engaged with the enemy; but overattentive to the humane duty devolving upon him as a human being, he relieved the pains of the dying, calmed the tormenting pangs of those who suffered with broken limbs, however exposed might be his situation, without one sign of dread or fear. If any man deserves the blessings of those poor wounded fellows, it is *Doct. McMath*; if any service performed upon that day is more worthy of remembrance than another, that of McMath merits the preeminence; if there was a duty performed worthy of the truely brave man, and the Christian, that duty was performed by McMath; and if there is one man who, for his deeds upon that memorable day, merits the praise of the Brave, the generous and the good throughout the world, that man is *Doct. Wm. F. McMath*. His reward will be greater than man can bestow; and though the accounts of that Expedition call *Doct. Sinixon* the *Surgeon* of the army, who never performed one of the duties of a surgeon, McMath enjoys the pleasing consciousness of having done his duty as such—of having administered to the comfort of his suffering fellow creatures when no one else would take that trouble; and may he long live to enjoy that reflection and finally meet the reward of the truly brave, the good and the Christian in a world eternal and beyound the grave.

13. William F. McMath was the assistant surgeon of the Mier Expedition but had been a private in Captain Jerome B. Roberton's company of the Somervell Expedition. Joseph Milton Nance, *Attack and Counterattack*, pp. 643–644.

Chapter V

The disposition of the wounded Texians made by Ampudia; The stay of the Texian prisoners in Mier; The Mexicans search for Vasques; Ill omens; But little to eat; Departure for Matamoras; Enterance into Comargo; Other incidents of the road; Arrival at Matamoras; Genl. Houston's two boys, Tom and Esaw; The conduct of many of the lower class upon the enterance of the Texians into Matamoras; The Texian prisoners are quartered; The conduct of Mr. Schatzell, a merchant of Matamoras; Noble, a negro man who had run away from a gentleman living on the river Colorado in Texas; The Texian prisoners start for the city of Mexico, via Monterey, under the conduct of Genl. Caneles, leaving six of their number behind.

The wounded Texians who were unable to travel were sent to what was *called* a *hospital*, but which in fact, from all accounts more resembled a *slaughter pen*, or *hog stye*, at the time, where they were consigned to the care of this before named *Doct. Sinixson* (would that there were no cause to refer to his name), and thus left for their wounds to heal, or carry them off, as the case might be.

The Prisoners were left in Mier a few days totally ignorant of what might be their fate, but there was every reason to fear a tragical termination of their career. Many of those who were best acquainted with Mexican char[a]cter thought it most probable that a very short alotment of time would cary out their fatal destiny upon earth; and, in truth, circumstances combined to make that supposition reasonable.

Two or three days after the battle the Texians were marched out from their different rooms—being confined in four separate houses—and collected into a body, were taken to the outskirts of the town to a strong and gloomy looking dwelling into which—or through which, into a back yard surrounded by a high wall—they were marched, each being carefully examined as he entered to see that he bore no concealed knives or weapons of any kind. In this back yard, a few feet—or perhaps, ten steps from the wall, all round, there was a double line of soldiers extended, while the Texians were mate [made] to forme themselves by the wall in a single line with their faces to the soldiers. This, the Texians knew to be a custom of the Mexicans when they contemplated shooting their prisoners, and therefore they viewed these portentious arrangements with no little dread, but still—their hands being free—with a resolution to sell as dearly as possible a life they could no longer keep! There was a manly resolve and firm determination written upon every face. The Mexican[s] pretended to be in search of this *Vasques*,[1] who had once been a notorious robber upon the rio Grande and to whom allusion has before been made, but this was evidently false. Though they may have desired to capture Vasques, yet it would not seem reasonable that they would have taken this laborious course when that object might, had he been among the Texians, have been far more easily accomplished by searching one room at a time. However, if it was their object to shoot their Prisoners, they gave it up and conducted them to prison. It was afterwards ascertained that at that time the officers were holding a Court Martial upon the lives of their prisoners; and it was said, and received as true, that the lives of the whole were saved by barely one vote! What a small thread upon which to hang the lives of two hundred and forty-eight men!

There were other omens equally ill, which seemed to prognasticate inevitable distruction; but as they all failed, it is needless to allude to them by farther remarks.

On the day of surrender, about twelve o'clock at night, the weary and battleworn Texians received a small allowance of beef, badly cooked, with some water to allay their thirst. When this scanty portion arrived, although hungered by thirty-six hours of fasting and parched by a thirst of near the duration, many of the poor Prisoner Soldiers had sunk upon the cold stone floor without covering—save the roof above them, and had blissfully forgotten their griefs in dreams of b[l]oody contests with their countries foe. Some, perhaps, were dreaming of a home and friends, never more to meet their view, while others were tra[n]sported back to the dinn of battle. And those stunning roars of cannon and deafening peals of musquetry were heard by sleepers among that ill fated band, for night after night, for weeks. Their waking hours would come, however, in which they became conscious of

1. The search for Vasquez was given as the excuse for lining up the Texans in a compound, but the real reason seems to have been that the officers were trying to decide whether to shoot the prisoners. General Antonio Canales seems to have been the leader in seeking a verdict of death for the Texan prisoners by court-martial, but General Ampudia was able to prevent such a decision. William Preston Stapp, *Prisoners of Perote*, p. 39.

the realities of their situation and the scantiness of their fare. The Prisoners received but two meals per day, one about ten o'clock in the morning, and another about ten at night, both of which would not have made more than enough for one meal to the whole number. These meals generally consisted in [of?] boiled beef, but an occasional varriance was m[a]de by substituting boiled beens instead, which were boiled with nothing much to season them.

The prisoners were kept in Mier about four days with quite a monotonous (if the expression is allowable) course of treatment; and on the morning, probably of the 31st of December,[2] they were put upon the march to Matamoras under an exceeding strong escort of both infantry and Cavalry, accompanied by one or two pieces of Artillery. The first days march took them a distance of eight leagues to the river *St. Juan*, upon which they were encamped for the night, opposite to the town of *Comargo*.[3] At this encampment the extreme cold and dampness of the night caused the Prisoners to suffer greatly, as they were almost, and some few totally, destitute of blankets. On the morning of the 1st of January 1843, they were marc[h]ed across the river and into the town.

The reception of Ampudia in Comargo was not as brilliant as he may have wished, but there was considerable clatter among the bells and he made some perade in showing of[f] the fruits of his victorious arms. This day (whether it was the first of January 1843, or the 31st Decem. 1842, is not remembered) was spent in Comargo (but it must have been the 1st of Jan.,[4] as the Prisoners were allowed a drink of *Agua dente*[5] shortly after their arrival).

There was not much to interest, but a great deal to annoy, upon the rout to Matamoras. At one encampment upon the road there was a bugler in the Mexican Army who introduced himself to the Texians as an Irishman who had been captured in western Texas while out on a

2. The date of the march from Mier was Dec. 31, 1842.

3. Camargo was located upon the southern bank of the San Juan River four miles from the Rio Grande. It had been founded on Mar. 5, 1749, by Colonel José Escandón as La Villa Santa Aña de Camargo and at one time was regarded by the Spaniards as having the best site for agricultural purposes on the Rio Grande; but in January 1843 it was a bleak city of some four thousand inhabitants. W. A. Crofutt (ed.), *Fifty Years in Camp and Field*, p. 234; Polly Pearl Crawford, "The Beginnings of Spanish Settlement in the Lower Rio Grande Valley," pp. 61–116.

4. The date was Jan. 1, 1843, when the prisoners entered Camargo.

5. *Aguardiente* (or *muscal*) was a strong spirituous drink made from the juice of the maguey or century plant.

cowsteeling expedition and forced into the Mexican service; he may again be spoken of. At *New* Rionosa[6] there was a magnificient reception granted to Ampudia; triumphal arches erected at various places along the street by which he entered with his train of captives; some small boys fantastickly dressed danced before him; every bell in the town, seemingly hundreds, gave forth a doubled tongued welcome, in thunder tones; and every voice in the place gave forth its "viva" for the "*heroe of the age*." Oh! that town should be razed to earth, and its hundred bells run into cannon, with which to batter down the pride of that self-conceited people. Either at this town or at Comargo, a young man by the name of McDade[7] was taken ill and left, where he subsequently died. And here there was meet given to eat which was suppose[d] by good judges to be the meet either of a *mule* or a *Jack Ass*. One or two days march from Matamoras there was an effort made by several persons to prevail upon the men to rise, as *one man*, and conquer their guard and escape to Texas; or die in the attempt; but those efforts were unavailing; the men were too much worn down by travelling upon foot, a custom to which very few had been used.

On the Evening of the 8th of January the Prisoners reached the vicinity of Matamoras, and were halted at a little village about five miles off, called *Guadaloupe*. Here Ampudia was met by his friends and many of the principle men of Matamoras, among whome came *Tom* and *Esau*,[8] two slaves who had runaway from their Master, *Genl. Sam*

6. Nueva Reynosa was eighteen miles below Nuestra Señora de Guadalupe de Reynosa (Reynosa Vieja or Old Reynosa) in the direction of Matamoros about a mile from the Rio Grande. Reynosa is sometimes written "Rhinosa."

7. Samuel McDade, who had been taken ill after leaving Mier, was by the time he reached Nueva Reynosa too weak to travel farther. When the prisoners left Nueva Reynosa, he was left lying upon a rawhide for a mattress and was soon dead. Israel Canfield diary, Jan. 4, 1843, Texas State Archives.

8. One version of the story of Tom and Esau is told by William Seale in *Sam Houston's Wife*, pp. 38, 44: In the summer of 1840 Esau was with Mrs. Sam Houston at her husband's farm at Cedar Point on the Texas coast near Galveston Bay. When Houston, owing to friction among his slaves, hired some of the male slaves out to other persons in the fall of 1840, Tom and Esau disappeared during the process of exchange and later turned up in Mexico. Quite a different version is that given by Noah Smithwick in "Recollections of General Sam Houston," Daughters of the Republic of Texas Library, San Antonio, Texas. In speaking of the log cabin used by President Houston in 1837 as a residence near the capitol in Houston Smithwick wrote:

> I dont know who presided over the domestic affairs of the establishment, but his office boy was a light Quadroon boy, Tom, who fully

Houston of Texas. Esau, a black fellow who would grace a cotton field most suitably, met Genl. Ampudia like an old friend; and he and the General remained *locked in each others arms for some moments*, with all the apparent signs of joy and affection that could have been exhibited in the meeting of two only and long separated brothers! Esau was a saucy puppy, and had he been placed at the mercy of some few of the Texians he would have been worth no more than his spiritless body—his carcas. Tom, a yellow boy, almost white, was rather more politely inclined towards the Texians and consequently could venture among them, but Esau feared to venture.

On the morning of the ninth, when approaching the town, the soldiers who escorted the Prisoners were often questioned by a mother, a wife, or sweetheart in relation to some face that was missing, and the general reply was a sudden stroke upon the forehead with the end of the forefinger and a significant shrug of the shoulders, which invariably produced a shreek of woe. There were numbers who met the band, only to hear the bad intelligence of their friends having fallen! Then were screams heard, and curse upon curse uttered upon those disarmed

---

realizing the dignity of his position, put on his airs of a whole government; he could read and write and had acquired in addition to these accomplishments quite a vocabulary of technical words and phrases. There was also a black man-servant, Shadwick. A few years later Tom concluded to shake off his shackles and with this end in view took Shadwick into his confidence, promising him his freedom if he would obey instructions. Shadwick promised implicit obedience and providing themselves with a couple of Gen. Houston's best horses and what money Tom could extract from the office till, the two set out for Mexico. Tom bore so little trace of African Ancestry that he had no difficulty in passing himself off as a gentleman of means traveling through the country attended by his servant, but he played his role of master rather too perfectly to be agreeable to Shadwick who often threatened to revolt, upon which Tom cursed him for a fool, pointing out the necessity of keeping up the farce till they were safely across the Rio Grande. They made the trip in safety and Tom, who introduced himself as Mr. Thomas Houston, son of the renowned general, was received with great respect. Some of the Texans who were taken to Mexico as prisoners met Tom and by one of them, Sam Norvell [a San Antonio prisoner], I think, he sent a letter back to Gen. Houston expressing his deep sense of obligation for the many advantages and kindnesses enjoyed during his sojourn with the general, and assuring him of his willing service in advancing his interests with the Mexican government, concluding by saying that he was expecting to get an office soon and if successful would send him a remittance.

Texians! Amid all the noise and confusion, in the midst of all that woe, under all those curses—where frowning brows and clenched hands—where the terrible aspect of thousands of infuriated enemies seemed to betoken a coming distruction—that little disarmed band of Texians stood as men whose bosoms had never known evil, and whose hearts had never felt a single pulsation of fear! They seemed insensible to all things around, for they felt that they had gone as far as possible towards the performance of their duty. The reception of the victorious Mexican General was splendid; but this pen cares not to be exercised in recording it.

After being peraded about the streets to the amusement and edification of the populace, for near two hours, the prisoners were marched to strong, but rather comfortable quarters, where they were lodged with little or no cerimony and still less eatables.

Though the eating was bad, and—worst of all—but little in proportion; and though their situation was uncomfortable; yet, under the circumstances there were many who had no great reason to complain, for Mr. Schatzell[9]—long be his name remembered—extended assistance and gave sucor to many. He was of Du[t]ch parentage, and born, perhaps, in the United States; and having lived long in Kentucky, he gave the amount of five Dollars to every Kentuckian present, besides loans which he made to others upon their good faith. Upon the generous, disinterested friendship of this man comment would be useless, for, though friendship that draws upon the pocket is a rare virtue in this cold, calculating world, yet the hearts of men are not so cold and blind to benevolent feelings as to exclude every spark of admiration for this generous man's conduct when they read of his acts.

There is one other whose name should be particularly mentioned, and whose little offices of kindness in behalf of that ill-fated band will

9. Joseph P. Schatzell was a German merchant who had formerly resided in Louisville, Kentucky. In all, he gave and loaned to the prisoners approximately three thousand dollars. Following the death, from "an epidemic fever," of Richard Heath Belt, U.S. consul at Matamoros on Oct. 11, 1844, Schatzell was named consul at that port. Canfield diary, Jan. 10, 1843; John R. Alexander, "Account of the Mier Expedition," Archives, University of Texas; Thomas J. Green to Gen. Felix Huston and Col. Bailey Peyton, New Orleans [dated] Matamoros, Jan. 12, 1843, in Domestic Correspondence (Texas), Texas State Archives; Stapp, *Prisoners of Perote*, p. 44; Jos[eph] P. Schatzell to John C. Calhoun, Secretary of State, Washington, [dated] Matamoros, Nov. 6, 1844, and same to same, Matamoros, Mexico, Feb. 15, 1845, both in National Archives, United States Consular Despatches, Matamoros.

long be remembered by every Texian who then were "*Mier Prisoners.*" *Noble,*[10] a negro man who had run away from his master residing somewhere on the Colerado in Texas, proved himself worthy of the name he bore; shortly after the Texians were placed in "quarters," Noble made his appearance with such provisions as he had been able [to] collect. He had summoned into requisition every Dollar of his scanty means, and purchased provisions with which to allay the hunger of the Prisoners! The act merits the same reward as though he had possessed hundreds and given it all to that benevolent purpose, for he had given all he could raise.

This place was the abode of the prisoners untill the Fourteenth of January 1843, at which time they were ordered upon the road to the City of Mexico. During this short stay here, their treatment had been quite severe, as far as eating was concerned; but otherwise their time was as easy as they had any reason to hope for. They received but two meals *per diem* and those quite light. They were now called to take up the line of a long and weary march, who could tell where it would end? On the morning of the 14th, upon complaint made to the Commandant that there were some who were unable to travel, *Votager*, the Mexican Surgeon General of the post, was sent in to examine the sick. He reported (this will be spoken of more at large in another place) that there were six unable to travel, whose names were as follows: *Ezekiel Smith,*[11] *Patrick Usher,*[12] *George W. Critenden,*[13] *Charles Wilson,*[14]

10. Noble is estimated to have spent as much as several hundred dollars in furnishing relief to the Texan prisoners.

11. Ezekiel Smith of Gonzales County was a private in Captain Mathew Caldwell's company of Gonzales Rangers (March 16, 1839, to June 16, 1839). Muster Rolls (Rangers), Texas State Archives; Gifford White (ed.), *The 1840 Census of the Republic of Texas*, p. 59.

12. Patrick Usher was born in Ireland in 1801 and came to Texas in May 1835 from Hanover County, North Carolina. He fought in Captain Moseley Baker's company in the battle of San Jacinto. He continued in the Texas army until May 28, 1836. Six weeks later he re-entered the army on July 2, 1836, as first sergeant in George Sutherland's company. He later resigned to become chief justice of Jackson County to which position he had been elected by the Texas Congress on Dec. 16, 1836. He resigned this position on Mar. 14, 1839. For a time between 1836 and 1839 he was the first president of the Board of Land Commissioners of Jackson County and from 1840 to 1842 he represented Jackson County in the House of Representatives of the Fifth and Sixth Congresses of Texas. From Mar. 6, to June 6, 1842, he served as first lieutenant in Captain John S. Menefee's company of volunteers commanded by Colonel Clark L. Owen in the Vasquez campaign and as a private in Owen's company in the First Regiment of Volunteers under Colonel

John D. Morgan,[15] (known among the prisoners as *John Day*, having changed his name from Morgan to Day on account of having been on the Santa Fe expedition) and *Joseph D. McCutchan*, that is, *your Humble Servant, at command*. Accordingly this little party was ordered to the Hospital, and the residue to the road, with the exception of three boys, *Gilbert R. Brush*, *Wm. H. Sellers*, and *John Hill*, who were left in Matamoras on parole. The latter of the three, John [Christopher Columbus] Hill was *adopted* by Genl. Ampudia. About 12 o'clock, M. the main body took up the line of march for Mexico, *via*

James R. Cook in the Somervell Expedition. When the Mier Expedition was formed he became a private in Captain Ewen Cameron's company. Militia Rolls (Texas), Texas State Archives; Muster Roll of Capt. Clark L. Owen's company, First Regiment Volunteers, Col. James R. Cook, in Sam S. Smith Collection, Archives, University of Texas; [Elizabeth LeNoir Jennett, ed.], *Biographical Directory of the Texan Conventions and Congresses*, p. 183; Walter P. Webb and H. Bailey Carroll (eds.), *Handbook of Texas*, II:826–827.

13. The name is George B. Crittenden. He was the eldest son of John J. Crittenden, prominent Kentucky political leader, U.S. senator from Kentucky, and U.S. attorney general under President William Henry Harrison. George B. Crittenden was born in 1812 and graduated from West Point Military Academy in 1832. In 1833 he resigned from the U.S. Army and, when his father was away from home, came to Texas, where he served as a second lieutenant in Captain William Ryon's company in the Mier Expedition. Joseph Milton Nance (ed.), "A Letterbook of Joseph Eve, Chargé d'Affaires of the United States to Texas," *Southwestern Historical Quarterly* XLIII (January 1940):372n.; Public Debt Papers (Texas), nos. 1197, 1785, Texas State Archives; *National Cyclopaedia of American Biography* XIII:6–7.

14. The name is James Charles Wilson, who was born in Yorkshire, England, on Aug. 24, 1816. Before coming to Texas in 1837, he had attended Oxford University. From Mar. 20 to June 20, 1842, he served as third sergeant in Captain John P. Gill's company of mounted volunteers, under the overall command of Colonel Clark L. Owen, who commanded troops in the Goliad-Victoria area. Wilson later served in the Somervell Expedition and the Mier Expedition as a private in Captain Charles K. Reese's company. Militia Rolls (Texas); James C. Wilson, Public Debt Papers (Texas).

15. John Day (alias John D. Morgan) had been a member of the Santa Fe Expedition but had changed his name to John D. Morgan in an effort to conceal that fact for fear of being executed for violation of the terms by which he had been released. He was born in 1818 and had been a resident of Bastrop County, Texas, since 1838 but had a record of military service in Texas from 1836 to 1843. He had been in the campaign against Woll. John Day Morgan, Pension Papers (Republic), Texas State Archives; John Day Morgan, Public Debt Papers (Texas).

Monterey and Saltillo, after having taken a hasty farewell of their sick companions. They were placed under the conduct of *Genl. Canales*, who, at first, refused to answer for their safe keeping, unless Ampudia would permit him to take them in irons. But the latter, being possessed of a glimmering spark of generosity would not grant his request; and the former, mean, traitorous, and dastardly, as he was, dared not disobey.

It is not improper to say before closing this chapter that Col. Fisher and Thos. J. Green were permitted to travel [on] horseback in advance of the main body under a separate escort.[16]

16. William S. Fisher and Thomas Jefferson Green were taken (they had no choice) under separate escort in advance of the main body of prisoners as security for the good behavior of the main body of prisoners. Besides Fisher and Green, in the advance party went Samuel C. Lyon, Daniel Drake Henrie as interpreter, Thomas W. Murray, and Dr. William M. Shepherd. Thomas Jefferson Green, *Journal of the Texian Expedition Against Mier*, p. 127.

[Chapter V-a]

[McCutchan's March to Mexico City[1]]

On the fourteenth, about twelve o'clock (at noon) the main body took up the line of march, for the city of Mexico under charge of Gen. Canales, leaving six men in Matamoros, myself among them. Permission for me to remain was gained through the intercession of Doctors Brenham and McMath; being wounded severely by a thorn which had lodged under the cap of my knee, they judged that if I was marched off, I would loose my leg and likely my life, the latter of which was preferable.

In the Hospital we were treated with more kindness than had previously fallen to our lot. The chief physician and superintendent of the hospital was a Frenchman, who had formerly lived in San Antonio, Texas. His manners were kind and friendly to men in our station. The names of those left in the hospital, six in number, were E. Smith, G. W. Critenden, Charles Willson, Patrick Usher, J. D. Morgan, and J. D. McCutchan. There were three youths left in the city (mear Boys) on their parole; these were Gilbert R. Brush, Wm. H. Sellers, and John Hill, the latter the *adopted* son of Gen. Ampudia.

At the end of nine weeks some of our wounded[2] came down from Mier where they had been left. I wish, in honor to Col. H. L. Kiney,[3]

1. McCutchan recopied portions of his diary. At this point there is an overlap and repetition that destroys the sequence of events. He did not get the story of the march of the main body of prisoners and of the overthrow of the guard at the *hacienda* Salado until after his arrival in Mexico City. The editor has transferred a portion of the diary found in Chapter V and created Chapter V-a with a title. What appears to be a first draft of the overlapping portion has been relegated to Appendix II and the information contained therein preserved for information to the reader.

2. From among those left wounded at Mier the following were transferred to Matamoros: David Allen, Lynn Bobo, James J. Barber, Jeffrey B. Hill, Frank Hughes, Edward Y. Keene, Malcolm McCauley, Theodore D. Maltby, Harbert H. Oats, and William Y. Scott.

3. Henry Lawrence Kinney was born in the Wyoming Valley, near Shusshequin, Pennsylvania, June 3, 1814. He moved to Illinois in 1830 and while there fought in the Black Hawk War (1832 to 1837) and later in the Seminole War (1835 to 1842). Then for a brief period he operated as a trader in Havana. His proposed marriage to Daniel Webster's daughter, Julia, in 1837

to mention here that about 6 weeks after we were left in Matamoras, this gentleman Col. Kiney came to see us and said that he would make arrangements for us to escape, but before he could effect his *Noble* and *Generous* purpose, *he was taken* and *thrown* into *prison*, as [and] accused of having assisted eight of our men off from Mier.[4] *This was done* the verry day on which Doctor Sinixson arrived from Mier.

About the first of March, ten of the men were marched off to Mexico. About the same time, I was sent from the Hospital to prison, where I remained six days, and was under the necessity of returning to the Hospital. During the stay which I had in prison (there were five in the room), we formed a project of escaping, but after diging a short time found that it could not be effected. To show the cowardice natural to

---

met with a decided, "no." In 1838 he came to Texas and in 1839 settled in the Corpus Christi area. On Jan. 4, 1840, Kinney purchased from Captain Enrique de Villareal, with the approval of the governor of Tamaulipas, ten leagues of land extending from the stream called the Oso to the Nueces River. On the west bank of the Nueces, at Flour Bluff, he established Kinney's Ranch and Trading Post in a commanding position on the high bluff, and associated with him William P. Aubrey, an English subject. From this point they carried on a clandestine trade with Texas and Mexico.

On one of his trips to Matamoros, Kinney, claiming United States citizenship, visited the wounded and sick Texans in the hospital at Mier and left five hundred dollars with James O. Rice for the purchase of food, clothing, and other necessities required by the Texan prisoners. Rice and seven others, who were able to travel, used the money to bribe the guard to supply them with ammunition, three guns, and provisions to facilitate their escape to Texas. Everything being ready for the journey, the eight Texans were taken from the prison by an officer of the guard and escorted to a point outside Mier and released. Kinney was arrested at Matamoros and charged with aiding the prisoners to escape. He was able to escape from Matamoros on the evening of June 13, 1843, after a confinement of several months, and made his way overland to Corpus Christi. From there he took the schooner *Santa Anna* to Galveston, and from thence to Houston where he arrived on June 20, 1843. Coleman McCampbell, *Saga of a Seaport*, pp. 4, 124–125; idem, *Texas Seaport*, p. [23]; idem, "Colonel Kinney's Romance with Daniel Webster's Daughter," *Crystal Reflector*, June 1939; Joseph Milton Nance, *Attack and Counterattack*, pp. 208–210; Walter P. Webb and H. Bailey Carroll (eds.), *Handbook of Texas*, I:962; *Morning Star*, Feb. 28, 1843; *Telegraph and Texas Register*, Mar. 15 and June 28, 1843.

4. The eight who escaped from Mier were Robert Beale, John Bideler, Lewis Hays, Nathaniel Mallon, George B. Piland, James O. Rice, William Ripley, and Henry D. Weeks. Thomas Jefferson Green, *Journal of the Texian Expedition against Mier*, p. 445.

all Mexicans, I will mention that when returning to the hospital, scarcely able to support myself with a stick, I had accompanying me three soldiers with fixed bayonetts and cocked pieces; one marching on each side, and one in my rear.

On the eleventh of March five more were started toward Mexico by the road to Tampico, I among the number. The names of them were E. Smith, T. Maltby,[5] Jeff Hill,[6] E. Y. Keen, and J. D. McCutchan. We suffered much on the road, being badly fed and making long marches. A great part of the time we got but one meal per day; in fact there were a fiew days in which we got but two meals in three days. Our food was bad, being nothing but a little rice or boiled beef. But through fatig[u]e and wretchedness, we at length reached Tampico on the twenty-third of April nearly naked, after having passed forty-three days of extreme destitution, marching, and countermarching. The day following our arrival, Mr. Franklin E. Chase,[7] the American Consul at that port, came in to see us. He evinced signs of distress at seeing men in such a wretched and desolate condition. Before leaving he gave us some money, which was quite acceptable to us. The sight of the Star Spangled banner opperated like electricity on our nerves.

The next day two American merchants came to see us, bringing money, clothes, blankets, towels, needles, thread, buttons, and tape. Enroled in the towels were the thread and needles with the following note penned by the blessed ha[n]d of angelic *Woman*,

"A Woman knows the value of such trifles to men in your

5. Theodore Dwight Maltby was a native of Connecticut. He fought in the Seminole War in Florida before coming to Texas. He went on the Somervell campaign and served as a private in Captain William Ryon's company on the Mier Expedition. At the battle of Mier he was wounded in the head. On Nov. 12, 1845, about a year after his return from imprisonment in Mexico, he married Mary Jane (Baylor) West, niece of Judge Robert E. B. Baylor, at La Grange, Texas. Maltby died in New Orleans at the age of 58 on Oct. 27, 1871, of yellow fever, after an illness of six days, and is buried in the Washington Cemetery. *Daily Picayune*, (New Orleans), Oct. 28, 1871; *Telegraph and Texas Register*, Nov. 8, 1843; Theodore D. Maltby, Public Debt Papers (Texas), Texas State Archives.

6. Jeffrey Barksdale Hill, son of Abraham (Asa) Webb Hill, was born in Georgia on May 7, 1814, and in the spring of 1835 moved to Texas with his father and settled in Fayette County, later moving to Gonzales County. His father and brother (John C. C. Hill) were also in the Mier Expedition. Webb and Carroll (eds.), *Handbook of Texas*, I:812–813; *Dallas Morning News*, Apr. 23, 1893.

7. Franklin E. Chase was the American consul at Tampico, Mexico.

> condition, therefore accept these with a woman's prayer. May God grant you a speedy release."

These fiew but Heavenly words instilled into me a belief that woman is an angelic being placed on earth to administer happiness to the World.

Two or three days following, Jeff Hill and myself gained permission to take a stroll over the city, with the honor of being followed by two soldiers at a short distance; that is, at a respectable distance. One of the soldiers offered to take his musquet, but the officer on guard refused, saying that he was not going with wild beasts, but men and soldiers. I only mention a circumstance so trifling to show that there are some of the *tribe*, who know a little of civilization.

I had some letters to present to the United States Consul, for Texas, and hence to his residence we directed our course. Mr. Chase was not in, and we waited his company. I am of opinion that in the person of Mr. Chase's lady we found the one from whom came the foregoing note. I judged this from the course of her conversation on our capture and the the agrievations which had led us to attempt the Expedition. After hearing the cause of the campaign, she justified by saying that "the impulse on which we acted was natural." "And that we were certainly in honor and humanity bound to revenge the fall of our countrymen." She concluded by asking if we were sufficiently revenged, and in the fall of the six hundred and fifty Mexicans, and the wounds of two hundred, which she informed me was the official report of Gen. Ampudia. I replied that it was enough for Dawson's Massacre, but that we might hereafter take satisfaction for our own sufferings. She "wished us speady release," but "hoped that in our next descent on the enemy, we would come in greater force."

In the ramble we met with a Negro, who grieved much to see white men in our condition and in his own language, "lamented dee pensation ob probidence in deliverin dee white Gemen into dee hands ob dee Sunburnt debels dat want fit to cook dee debels Supper, for he self." Our coulored acquaintance was verry affable in his manners. We also met with Mr. Denton, Mr. Fleming, and two or three others whose names I disremember, whith whom I conversed for some time previous to returning to prison. They all seemed willing to show the justness of our cause; indeed they could not do otherwise. How could they?

In this place, we received near twenty Dollars each and a considerable quantity of clothing; the latter, however, was nearly all stolen from us by the Mexicans.

Let the proud and haughty sons of opulence say that they would not accept aid offered to them, but to such, I say, go seak common service in a Mexican dungeon.

In this place, where we remained about 72 days, we received the treatment due to prisoners of War.

Either the fourth or fifth of May we bid farewell to Tampico, and the kind friends we had thare not with, and found ourselves on the road to the city of Mexico under charge of a lieutenant and seven sargents who were on their way to join their regiment at the capital. The Lieutenant and one of the Sargents had been prisoners in Texas. After pledging our word of honor as Soldiers and gentlemen of Texas, there was no restraint placed upon us as we only bore the name of prisoners. Our first night from Tampico we stoped at a small town called Puebla Biejo,[8] where we visited in company with the officer a rope performance and Theatre, which was verry good. Here we met with a Spaniard who spoke good English, educated in England, and a verry intelligent man. He conversed for some time on the condition of Mexico, and judging from the tenor of his conversation, he thought she would have been better in condition under the Spanish Government. The people are falling into darkness fully as fast as other nations are gaining light, and all the edifices and public works erected by Spain are going to ruins. In short, Barbarism is spreading her sable mantle over the *country fast as time can move.*

On our march to the city we passed through a defile near eight leagues for twenty fore miles in length. This valley, or pass, was from one hundred to one hundred and fifty yards in breadth—no place, more than that, and at some giving barely sufficient room to pass, with a beautiful stream running down it, which we crossed and recrossed fifty-eight times. On each side of this pass is a perpendicular wall, or rather projecting [*sic*] than otherwise, which varys from one to five hundred feet in hight, reasonably speaking. In one part of the pass I saw a stone or mass of stones firmly united, which had fallen from a hight of near two hundred feet; it was globular in form and would have measured near one hundred and fifty feet in circumference, nearly obstructing the passage. It appeared that this might have been, at one time, the center of a chain of large mountains, and that they had by some revolution of Nature been burst asunder, leaving a pass, with cliffs overhanging each side. This part of the country was chiefly in-

8. Pueblo Viejo was situated a short distance south of Tampico, not far from the Gulf of Mexico. Alexander von Humboldt, *Atlas géographique et physique du royaume de la nouvelle-espagne*, map 23.

habited by Indians. Speaking of Indian dialect, and it was not a sight uncommon to see their huts situated at the verry verge of the pricipice apparent as though a light breeze would precipitate it into the yawning abyss beneath.

We stoped at a mining town to rest a short hour or two called Real Del Monte,[9] where there are many English and Irish, among whom was an Irishman by name Lynch, and by nature a gentleman, who politely invited us and our officer to dine with him. We at first refused, but he pressed the invitation, and it was at length accepted by four of us, and the officer, Jeff Hill remaining at the quarters we had taken. We repaïred to his residence at half past two, where we found an excellent dinner awaiting us with the best of wines, brandies and cigars. The dinner passed in anecdotes and abuse of Santa Anna, and in the latter Padr[a]jo was equal to the best of us. In the course of the time we stayed, Lynch requested the native state of each individually, upon hearing which, he made some remarks indicative of an Irishman. At length he questioned me. I replied that I was by birth a Tennesseean. "Ah," said he, in his Irish way, "you are from the State of marksmen, where a man is laughted at unless he is good for a Squrrel's eye one hundred yards distant, and I suppose you came to this country to try your Skill." Yes, said I, I am a good marksman in a good cause. He said he was ever partial to Crocketts countrymen. On taking our leave he presented us with a basket, a leg of mutton and a loaf of fine bread, and a bottle of most *excellent brandy*, and beged our acceptance of it, and luckily for us we did so, in as much as the place we put up at for the night could not even furnish us with tortillas.

We visited the splendid Church of Guadaloupe,[10] situated about

9. Real del Monte was about 160 miles southwest of Tampico on the road to Mexico City. Hubert Howe Bancroft, *History of Mexico*, IV:340.

10. The church of Guadalupe was located upon Tepeyac Hill where a temple to the goddess Tonantzin (Our Mother) had been built by the Aztecs. The dark-skinned Lady of Guadalupe was the patron saint of the Mexican-Indian and mestizo. Jesus was accorded secondary place to the Virgin of Guadalupe, who was early included in the Catholicism of Mexico as the patron saint of the Mexican Indian. According to Hubert Herring, in *A History of Latin America*, p. 178, the legend of the Virgin of Guadalupe developed as follows:

> On December 9, 1531, an Indian, Juan Diego, was passing the hill of Tepeyac on the northern outskirts of the Mexican capital when an Indian maiden appeared in a half-moon of dazzling light, announced herself as the Mother of God and the mother of all Indians, and bade Juan Diego carry a message to the bishop begging that a shrine be built upon the spot. [Bishop] Zumarraga was properly cautious. The virgin ap-

three miles from the city of Mexico. It is really a super-splendid edifice. The outer appearance is nothing extraordinary, but on entering you are at once amaised and overpowered with the extensive display of Gold and Silver. I passed entirely through the whole structure, examined minutely every part of it, and although I have heard what I thought exagerated accounts of its splendor, yet when I beheld it with the eye my feelings were rather a mingled sensation of wonder, awe, and respect. Many of the paintings on the wall seemed to be gifted with life. I felt that I was in a consicrated place. I felt, I must confess, that there was something supernatural in the appearance of the house. This edifice stands near the spot where the Saint Guadaloupe made her appearance. Where she descended there stands a statue. The story of her appearance, as related to me by the officer in charge is, in his own language, by me translated as follows: "Some years ago, I disremember the date, an Indian of the Old tribe of Montezuma, met with the misfortune attending many, that of having a sick family. His wife was worse than any, and he thought she would die. One morning she became so bad that the Indian thought it best to go into the City to seak assistance. He started before day light; when he reached this place, he was startled by an extraordinary light apparently descending from heaven. Droping on his face, he there lay untill called by a voice whose tones were sweeter than music. At the summons he arose and beheld near him and standing on that" (here the officer pointed to the statue) "very spot of ground, a beautiful lady arrayed in glorious light so bright that the eye could scarcely look on it." This lady was Santa Guadaloupe. She spoke to him "Saying 'Go thy way to thy own house, bear this' giving a paper" (the contents of which the officer could not tell me,) "and when thou shalt reach thy house, thou wilt find thy wife and little one well." "The lady also presented him with a certain shrub, which would act as a preventative to all diseases, with many words of council."—This was the circumstance which induced the erection of the church, or so says Francisco Padrajo. He related many

---

peared to the Indian a second and a third time. On the third occasion she gave him a miraculous sign: roses suddenly appeared on the slopes of barren Tepeyac. Juan Diego wrapped the flowers into his mantle and hurried to the bishop. When he unfolded his mantle, the roses had disappeared, leaving in their place the painting of the Virgin of Guadalupe, which now hangs over the high altar of the basilica near Tepeyac. The story, long debated by churchmen, conveyed the dramatic message that the religion of the Spaniard was not an alien faith, that it belonged to Indian Mexico, that the Mother of God could rightfully appear with the dark hair, golden skin, and somber eyes of a Mexican maiden.

other anecdotes indicative of the superstitution of the Mexican people. We arrived at the long wished for city of the Montesumas on the 27th of May. This place is not as handsome as I had thought. It is built after the fashion of all Spanish or Mexican towns—flat roofed houses and very narrow streets. If the breadth of street was greater it would present a fine city, as the houses (or a fiew of them) are quite splendid.

On our arrival we were taken to the quarters of the Fourth Redgement of Cavalry to which belonged our friend and conductor Lieutenant Francisco Padrajo. I will relate a little circumstance which hapened this day before we reached the city. When near three miles from the place, Padrajo said to me (we were riding), "It will be best for you now to dismount; let me send the horses back and you walk into the city, all of you." "For were you to ride into the presence of the Commanding General, he would say to you—'You are not fatigued, therefore go immediately to work,' and you would be put in chains and made to work tomorrow. But if you walk in, he will think you verry much fatigued with the journey and will give you a fiew days rest." This arrangement we all readily agreed to, as it was an object worth our attention, to keep out of chains and from work as long as possible.

We remained with this redgiment the night of the twenty-fourth, the twenty-fifth, and on the twenty-sixth we went to the old convent of Sandeago, where we met with two of our men, James C. Wilson and Joe Smith[11] (not Mormon Joe Smith, nor a relative) from whom we learned that the main body of prisoners were about three miles out of the city at Tacubaya[12] making a road leading from Santa Anna's palace towards the city, and that they were quartered at an old powder Mill[13] one mile from the place of their labours.

11. Joseph F. Smith came to Texas from Arkansas and was "well known as a locator of land in Refugio County, Texas, and one of the meanest men God ever put breath into," Israel Canfield recorded on Jan. 23, 1844, in his diary, Texas State Archives.

12. Tacubuya was a small village about four miles southwest of the capital and a mile south of the hill of Chapúltepec on the slope of the Sierra de las Cruces. Some six or seven hundred yards to the southwest overlooking the village stood the Archbishop's Palace. Thomas Philip Terry, *Terry's Guide to Mexico*, p. 417.

13. The Powder Mill or King's Mill (Molino del Rey) was situated about one and a quarter miles north of the Archbishop's Palace and behind Chapúltepec forest. It was a mile from where the prisoners worked on the road. The mill had been constructed in colonial times by the Spanish king and consisted of a complicated range of low stone buildings with a flour mill at its south-

We remained here[14] untill the 30th on that day, after having received each a suit of clothes made of verry course and thin blankets, we went to "El Morleno Del Rey," the quarters of the main body, where we met with our friends. Sweet is the meeting of fellow soldiers, suffering in the same sacred cause. Holy and blessed is the meeting of friends in adversity. We were one and the same people, enduring hardships in the same glorious cause of liberty; we had fought and suffered for the same ungreatful country, and our feelings towards each other were the same. The grip of the hand of a fellow soldier in the same cause, and a fellow sufferer under the same cruelties, is fare more prefferable, and gives more real joy, than the feigned harty *embrace* of pampered monarchs, or even the wellcome embrace of friends in prosperity. *We were one and the same family.* Then were words of consolation from one to the other said. And the battle fought o're and o're again.

---

ern end and a foundry (formerly a powder mill) at its northern end. Bancroft, *History of Mexico*, V:497–498, 498n.; José Fernando Ramírez, *Mexico during the War with the United States*, p. 155.

14. "Here" means the Convent Santiago.

Chapter VI

March of the main body of prisoners towards the City of Mexico; their arrival at and departure from Monterey; and arrival at and departure from Saltillo; their arrival at Rancho Salado; the plan, and consumation of the "Rescue": the Battle of the Rescue, and triumph of the Texians; the Texians turn towards home, leave the road and take to the mountains; kill their horses for sustainence; their sufferings; they disperse; are captured in different parties, and taken to Saltillo; where an order is received commanding them to be put to death; conduct of Genl. Mahier, to whom this order came; the Texians leave Saltillo in Irons, and arrive at the Salado; where an order is received, commanding every tenth man to be put to death; the order is obeyed; the Been Drawing; the names of the decimated; the cruelty of the decree! the Texians are marched off towards the City of Mexico; the cruelty of their treatment; the murder of Capt. Cameron; the Texians arrive at the City of Mexico, where they are Ironed and put to Work.

As the writer was one of those "poor unfortunates," who were left at the city of Matamoras unable to travel, he is brought to the necessity of depending upon oral knowledge relating to those events which he is about to record in the present chapter. This knowledge, however, has been derived from the very best authority, among those who were eye witnesses of, and partakers in, those scenes about to be depicted and for whose integrity the writer would willingly vouch were it probable that such a voucher would fortify or assist in the least the truth of the record. Or, at any rate, the writer feels fairly convinced of the truth of what he writes.

On the 14th of January 1843, the main body of prisoners left Matamoras for the City of Mexico under the escort of Genl. Canales and seven or eight hundred of his *Rancheros*, or citizen soldiers taking the road to Monterey. On the march, while they were yet in the vicinity of the *Rio Grande*, there was an effort made to induce the Prisoners to attempt a Rescue; which, however, proved fruitless. After a fatiguing march, they arrived at Monterey on the 1st of February.[1] After a short rest of two or three days, they were again put on the road and arrived at Saltillo on the 6th,[2] without the occurrance of any thing worthy of note. On the 7th they again took the road, pursuing their march without any occurrence capable of giving interest and reached "*El Rancho Salado*"[3] (The Salt Farm) on the evening of the 10th of the same month.

There, the writer takes pride in acknowledging it his duty to record one of the most glorious achievements that adorns the annals of National History. It was on that night, while the Mexican sentinel dozed at his post or drowsely uttered the occasional "*Sentinella alerto*!"[4] and the Mexican officer slept quietly in his "*Serape*," that a small band of prisoners resolved to free themselves, though unarmed and five hundred miles within the bounderies of an enemies country. The treatment which they received, the harsh abuses heaped upon them, the insults which were continually offered to their high and freeborn souls had become to grevious to be borne by such spirits; therefore, though Death in its most awful forms and Dangers of every kind hovered near to deter them from the step, a large majority of the Texian prisoners resolved to free themselves—to enjoy one moment's liberty—although Death might quickly follow—or perish in the attempt. They understood the hazards that were to be run. They were not quite two hundred and twenty strong, without arms—not even a pen knife with which to offend or defend; while their guard numbered something over Four hundred well armed men, a part of whom were Cavalry. The[y] had difficulties to surmount, which would, under other circumstances, have detered any but Texians from taking such a step. To make the necessary charge, they must pass through two doors, the first of which was not wide enough to admit of two men passing through at the same time. On each side of this narrow entrance stood a sentinel. Between that and the second door was a strong guard. There

1. The prisoners entered Monterey on Jan. 29, 1843, where they remained until the afternoon of Feb. 2, 1843.

2. On Feb. 5 the prisoners entered Saltillo, the capital of the state whose name was still Coahuila y Texas. The city's population at the time was estimated at 18,000.

3. El Rancho Salado (the Salt Ranch or the Salt Farm) was a small establishment in a desert plain twenty miles from San Salvador and ninety miles from Saltillo on the road from Saltillo to Matehuala.

4. *Centinela Alerto*: Sentinel is alert!

seems to have been a traitor among the prisoners, for the conduct of the Mexicans clearly proved that they entertained some idea that all was not right, which was seen by the alertness of the guard, and more satisfactorily, by the guard being doubled. (The writer will not say *that there was a traitor among his countrymen,*[5] for he wishes not to accuse unjustly; and least he might, he lets the matter rest.) But the Rescue had been determined upon, and *Capt. Ewing Cameron* chosen as its leader; and on the following morning, when the hour drew near at which the fearful trial was to be made, although these difficulties and dangers were clear to every mind, no one that had resolved gave back; not one that had set his hopes upon his own prowes trembled; and all who had the night previous given their voices for the rescue, now stood ready to lend it their hands; aye, and surrender to it their lives! The time of receiving breakfast had been fixed as the moment for the outbreak. They formed as usual to receive their morning rations. Cameron stood foremost; an unbroken silence reigned over that daring band; every eye is turned to the noble Cameron, who stans like a statuė, his head erect, his eye fixed upon vacancy, his nerves steady; no one moves, none seem excited, but anxiety has a place upon the features [of] all save Cameron. The moment arrives; his piercing eye lights up, and throwing his timeworn hat far above his head—the preconcerted signal—he utters the word; the door is reached placing a hand upon the breast of each sentinel at the narrow doorway the Lionlike Cameron hurls them far away in opposite directions as the wirlwind scatters chaff, and with a bound he rushes through the remaining door. The Texians pour out after their leader. The Mexicans rally for a few minutes, but it is useless; for the whirlwind impetuosity of the Texians bears all before it. In a very short time the Texians were masters of the field, and the Mexicans were scampering away for life. They fought hand to hand, but the struggle was to deadly to last long. Cameron had instructed his men to kill none of the enemy if they could avoid it; consequently, there were only five or six Mexicans killed, and a very few wounded, while the Texians lost five killed and

5. According to Samuel H. Walker, one of the finest spies in the Texas Ranger force and one who was especially noted on the frontier for his great coolness in difficult situations, the Mexicans were "befor[e] hand apprised of our intention it is supposed by Capt Reese of Brazoria whose conduct has been dishonorable." Capt. S. H. Walker to A. Sidney Johns[t]on, [dated] Prison Santiago, City of Mexico, May 4, 1843. Army Papers (Republic), Texas State Archives.

three wounded.[6] This act prehaps has no precedent; it is unparaleled in historical annals but it was nevertheless effected by two hundred Texians against four hundred Mexicans, when the former had not as much as a pocket knife with which to make defence, or give offence, whereas the latter were well armed, and a portion of them cavalry.

Not more than a fourth of the Texians were enabled to enter into the engagement, from the cause that the door through which they passed was only sufficient in weadth for one man to pass at a time; consiquently, the enemy had taken a *Stampeda* ere more than a quarter of the Texians could gain admitance to the Scene of action, and it is probable that a fiew did not wish to enter on the stage untill the act was closed and the curtain droped. I mention this from several well directed hints which I have received from those who did engage *heart* and *hand*, *soul*, *body*, and *strength* in the struggle for liberty.

Some of the Texians, refusing to take advantage of this victory, remained with the Enemy. A fiew of these were compelled to do so by wounds and disease, but others, I shall not attempt to speak for "*Actions speak louder than words*," is an old, and, I think, true saying.

On the same day of the fight, they began their retreat towards the Rio Grande, from which they were distant about five hundred miles. Knowing well that their only safety was on the east of that river, they, of course, delayed no time. The idea of retreating that distance through an enemy's country under such circumstances is a thing before unthought of. It is true that the gallant Col. Jourden[7] performed a good and glorious retreat from Saltillo to the [Rio] Grande, a distance of four hundred miles, with 110 men, but he was retireing from an enemy who were not anxious to come up with him from the fact that the enemy were aware of the body being well armed with rifles. But Cameron's men were badly armed, having nothing but arms which they

6. Those who were killed were Dr. Richard Fox Brenham, John Lyons, Archibald Fitzgerald, John Higgerson, and Lorenzo D. Rice; and those who were wounded were Captain John R. Baker, John Harvey, and George Washington Trahern. Fitzgerald was captured by Woll at San Antonio, and Higgerson was one of the wounded Dawson men taken near the Salado in Texas. See Appendix II for McCutchan's further description of this incident; Thomas Jefferson Green, *Journal of the Texian Expedition against Mier*, pp. 444, 447; Joseph Milton Nance, *Attack and Counterattack*, p. 623; Israel Canfield diary, muster rolls, Texas State Archives.

7. For an account of Colonel Samuel W. Jordan's masterful retreat from the vicinity of Saltillo to the Rio Grande, see Joseph Milton Nance, *After San Jacinto*, pp. 358–360.

had taken from the enemy, the efficacy of which and the fear which the[y] impose on the Mexican people is far inferior to the arms with which Texians go to meet liberties foe. But we will, hereafter, say more on this subject.

On the twelfth, they, misjudging their policy, left the road and took to the mountains. To this Cameron was bitterly opposed, but it appeared to be the general wish of the men and he consented. In that he was to blame, for he should have assumed the *entire command*, as he had been chosen for that purpose, but he was too much given to acceding to the propositions of his men. Still Captain Cameron cannot be censured; he must not be answerable for the acts of others. There were two (perhaps more) of the captains who went to Cameron telling him that if he did not leave the road that they would draw off their companies and leave the command. Here Cameron was placed in a dellicate and critical position; he saw that he must either go directly contrary to his own will, or that he must see a band of brave men, already to small for the undertaking bursted asunder and cast apart in an enemy's country, where distruction would soon overtake them. Here were two verry great evils presented to his view, and he finally concluded to give the reign to his men in preference to seeing the[m] disunite. Of the two evils he chose the least. No man can be found who would not have acted the same way under similar circumstances.

On the fifteenth, being in great want of food, and finding a water hole convenient, but small, they killed their horses and dried the flesh, or a portion of it. This place furnished them the last water they received, some for six days, some seven, and others were eight days without a drop of water. From this place they moved on to gain the pass through the mountains; but, finally, from exhaustion and want of water (food they had but could not eat) the desparate became unable to stay in a body. Water was the only wish—the only cry—*Water*! *Water*! *Water*!!! But none was to be had! They scattered over the small valleys in serch of water, and *thus* were taken, *unable to resist*. The largest body of them with Cameron at their head were taken on the 25th of Feb. *Poor fellows*, they were willing to sacrifice their life! nay *more* their liberty, for *one sup of water*. They were all taken, save sixteen, four of whom came in—the remainder were missing, and supposed dead. After the recapture they were marched to Saltillo where they arrived on the second of March.

Conduct of the General Government of Gen. Mahier, Governor of the State of Saltillo.[8] *The cause for the conduct of the General Government.*

When they reached Saltillo, the President, Santa Anna,[9] sent an order to Gen. Meheir,[10] the governor, to shoot every man without distinction. This was a peremptory order, but the *Noble* and *Generous* Meheir refused to execute it, saying that he would be murderer for no man or government, for which generous resolution he was removed from his office. Thare, among those people, was he dishonored for an act which would have raised him in the estimation of any other people on the globe who bear the credit of civilization.

It is the belief, and it is my opinion, that the cause which, in a great measure, is to be attributed this determination of the General Government was that about this time Sam Houston caused Capt. Elliott,[11] the English Chargé d'affaires to Texas, to write a letter to Packingham,[12]

8. The name of the state was Coahuila y Texas.

9. Antonio López de Santa Anna.

10. Francisco Mejía was a native of Ixtapan who began his military career Feb. 18, 1811, in the squadron of Tulancingo. In 1843 he held the rank of general of brigade and was governor and commandant general and inspector of the state of Coahuila y Texas. He refused to carry out the order of the government to execute the recaptured prisoners and for doing so was arrested and removed from office. With a change in political climate in Mexico, he was named commandant general of Durango in 1849 and of San Luis Potosí in 1852. Alberto M. Carreño, ed., *Jefes del ejército méxicano en 1847*, pp. 118–120; Hubert Howe Bancroft, *History of Mexico*, V:237; P. D. to the editor, [dated] Monterey, March 24, 1843, quoted from the *New Orleans Bulletin*, Apr. 22, 1843, in *Telegraph and Texas Register*, May 3, 1843.

11. Charles Elliot was born in 1801 and in 1815 entered the British Royal Navy for service in the East Indies and on the coast of Africa. In 1828 he retired from the navy and entered the British colonial service and was in charge of English trade relations with China from 1834 until the outbreak of the Opium War in 1840. On Aug. 6, 1842, he arrived in Texas as British chargé d'affaires for the Republic of Texas. Walter P. Webb and H. Bailey Carroll (eds.), *Handbook of Texas*, I:556–557; Sam Houston to Captain Charles Elliot, [dated] Washington, Jan. 24, 1843, and notes thereto in Amelia W. Williams and Eugene C. Barker (eds.), *Writings of Sam Houston*, II:299–304.

12. Sir Richard Pakenham was born in 1797 and spent most of his mature life in the British diplomatic service. After receiving his education at Trinity College, Dublin, he was, in 1817, attached to the embassy at the Hague and later sent to other European posts. In 1826 he became secretary to the British legation at Mexico and in 1835 minister to Mexico, which post he held

the English Minister to Mexico, stating that although we had entered on the Expedition contrairy to the wishes of the Texian government, he (Sam Houston) wished him (Packingham) to see that we were treated with all the lenity that could be possibly extended to such men. This gave Santa Anna the power to act as he thought propper. But we will speak of this hereafter.

* * * *

We will now return to the narrative. They left Saltillo on the 22d, handcuffed two and two, and arrived at the Salado on the 25th, where an order met them for the shooting of one tenth. This was effected in the following manner; thare being 176 men, thare were 176 beans put into a small pot, 17 of which number were black—the others of a yellowish cast. Those who were so unfortunate as to draw the former were shot that evening within hearing of their companions, who were handcuffed and made to set down, and sentinels drawn up in front of them with arms presented and express orders to fire on the Texians if one of them attempted to rise from his position. What an aweful crisis! What a solemn, heart rendering position for men! They knew that seventeen men *must die*! The dread edict had come from the Despot! and they must *die*! The drawing was over; the doomed were marched out to receive their *death*! The only dry eyes in that little band of Warrier Prisoners were those of the doomed ones! They said they were willing to die in the cause in which they had fought and which they loved. The observation of one of them was in effect this—"They murdered my uncle! they butchered my brother! and now they call for my blood! Let them have it! Ere this have I seen them drop before my rifle! My death is already well revenged! *Farewell Soldiers of liberty I die content*! *Farewell*!" So went the brave, the sacrificed men to slaughter, with cheeks unblanced and lips that quivered not! Thare escaped not a tear from their eyes, nor a sigh from their lips! but they went like the bridegroom to his bride, the soldier to battle, or the Saint to Glory.

On the following morning one of the bodies was missing, the name of which was Shepherd.[13] We afterwards learned that he had recieved

---

until December 1843 when he returned to England. Ephraim Douglass Adams, *British Interests and Activities in Texas*, p. 23n.

13. James L. Shepherd, a lad of about seventeen years of age, had received a ball through the side of his cheek, "cutting his face severely, but inflicting nothing more than a bad flesh-wound." One of his arms was also broken by another ball. At the first volley he fell upon his face pretending to be dead.

a ball in each arm breaking the bone and one in the neck, thus he lay untill dark, and then cralled off. He went to the home of a sheapherd who cured him of his wounds. He then erroniously went to Saltillo where he was recognized and shot in the street.

Poor fellows! Yet better to die than endure such misery as we have suffered. We know not that they were buried.[14] They lie neglected by friend and foe; but now car[e]less of the storms of life, they are in a better world.

The Cause why we were not all *Shot*

The circumstance of Gen. Mehier's refusal to obey orders saved the Mier prisoners from an untimely and bloody death. When Gen. Wady Thomson,[15] the United States Minister heard of the order of Santa Anna for the death of every Texian prisoner, he immediately went to Doyl,[16] Her Britanic Majesty's Minister, and requested his cooperation

---

As soon as night descended, he made his escape into the mountains. Canfield diary, Mar. 25, 1843.

14. The bodies of the decimated Texans were buried at Cedral by Padre Luis G. Medina.

15. Waddy Thompson, son of Waddy and Eliza (Blackburn) Thompson, natives of Virginia, was born at Pickensville, near Easley, South Carolina, Sept. 8, 1798. He graduated from South Carolina College (now the University of South Carolina) in 1814 and in 1819 was admitted to the bar. He practiced law for five years in Edgefield and then moved to Greenville, where, in 1826, he was elected from the Greenville district to the state legislature, serving until 1830. Thereafter he became solicitor for the western district. In the controversy with the United States over the protective tariff, he was an ardent Nullifier and was made a brigadier general in the state forces to defend the state against the United States. This position he held to 1842. From 1835 to 1841 he served in the House of Representatives of the United States Congress as a Whig. Early in 1842 he was named by the Whig administration minister to Mexico, where he ably represented the United States. In Congress he had strongly advocated United States recognition of Texan independence and the annexation of Texas, an advocacy which did not seem to impair his effectiveness in Mexico. He returned to the United States in 1844. *Dictionary of American Biography*, XVIII:473–474.

16. Percy Doyle succeeded Pakenham as the British diplomatic representative in Mexico, holding the rank of chargé d'affaires. The assignment was a temporary and unfortunate one, and he never became the British minister to Mexico. Furthermore, Thompson made his appeal to Pakenham rather than to Doyle.

in saving the Texians. Doyl, at first, refused to comply, alledging as his reason that "he as the Minister of H. B. M. at Mexico had no right to interfear in the coarse of Justice for men who were outlawed by their own country," which he said we were, and as a proff he produced the letter which I have beefore mentioned from Elliott to Packingham. Thompson then produced the order under which we left our homes, and proved clearly to Doyle that we had acted under the authority of the Texas Government. From this he agreed to cooperate with Thompson. They did do so, and we were saved from death to live a life of misery. The French Minister[17] also told Santa Anna that if he dared shoot another of the Texian Prisoners he would immediately demand his papers and return to his Government, for he could not stand a silent spectator of the most barbarous acts that ever did disgrace civilization. They were acts, high acts of murder, worthy of barbarians alone. It is probable that the words of the Minister of France had more influence over Santa Anna than both Thompson and Doyle, for he well knew if the Frenchman went home it would be but little time before the Fleet of France would commence opperations on Vera Cruz. He had previously had ample proof of its efficacy.

But there are many officers in Mexico to whom, if the order had been given, which was given to Mehier, they would have executed it with such promptitude that foreign powers could not have effected any good in our behalf. But Mehier, with that spirit of bravery, that soul of *man*, said, "So far from these men deserving death, if I had it in my power, they should have their liberty."

On the morning of the 26th of March they took up the line of march for San Louis Potosí, where they arrived on the sixth of April.[18] From hence, they started for the City of Mexico. They arrived at Huehuetoca, on the twenty-fourth. On the 25th Capt. Ewing Cameron was shot by order of the general government. I will take occasion to speak more explicitly on this hereafter. On the evening of the 26th they arrived at the City of Mexico and were put in the convent Sandiago.[19]

17. The French minister to Mexico was the Baron Alleye de Cyprey. He was appointed envoy extraordinary and minister plenipotentiary on July 11, 1839, and presented his credentials in Mexico on Feb. 20, 1840, and served until 1845. Luis Weckmann, *Las relaciones franco-mexicanas*, II (1839–1867):401.

18. San Luis Potosí was reached on Apr. 5, 1843.

19. Although the Convent Santiago still housed a few monks in 1842, it was principally used as a common prison. It was here that the able-bodied men of the Santa Fe Expedition had been incarcerated. George Wilkins Kendall, *Narrative of the Texas Santa Fe Expedition*, II:288–289.

About the first of May, they were chained, *two* and *two* togather, taken out to Tacabaya, and there put to hard work, where we, five in number, found them, on our arrival at the same place on the 30th of May. They were at work on a road leading from Santa Anna's place[20] towards the city.

Captain Cameron's Death

This great and brave, but neglected man, was Scotchman by bearth. He came to Texas, enlisted in the service of the country, and well did he do his duty. He resided on the western frontier at or near Victoria. It mattered not at what time or in what force the enemy came, Ewing Cameron was ever in the front rank of her defenders. His breast was ever placed to the foe, and ever ready was his arm to strike the blow in defense of the liberties of his adopted Country. He had been in several engagements previous to that of Mier, and had ever, as he did thare, show a determined, firm, resolute bravery, not to be excelled by heroes, either ancient or modern. Yet he had never been noticed, save by those immediately around and acquainted with him. He never made any boast of his own actions but showed himself by his acts to be a modest, unassuming, brave, and determined man. In the Battle of Mier he was captain of the Victoria Company, and he and his men did honor to themselves and their country in that well fought but badly ended battle. I once heard him say that he did not expect the Mexicans would let him escape. He was well known to many of the rio Grande Mexicans personally, and known by character to all. Canales was a personal enemy to him. It was partly through his personal exertions that the "*break*" was attempted, and dearly did he pay for it. He was unanimously chosen to lead them in the charge at the Salado, and well did he fulfill the duty placed upon him. He gave the word, lead the charge, and acted as cool and heroic as ever man could act. He drew the first bean at the Salado on the twenty-fifth of March. It is said that the Mexicans placed the white beans at the bot[t]om and the black at the top, and did not shake them up till Cameron had drawn, thare by plainly showing that it was their wish to murder him, and do it with

20. President Santa Anna's residence was the Archbishop's Palace at Tacubaya, about four miles from the capital and about a mile directly south of Chapúltepec. The residence for the archbishop had been erected by order of Archbishop and Viceroy Juan Antonio de Vizarron y Eguiarreta in 1739. W. A. Croffut (ed.), *Fifty Years in Camp and Field*, p. 280; Thomas Philip Terry, *Terry's Guide to Mexico*, p. 417.

some show of right. Even a people so base as they wished to have some pretence for an act so barbarous. On the night of the 24th of April 1843, at the solemn and awful hour of midnight he was taken out from his companions, and on the following morning was *shot.* Why did they not commit the horrid deed by night? It was too murderous for the light of day! Oh! Why could not some saving hand have interposed to snatch the brave, the noble victim, from his barbarous enemies—hurling them into eternity, and thus have saved *one* brave Texian. The murder of Cameron was an act which should have called fourth the vengance of the world on an insolent and savage race! It was a high, a *horrid* act of barbarity! It was an awful act! enough to make *angels* weap! *Devils* laugh! and man lament! When the Mexican Government saw that he did not draw the "*Black bean*," it then had him taken out and shot like a *dog. May the blood of Cameron and his companions be on the heads of their murderers.* We did not see him shot. The following is told by a Mexican who saw it. "They lead him out, and wished to blindfold and tie him; he refused saying that he feared not death, and he would die as a man and a soldier should *die, free and* unfetered. They then shot him, but not to kill, only to cripple. After wounding, they tied, blindfolded, and shot him as if he had been a *dog*! but he received his death *bravely*, without a murmur or shudder. Thus died your leader." This was, recollect, told by an enemy. Even they could not but give credit for his heroism. Even though they murdered, they could not but admire him, for the calmness with which he met his death.

Parents teach the name of Cameron to you[r] children! May his name live! Nay it will live while time lasts, and when *time* shall *be no more*, Eternity itself shall catch and dwell with increasing rapture on the name of *Cameron*, a man neglected while living, but lamented and revered, now *dead.*

That Noble man met an untimely and bloody end. But he met it with that cool and laudable front which he had ever presented to danger. His acts speak volums more for him than all writers of the world could say. *Long last the memory of butchered Cameron*!

Sam Houston and his letter through Elliott to Packingham

In the first place I will speak of the causes of the Expedtion. Our frontier was continually lyable to the attacks of the enemy. Wall[21] had just

21. Brigadier General Adrián Woll.

been into Sanantonio, and every one knows what was his conduct, and that conduct lead Gen. Sam Houston to give an order in which he plainly said "pursue the enemy, even into his own territory, and chastise him there." Then I ask, why is it that Sam Houston president of Texas, has denyed giving this order, when the evidence of his fals[e]-hood stands plain to the face of the world? It is true that we left the command, but it is not less true that we had General Sommerville's acquiescence in the separation. We had his consent.[22] He was placed in the command by the President, and we had an incontestible right to do that which he would permit. Houston sent us out, and after we had, by hardships encountered and daingers overcome, reached the Rio Grande, the territory of the enemy, he ordered the command back to the settlements. This order was not to us, but to our Commander, and if that commander, then in the face of this order, gave us permission to cross the river and do service for Texas, *we are not to be held responsible.* The soldier is not to answer for the acts of his commander. Sommervill acted just also, for many of us were on foot having lost our horses; those who were on foot needed the protection of horsemen. Tharefore, he gave those dismounted permission to go down the river and procure horses, with a grant to all who were mounted and wished to go to follow their example, and act as a protection to them. Now why has Sam Houston thrown us on the *mercy* of an enemy to whom he knew belonged no such heavenly feeling? Why did he at the verry time when we most needed a word to show that the expedition was authorised by our government, in the face of a paper bearing evidence of his own falsehood, say to the world that we were robbers; but nevertheless, *he* prayed that our captors would be merciful to us? Yes, he prayed for mercy towards us, and had it not been for the interfearence of foreign powers, that prayer would have had its designed effect; it would have sealed the fate of every man so unfortunate as to be taken in that expedition! His letter, had it have been allowed to take it[s] full force, would have been neither more nor less than our death warrent! It was proven that he did give this order. Then why did he, we we [*sic*] stood in need of his assistance, deny it to us, thus cutting off all hope? When, by the cruel fate of war, we were made prisoners, why did he deny us that protection to which only we could look with hope for life and liberty? *Because we were unfortunate, and unsuccessful.* But the design, *deep, dark,* and *base,* which he had in view by that *awful,* that *bloody letter,* his actions plainly show. I will not accuse him directly, *but his conduct was suspicious! Suspicion is on him!* and there let it rest, it is *well* placed.

22. See Chapter II, footnote 12.

If we had been successful at Mier—if we had captured a fiew of the enemy—carried them home as trophies gained, then would Houston have addressed us, calling us "the heroes of Texas—Glorious sons of Liberty—soldiers deserving honor, trust, and glory—worthy of the nation's praise, and the t[h]anks of the Nation's Congress";—and would finally have wound up by taking all the honor and thanks to himself, because *he had ordered the expedition*. But as it is, Houston swore he never gave the order, and has been heard to say—"They are better thare than at home." *He not only aimed to take our lives, but to Blast our honor*. Had he have only aimed to murder us, we could possibly have forgiven that, but the attempt to blast our reputation has placed an impassable abyss between Sam Houston and the Mier Prisoners.

The Old Powder Mill—Tacubaya—Santa Anna's Palace—City of Mexico and its vicinity—The country surrounding Mexico, and the character of the inhabitants—Montezuma's Castle and Subteranian Passage.

The Old Powder Mill, or Morlino del Rey, is situated three miles from the city, and one mile from Santa Anna's or the President's Palace. It is a large and has, in time, been a good building, but the walls are now dilapidated. It is verry extensive, and in the center of the inner court thare is a fountain of water bursting up—it is artificial, yet it is beautiful and good water.

Tacubaya is a small village four miles from Mexico in which is the President's Palace. It is a place of no particular note save that it is the residence of the President, and thare is a road made by Texian Prisoners taken at Mier.

The Presidents Palace is a large and fine building two stories in hight with windows opening on all sides. Adjoining it is a park, in one part of which are many fruit trees. It is situated on an eminence overlooking the whole valley of the city of Mexico.

The City of Mexico is situated in a valley nearly circular in form and about twenty miles in diameter. This would be a splendid city if it had breadth of street, but it has not. Thare are many fine buildings, beautiful in appearance, but greatly darkened by their proximity to each other. There are about one hundred and fifty thousand inhabitants in the city, some say more. Though at first glance one would suppose that it was impossible for that number to exist in a city of that dimension, but the Mexicans live, many togeather. This valley is rich and fertile, producing corn and wheat mostly though any grain would do well. The city is situated within thirty miles and in sight of two extraordinary high mountains, who's sumits are clothed in perpetual snow, and when the sun is rising or siting, his rays just tiping these snow and cloud caped mountains it presents a sublime and beautiful sight. The whole country surrounding the city, save this valley, is mountainious. Thare are four different passes leading into the valley of the city of the Montezumas.

The inhabitants are generally verry dark, though many of the ladies are fare and beautiful as the lily. The higher class are of Castillian descent, and the lower class are of Indian orrigin. The men are cowardly, treatcherous, and thieving; the women are pretty, modest, and loving. The Spanish women, or those of Spanish orrigin, are beautiful, being faltless both in form and feature, with black glossy hair and dark flashing eyes, sufficient to set man's soul on fire at one glance. But the men have no redeaming trait. Situated two or two and a half miles from the city is what was once the castle of Montazuma, but now chainged and so remodeled that was its old proprietor to return to earth, he could not recognize his ancient and trusted strong hold. It is now a military college. It was once the seat of a powerful prince, and its battlements gleamed with steal, but now it is not an immage of what it was in former times. From this castle thare is a subterranian passage of about three miles to the palace in the city. This passage was once large enough for two men to go abreast and about six feet in depth, but it is now nearly filled up with fallen stones and earth.

Every thing is fast dilapidating, even the churches for which they pretend such reverence are going to ruin. And judging from the past, ten years will not roll round ere the splendid edifices for which Mexico had been justly cellibrated shall have m[o]uldered to dust and the whole country present one mass of ruins.

Labour at Tacubaya

When we, five in number, reached Tacubaya on the thirtieth of May eighteen hundred and forty three we found them [the Texan prisoners] employed making a road from the palace towards town. This road was formed in the following manner, three lines of pavement were run one foot wide, one of these on each side and one in the center of the road, the intermediate space was then filled in alternately earth and pebles, untill raised to a level with the part paived. The center line of stones was something higher than the other two, thus giving a sufficient decline from the center [to] each side to drain it clear of water falling on it. We made six hundred yards of this road in five months, but it could have been done in much less time. We laboured harder in opposing them than we did for them. Our policy was to do as little as possible, and spend as much time at it as was convenient. The labour which we performed, though extremely rough and hard to us, was of but little advantage to the Captors. We frequently burried crowbars, shovels, trowels, and other instruments under the earth thrown upon the road; this the overseer was responsible for, so it interfeared not with us. Some of us were a part of the time engaged in packing sacks a distance of half a mile and we frequently moved so slow that it was hard to perceive whether we were stationary or moving. We had tin knives with which we cut our sacks and let out our rocks, thus managing to release our nerves from the weight and so to dispose of our cargo among the shrubs and grass that when reaching our place of destination, we would have not one pound. By this and many other plans, we managed to be kept hard at work, but doing in a manner nothing for our ignoble, barbarous, and treacherous enemies.

About the first of June we were looking with anxiety to the thirteenth. Thompson[23] said that he thought it probible that on that day we would regain our liberty. But before that looked for day arrived, the news of Col. Snively's expedition[24] to Santa Fe reached the capital, then Santa Anna said that he would not release us while our country-

23. General Waddy Thompson, United States minister to Mexico.

24. The Jacob Snively Expedition was authorized by the Texas War Department on Feb. 16, 1843, to retaliate upon the New Mexicans for the indignities heaped upon the Texan prisoners of the Santa Fe Expedition of 1841 and for the recent Mexican raids upon Texas. On May 27 the expedition reached the Santa Fe Trail where it crossed the Arkansas River. The Snively Expedition ultimately proved to be a failure, as had the earlier Charles A. Warfield Expedition authorized by the Texas government on Aug. 16, 1842, as a private freebooting enterprise.

The Mier men had been led to believe that they would all be released on June 13; but the proclamation issued by Santa Anna on that day, because of the Texan aggression against New Mexico and Commodore E. W. Moore's appearance with the Texas navy upon the Mexican coast, was confined to those who had committed political offenses and was not extended to the Texan prisoners. *Telegraph and Texas Register*, Aug. 2 and 23, 1843; Webb and Carroll (eds.), *Handbook of Texas*, II:632–633, 863; H. Bailey Carroll, "Steward A. Miller and the Snively Expedition of 1843," *Southwestern Historical Quarterly* LIV (1950–1951):261–286; William C. Binkley, "The Last Stage of Texas Military Operations Against Mexico," *Southwestern Historical Quarterly* XXII (1918–1919):262–266.

men were carrying on a war against his domain. This, it is true, was a plausable pretence; yet, I only can look on it a[s] pretence, for it is my belief that he never did intend releasing us on that day, though I have no right to say that he *did not intimate* as much to Gen. Thompson, the United States minister. He had made this intimation for some purpose. I do not pretend to say what, and then this afforded a good opportunity for him to make an absolute refusal to any proposition that had been or might have been for our release.

Sic[k]ness was prevalent about this time—mostly feaver and Rheumatism. Many of the men died, but their names I do not at this time recollect, but they will be easily found by refering to "the muster roll of the command, with the fate of each man," which will herewith be found. Also, there were some who died previous to our arrival at the capital—their names likewise will be found in the before mentioned muster roll.

In this month (June) a man by the name of Copeland[25] made his escape by night. It was not known, even by many of his companions, untill the following morning (Copeland was retaken about three weeks after near the rio Grande, but his recapture was not made known to us untill in April 1844, when he was brought to Perote. He then informed us that he had met with one of the officers who fought us at Mier, and this officer recognised him as one of the Texian prisoners. He was taken to Monterey, thare tried and found "*guilty*" of being one of the Texiano Diablos. Thence he was conveyed to Saltillo, and thare remained untill the time of his starting to Perote.)

Thare were, I think, eight others who escaped from the old powder Mill, but their names and the date of their escape will be found on the muster roll. If the foreign ministers (and more particularly Thompson) had not have held up continually the prospect of release to *all*, many more of us would have availed ourselves of oportunities which *did* offer for our escape. But we foolishly clung to a vain hope that all would be released! We let opportunities pass—chance after chance to escape went by, leaving us to our false hope, untill it was everlastingly too late! It is true that in escaping we ran a great risk, both of being shot in the attempt, and of being retaken after escape and then likely shot, but these are small considerations when compaired with the

25. Willis Copeland on the night of July 29, 1843, escaped over the prison wall, using blankets torn into ropes. He was a private in Captain Gardiner Smith's company in the Somervell Expedition but refused to return with Somervell. See a copy of Muster Roll of this company in Sam S. Smith Collection, Archives, University of Texas. Canfield diary, July 30, 1843, gives the name as William Copeland.

chances of liberty. Contrast liberty with slavery, and who will not take Ninety-nine chances of death to one of life in an attempt for his freedom? But we let all[26]

26. Book One abruptly stops at this point at the bottom of page 96, possibly with a portion missing. This page is numbered by someone as page 116; and page 117, being the beginning of Book Second, follows as a separate "volume"; but these are apparently not page numbers assigned by McCutchan.

BOOK SECOND

More of Tacubaya, and our pursuits

In making this road at Tacubaya (or Tacuballa, some spell it, though the pronunciation is the same) we were much retarded by the ficleness of the Mexicans. They would begin on one plan, and after having made probably one or two hundred yards would take it all up and commence it different. But the main cause was our unwillingness, which made itself verry apparent in more than one instance and under many different circumstances. One method on our part was a determination to moove as slow as possible, even to our own inconvenience. As, for example, I need only refer to the sand and stone packers and explain their conduct. To this *honorable* and *august* body, I, myself, had the *extreme gratification* of belonging. I received the honor of a membership in that aseembly, and *faithfully* did I perform my duty tharein. For the sake of good order and a perfect obedience to our best interest, we rather organised ourselves. As we were chained two and two for convenience, and thus compelled to march in double file, we chose, for advantage, two of the *most absolutely* lazy men that could be found among us for our "leaders." These two men invariably took the advance, and ever faithful to the trust which their constituents had honored them with, they mooved *so slow* that the moovement was scarcely perceptible. For this judicious management, we recieved praise from our companions, curses from our oppressors, and gratification from consciences. And while thus marching, one after another, we would watch an opportunity and catch the guard inattentive; seize the moment to thrust our hand into the sack of our neighbour in advance of us; pluck tharefrom a stone and *innocently* hurl it into the grass or any other convenient place that might present itself. This was our only real amusement. Though we were often even gay in appearance, yet thare was a something which caused continual sadness at the heart. A man may appear lively and even happy, when in reality if you examine his heart you find him the most miserable man on the earth. "That is not all gold which glistens." That is not all happiness which appears so. I shall say nothing more in this strain for it is evident that I am no morralizer. Some of the men took rather a singular method of raising "funds," as follows: they would procure a coldchisel, cut off their chains, smuggle them out, and sell them at a verry low rate; or after having cut their chain, wear it to their work, watch a opportunity to hide it in some convenient place and sell it at some future day. Thus did some of us manage to keep a little money.

About as little work as could be done in so much time did we do. We were not disposed to do that which could be avoided; tharefore we caught at every pretence to avoid a labour which was extremely disagreeable to our minds and bodies. Also when we quit the road we had the extreme gratification of leaving some of our overseers to "taste the pleasures of a *prison life*," for the loss of tools which we had distroyed or hiden. This was our sweetest consolation: I hope they had a fine time.

About the 7th of September 1843,[27] we finished the road, and on the 9th were moved to Sandiago,[28] which is a convent, now used as a prison, situated in the edge of the city. We were huddled into one room here on the night of the 9th.

The convent of Sandiago is said to be the first edifice erected in the city by the Spaniards; consiquently, it is one of the oldest buildings in the country. It is well adapted to the purpose for which it is now principally used—that of holding criminals of all classes. It is built in the form of a Square with an inner court, or Square, surrounded by a tier of cells which all open into the court. The only enterance to this inner court is through a corridore or hall in which stand[s] the main guard to the prison.

During the whole time of our confinement in the city of Mexico and its vicinity we were chained two togeather with a chain ten or twelve feet in length weighing about twenty-five or thirty pounds. These were fastened to our ancle by a ring rivited hard down.

On the eleventh our chains were cut off, and after recieving each a thin blanket we were started off towards the castle of San Carlos de Perote. We were told that we were to be released as soon as we reached Perote. Though this was told to us by the foreigners, and even hinted by Gen. Thompson, we did not place much confidence in it, for, though we were as drownding men, we had been too often duped by false illusions to catch at a straw. Our frail hopes had been too often hurled down from their assumed highth to the lowest habitations of dispair—hopes which had been raised by some flattering illusion of

27. On Sept. 5, 1843, President Santa Anna's secretary informed the Texans that the road had been finished and that the government was satisfied with their work. Canfield diary, Aug. 26–Sept. 5, 1843; Thomas W. Bell, *Narrative of the Capture and Subsequent Sufferings of the Mier Prisoners in Mexico*, p. 69.

28. Convent Santiago.

fancy, then blasted by the aweful realities of a horrible fate! Often did we raise hopes to have them blasted by the next hour! Then, I hope, no one will blaim us for our doubt, or censure us for incredulity, even when we had the word of many good people. We had a verry fatigueing march to Puebla through rain and cold, and arrived at that place on the fifteenth, where we were put into a prison, which was full to overflowing of criminals. This was one very disagreeable occurrence which ever followed us, go where we might. We lef[t] this place on the 17th[29] in Company of two hundred of the lowest and basest criminals. With them we were compelled to remain untill our arrival at Perote, which was on the twenty first. In the town of Perote we left the thieves —they for Vera Cruz and we for the Castle. These criminals stole nearly everything we had. From me they stole the only pa[i]r of pants I had deserving that name, which was truly an unfortunate circumstance.

On our arrival at Perote we found Col. Fisher and those who were marched on with him from Matamoras; also, the prisoners taken by Gen. Woll at San Antonio and the Salado in Texas in September, 1842. They were all in verry good health on our arrival, though *we* could not boast of being so. It is one of Misfortune's Sweetest pleasures to meet friends in adversity and recieve and return their warm greeting. But I will not morralize.

29. The correct date for the beginning of the march to Perote Castle was Sept. 12, 1843; see entries for Sept. 12, 1843 in Canfield diary and James A. Glasscock's diary, Texas State Archives; William Preston Stapp, *Prisoners of Perote*, p. 103; Bell, *A Narrative of the Capture and Subsequent Sufferings*, p. 103.

[Chapter VII]

An account of the march of Col. Fisher and his companions (also, of those who refused to take advantage of the victory gained over the Guard) from the Salado, on the 11th of February 1843.

These men who were with Col. Fisher—four in number,[1] were started from the Salado on the morning of the 11th verry early. It is presumeable that the officer in command had been informed that the break would take place, and that he started these men off to save them in as much as one of them was our commander, a Colonel, by the enemy commonly styled General. There were many other sources from which we may draw a conclusion, that thare *was a traitor* among the men, but he is not definitely known. I have been creditabley informed that one of the Texians was heard to make use of an observation, in purport, as follows "*This can be stoped, and I will do it.*" This was said on the night of the 10th previous to the insurrection. The man who is said to have made use of it went and asked permission of the officer on duty to go out; the permission was gained, and the Texian was out untill late at night, and next morning thare was a double Guard around the prisoners. This is *circumstancial evidence*, but I think sufficient, at least, to lay suspicion upon the man who thus acted. I would not assert this as *true*, for I did not see it.[2]

After the charge had been made on the guard, and that effectually,

1. Those who started with Fisher from *hacienda* Salado early on the morning of the overthrow of the guard were Thomas Jefferson Green, Samuel C. Lyon, Daniel Drake Henrie (interpreter), Thomas W. Murray, and Dr. William M. Shepherd. Matías M. y Aguirre to Sr. gobernador y comandante general del departamento, [dated] Matehuala, Feb. 12, 1843, in *Diario del Gobierno*, Feb. 24, 1843, says that there were seven Texans; but Thomas J. Green to Dear Friends, [dated] Castle of Perote, Mexico, Apr. 15, 1843, in *Telegraph and Texas Register*, May 17, 1843, says there were six in all and gives the foregoing names. Thomas Jefferson Green, *Journal of the Texian Expedition against Mier*, p. 127, gives the same six names. Canfield recorded on Feb. 10, 1843, in his diary, Texas State Archives, that the main body of prisoners found upon its arrival at Salado Fisher, Murray, Shepherd, and two or three others.

2. See Chapter VI, footnote 4.

thare were some who refused to take advantage of the victory. All of those who were able were marched off, and if I mistake not joined Fisher, Green, and others.[3] The wounded and those unable to march were removed to a place for recovery, and thence on to join their companions.

These men were marched to Perote, where they found the San Antonio Prisoners, and thare we found them.

In July 1843 Gen. Green and fifteen others[4] made their escape by enlarging a window. Eight[5] of these were retaken; the remainder reached their homes. Col. Fisher could have taken advantage of this, also, but he refused to do so, asserting as his reasons that he had brought the command into the "Scrape," and that he thought it his duty to stay untill all could go. This was truely Generous and noble on the part of Fisher. In fact the conduct of Fisher was ever such that if we had been otherwise disposed, we could not but have respected him as a Soldier and a man of honorable intentions. Such intentions were ever his.

The Castle of San Carlos de Perote,[6] situated near the town of Perote, Mexico.

This Castle, built about 75 years since, began in the reign of Charles V, finished in the reign of Ferdinand VII, Kings of Spain, is situated in a verry beautiful valley, and is one of the strongest fortifications in Mexico. The first intention of it must evidently have been a retreat for

3. Those who refused to escape were Captain Charles Keller Reese, Daniel Davis, Richard Y. Keene, George W. Bush, Andrew B. Hanna, D. R. Hallowell, Charles Clark, Milvern Harrell, Simon Glenn, William Reese (brother of Captain Reese), Leonidas Saunders, and D. F. Barney, who eventually joined Colonel Fisher and those in the advance party. Canfield diary, Feb. 10, 1843.

4. The sixteen who escaped through the tunnel were Richard A. Barclay, David Smith Kornegay, John Dalrymple, John Forrester, Thomas Jefferson Green, Daniel Drake Henrie, Charles Keller Reese, and those listed in footnote 5 below. Joseph Milton Nance, *Attack and Counterattack*, pp. 601, 623; Green, *Journal of the Texian Expedition against Mier*, pp. 446–447.

5. Those recaptured were Isaac Allen, Truman B. Beck, David J. Davis, Augustus Elly, Thomas Hancock, Duncan C. Ogden, Samuel Stone, and John Young. Green, *Journal of the Texian Expedition against Mier*, p. 447.

6. A disappointing description of the Castle of San Carlos de Perote published, with photographs, in 1945 by recent visitors may be found in J. J. McGrath and Walace Hawkins, "Perote Fort—Where Texans Were Impris-

forces when overpowered, though some contend that it was built to defent the pass, and thus to prevent an enemy from passing into the interior of the Country. But this, I think, is an incorrect supposition founded upon mear conjecture. One evidence of its falicy is that there are many other passes that would be much more eas[il]y defended; the most easy of which, and consiquently the propper place for such a fortification, is the Puente National, or National Bridge, a place well known to travellers in that country. Whereas the castle of Perote is in the center of a pass, or valley at least six miles in breadth, consiquently an enemy might pass on either side of the fortress without being materially injured by the guns of the battery. Upon a consideration and a view of the road from Vera Cruz to the city of Mexico, which is the only road by which communication can pass directly, I am lead to believe that the main first cause of the erection of that fortress was that they wished a strong place in the interior for internal protection and a place in which to confine prisoners. But it would of course opperate as a check upon an invading foe, for no general in an enemies country would pass and leave in his rear a fortification so strong in appearance without making more than one effort to reduce it.

This castle is apparently of great strength. The walls stand on and enclose twenty-six acres of ground. Around the wall is a ditch of about fifteen feet in depth, and enclosing this are the picketts which stand on and enclose forty-four acres of ground. The picketts are made of ceder firmly set in ceament. They measure about six-inches square.

The battlements are pierced for ninty-six guns—24 on each side or end. The main bearing of the general form of the Castle is nearly square, with a wing or butress projecting from each corner. The building is verry ingenious, also the form, and indicates its projector to have been a great engineer and a great genius. It is so formed that they can cross fire upon an enemy let him approach from which way he will. From the bottom of the mote or ditch, the wall is forty feet high, twelve or fifteen feet thick at bottom and eight at top, causing an average of eleven feet from bottom to top. As to the shape and general form refer to the plan at the conclusion.[7]

Upon the top of the battlements thare is space sufficient to muster five or seven thousand men with all convenience. The place or square

---

oned," *Southwestern Historical Quarterly* XLVIII (January 1945):340–345. Better descriptions of the castle may be found in Green, *Journal of the Texian Expedition against Mier*, pp. 235–243, and Philip Young, *History of Mexico*, pp. 318–319. During World War II Perote Prison was used as a concentration camp for German and Japanese nationals.

7. No plan of the fortress accompanies the McCutchan diary. A diagram

of the castle in the center is about one hundred yards square, which is completely hollow underneath, being arrainged into two distinct and separate vaults to hold water. The water is kept in one of them three years and then three in the other, thus giving chance for repair. Around the square is a tier of buildings, the Governor's house, the officers' rooms, and soldiers quarters; then a street; then a tier of rooms for provisions, prisons, &c.:—in this part we were confined. Our officers were kept in a building on the square.

The Moat surrounding the castle was constructed for the purpose of filling it with water, but I am disposed to doubt the practability of this, for which I have several reasons, one of which is the distance from which all water is brought, and the force of the fountain head from which it is derived. I have been to and examined the fountain head, which is distant from the castle five or six miles. This fountain is not able to afford a stream moore than three inches in diameter. Supposing they would be able to draw into the moat 100,000 gallons of water in 24 hours, which is as much as can be done, it would thus require 90 days to get water enough to serve their purposes, or 100 days to fill the moat, or possibly they could never fill it, for it is reasonable to suppose that the earth would absorb as fast as the water can, with their present conveniences, be put on it. It is clearly evident that it was so intended at first to be filled though it never has been so.

If this Fortress was garrisoned with good soldiers, Americans, English, or French, it would be blood work to take in any manner, but as it is garrisoned with Mexican immitation of Soldiery, it could be easily taken. Storming would be amusement sought after by good soldiers.

Another disadvantage is—the guns of the battery are all too small for a fortress. The largest guns are sixteen pounders, and but fiew of them. The general sizes are sixes and twelves. There are four mortars; one on each corner. Those on the front are large and good, but those on the rear are too small to take much effect at a great distance.

The fort fronts South East, and to the town—here is the gate or entrance, and in the rear is a secret passage.

The place is well sufficient for 10,000 men, but not more, with convenience, and also to hold a sufficiency of provisions for a long siege. They could not be deprived of water, for the reservoir in or *under* the square contains enough to supply them for a great length of time.

Upon the whole it is admirably constructed for defence but it lacks

---

made by Charles McLaughlin, one of the Mier prisoners, is found in Green, *Journal of the Texian Expedition against Mier*, p. [239].

the *heart*, which renders a fortress insurmountable—*Good Soldiers*; and without which it is worth nothing.

All, in the Castle of Perote.

On the day of our arrival at Perote, after having exchanged Salutations with our old friends, we were shown to our rooms and lodged for the night under lock and key.

About the 25th of this month (September) symptoms of an epedemic made themselves apparent. I was the first who suffered from it. The first October, it was a general thing among us. There were, at one time, eighty-six in the hospital, including Mier and San Antonio prisoners. There were but three men in the whole number of both bodies of prisoners who did not have this horrible disease. Something simelar to a Typhus and jail feaver. Of our number, there were eighteen men died,[8] and now rest in the ditch surrounding the Castle. Also two or three of San Antonio prisoners who were layed in the ditch to take their *last long rest*![9] That disease! how can I find language to describe it? The sufferings of others, I could only judge by sight, but mine, I know from experience. I felt them! I lay in the Hospital thirty days, and fourteen days of that time entirely insensible to all earthy things, even to suffering itself. On partial recovery from this sensless

8. McCutchan only gives the names of fourteen Mier men who died in Perote Castle, and there is no indication that all of these died of the epidemic. Green, ibid., pp. 444–445, lists thirty-five Texans who died "from Sufferings and Starvation in Mexico," but, again, not all of these necessarily died of the epidemic. Canfield, in his diary, lists twenty-one San Antonio and Mier prisoners who died at the castle between Oct. 9, 1843, and Mar. 8, 1844.

9. The San Antonio prisoners taken by General Woll who died of the epidemic were Joseph A. Crews and French Strother Gray. According to Albert M. Gilliam, Crews was "a young man who had been raised to the mercantile business at Lynchburg, Virginia." Crews was not bearing arms when Woll seized San Antonio on Sept. 11, 1842, but, nevertheless, had been made a prisoner. He had gone to Texas for the purpose of recovering his health and was at San Antonio as clerk of the district court at the time of Woll's invasion. Albert M. Gilliam, *Travels over the Table Lands and Cordilleras of Mexico*, p. 67. Gilliam, who was from Lynchburg, Virginia, recalled when he learned of Crews' death in Mexico that the aged parents of the youth were still living at Lynchburg; he gives the name as Joseph E. Cruse. Nance, *Attack and Counterattack*, p. 601.

Gray was a lawyer and assistant district attorney in the Western Judicial District of Texas in 1842. He was listed by Woll as a colonel and lawyer.

state or stupor, and before I had regained my intellect, I immagined myself many, many miles away from misery, among friends! But Alas! I lay on a sick couch unattended! And Oh! Such sickness—such misery! To endure it, and recover, *death* itself, though in a different, more horrible shape. Give me death in any shape save from that disease! On the battle field—it would be glorious! On a sick bead among friends who loved me, it would be relieved [relief], but in a land of enemies and in a *prison*, among those who hate and insult me, unattended and unnoticed, it is dreadful! Though I scarcely thought of it, I never thought but that I should live for *revenge*. Those who endure sickness among friends, never having suffered, neglected, and forgoten on a miserable bunch of straw in a prison know not the horrors of *any* disease, and less than all of a disease such as raged among us in Perote. Those poor fellows who lie in the ditch forgoten, save by those who suffered with them. Let all the world forget beside—we never can forget those of our fellow soldiers and prisoners who layed down their lives in a glorious cause dearly loved by us all. Long, long may their memory live in each soul that loves liberty. They died! and we could not give them a deacent burrial! Their bodies were insulted before us. *We could not resent it*! They are gone hence—gone to a place from whence no traveler returneth.—Peace be with them.—Here let me drop a *tear to* the memory of one whom I can not forget and to whom I must do justice—Campbell Davis![10] He is *gone*! He commited *Suicide* but was justifiable! The cause and result were these:

About the first of October he took the epedemic and was verry low. He lay at the Hospital about forty days, but finally became able to return to the Castle, where he stayed for some days without any apparent sign of recovery. He returned to the Hospital, thare remained a short time, and then again returned to the Castle disheartened and

10. Campbell Davis was a member of Captain William S. Fisher's company in the Somervell Expedition. On Feb. 15, 1844, Davis, sick and despondent, took two ounces of laudanum about daylight, and it was some time before his companions realized what he had done. James L. Trueheart says that they had supposed "that he was enjoying a fine sleep, and would not disturb him; it was found out near the middle of the day that he had taken laudanum and was laboring under its effects. Other medicines were administered immediately," but to no avail. "He laid in a torpid state and apparently lifeless the whole day, . . . [and died] early in the morning [of the 16th] before our room was opened. He had been suffering from diarrhea for the last six months and was reduced to a mere skeleton. On his arrival from Mexico [City] he was sent to the hospital, but could obtain no relief." Frederick C. Chabot (ed.), *The Perote Prisoners*, pp. 285–286.

almost desperate. He had given out all hope of recovery. About the close of November, or enterance of December, he was heard to say, in amount, about the following—"I have lost all hope of recovering, I cannot recover—and in fact either a life of sickness or health, is not to be covited here. I wish I could die!" This was said with that calm resignation bordering on dispair, but little or no notice was then taken of it, as they were the thoughts of many! He was, by far, *not alone*! But either that evening or the next, he ascertained the whareabouts of Doctor McMaths medicine, and that night! at the dead and solum hour of night, he arose; went to the medicines, procured, and drank a common sized viol of Laudnum, which did not take immediate effect, as he had taken too much for suden and easy death! He died next day about one o'clock, lamented and mourned by all! He said after he had taken the Laudnum, that if it was to do over, he would act the same way. I knew Davis well; he was a good man, a brave soldier, and a warm friend, deserving a better fate. *He* is gone! and the *best* and *only tribute* which I can pay him is—to drop o're him a soldier's tear. By his death, we were bereaved of a boon companion and Texas of a noble defender! by it he cleared himself of undergoing many hard, dark, miserable humiliations, which we his unfortunate companions had to undergo.

This is sufficient of a sad story. One which has made a deep impression on my mind—an impression which time and means will fail to obliterate.

As a casual remark I will state that our eating was none of the *best*, but to the reverse, it was of the worst; little of nothing cooked in the most horrible manner immaginable; neither fit for man or beast, yet we eat it, and do not even get enough, bad as it is.

On the 24th of March 1843 [1844?], the remnant of prisoners taken by Gen. Woll, numbering 33 or 34,[11] were released to Gen Waddy

11. The thirty-five Bexar (San Antonio) prisoners, including some of the Dawson men, were all released by President Santa Anna upon General Waddy Thompson's request made at the time that he was leaving Mexico as the United States minister. Their names were as follows: H. Alexander Alsbury, Isaac Allen, Truman B. Beck, Edward Brown, James H. Brown, William Bugg, Ludovic Colquhoun, David J. Davis, Augustus Elley, Nathaniel W. Faison, Simon Glenn, Thomas Hancock, Nathaniel Herbert, Milvern Harrell, Chauncey Johnson, John Lehmann, A. F. Leslie, John Lee, Edward T. Manton, Allen H. Morrell, Joseph C. Morgan, Francis McKay, Robert S. Neighbors, Samuel Nobles, Duncan C. Ogden, John Perry, Cornelius W. Peterson, Marcus L. B. Rapier, George P. Schaeffer, Johann George Andreas

Tomson as a personal favor. On leaving the castle, many of them shed tears of sincere regret at parting with those who they regarded as s[a]crificed to Texas. The following will show the estimation in which they held us:

I was standing in a collection of six or eight of the Mier men talking over our prospects, when one of the Bexar men came up saying, "It grieves me to leave you hear; you, who, when you heard of our capture, readily took up your arms, and, though you had but a handful of men, came boldly against the enemy, that thus you might release us; but you have also been unfortunate and we must leave you behind. If ever men did deserve liberty, you are those." His tears told that this was from the heart. This prooves how a man can feel for his fellow man. But *they* are gone and we are still here—likely *for life*!

God only knows when we will recieve our "*free papers*"—a Yankee could not even "*guess*" when our time for liberty will Come. I think we diserve a better fate. Ill luck and Disappointment have followed us from our homes, and formed a coopperation for the purpose of sowering every sweet that Mad'me Hope is pleased to throw in our way. And by the by, Ill Luck and Disappointment are far more lavish in their dispensations than Md'me Hope or any of her cooperators.

Amusements in Perote are exquisite!

Our amusements are various. Through the day we are greatly anoyed by the curses, abuses, of the Mexicans with their "*crajo*"[12] uttered hard between the teeth, and a sentence like the following: "Anda a travara Señores"[13] (go to work Sirs) with many other sayings equally oppressive to our sense of hearing.

At night, after being locked up, some begin to sing—a cainary bird in a cage, in resemblence; some read an old novel or old newspaper;

Voss, and John Young. Nance, *Attack and Counterattack*, pp. 600–603, 621–623; Green, *Journal of the Texian Expedition against Mier*, pp. 447–448. Green has misspelled many of the names, and he has listed "James H. Robinson" as being released earlier by Santa Anna, and a "Joseph Robinson" as being released later with the remaining Bexar prisoners. In both cases he wrote the wrong name and was referring to the same person, James W. Robinson, who was a lawyer and had been lieutenant governor of Texas from 1835 to 1836.

12. The word is *carajo*: damn it.

13. Should be *Anda á trabajar Señores*: Go to work, Sirs.

while others occupy their time at cards, in some game of amusement—in short, anything to kill time. Any thing that will cut to the heart the base sons of Mexico suits us best.

During the nois[e] after locking up is the time we choose to cut off our chains—a perfect Blacksmith shop at times. We will clear our ancles occasionally. After cuting off a chain, we generally bury it, or manage to destroy it in some way. Many are the chains we have destroyed for Mexico. But they never fail to rechain us, each time harder than the first, but custom makes all things agreeable, or rather, *fashionable.*

This is our motto: "We will *live* in hope, if we die in dispair."

During a dance we step to the music of a violin and chains, in conjunction. The irons keep up a clatter that would be dismal to others, but we are well acquainted with it. The clank of a chain once so dreadful is now nothing.

In singing, we are at times so loud and harsh that it causes the guard to quake with fear. Rawsin the Bow is sung divinely, *Excellent.*

Our laugh is at times so loud and long that the officers on guard even order us to "*Silencio*,"—Keep Silence.

But these amusements and laughs are not of the heart. We go to extremes in gaiety to prevent dispondency.

General Remarks

This Expedition was set on foot for retaliation toward Mexico for depridations commited on our frontier by the[i]r ignoble soldiery.

First.—*Sam Houston*, President of the Republic of Texas, issued a proclamation Bravado to all the Militia belonging to the first and second classes to repare forthwith to San Antonio, thence "to pursue the enemy even into his own Territory and chasise him thare for his insolence."[14]

14. This is not a direct quotation; but there is enough in the orders emanating from the president and the secretary of war and marine to cause men bent upon revenge and retaliation to believe that their invasion of Mexican territory was sanctioned. What they forgot was that the orders were couched with such statements as "submit to your [Somervell's] orders," "march across the Rio Grande under your orders," advance into the enemy's country was left "to your own discretion," and "you leading them into the enemies country." Upon the fall of San Antonio to Woll, M. C. Hamilton, acting secretary of war and marine, stipulated on Sept. 16, 1842, as quoted in Amelia W. Williams and Eugene C. Barker (eds.), *Writings of Sam Houston*, VII:6–7,

In accordance with this bombastic proclamation, the Officers of Military ordered those indicated to rendesvous at appointed places,—tare [there] to organize and take up the line of march for San Antonio. Thare we were ordered under the command of Brigadier Gen. Sommerville a man designed by Houston to ruin the expedition and well calculated in every respect for that purpose. We remained with this officer as far as Gurarro [Guerrero], the point at which the second division took place. Thare thinking that he had gained sufficient *honor* and glory by taking two defenceless towns, he determined to return home with a *whole body* and a *Hat full* of glory while it was yet time. He thought, "Now is the time before it is everlastingly too late!" He could see if we stayed thare much longer we would *have to fight*, and

---

"If the enemy [should] evacuate and fall back, the troops are authorized and required to pursue them to any point in the Republic, or in Mexico, and chastise the marauders for their audacity." On Oct. 10, 1842, President Houston, at Washington-on-the-Brazos, addressed the Montgomery County militiamen on their way to San Antonio and "urged them to cross the Rio Grande" with other forces to be found at San Antonio. *Telegraph and Texas Register*, Oct. 12, 1842. Sam Houston to Thomas M. Bagby [dated] Washington, Oct. 6, 1842, in Williams and Barker (eds.), *Writings of Sam Houston*, III:171–172. On Oct. 3, 1842, Houston ordered General Alexander Somervell to "proceed to the most eligible point on the Southwestern frontier of Texas, and concentrate with the force now under your command, all troops who may submit to your orders, and if you can advance with a prospect of success into the enemy's territory, you will do so forthwith. . . . You will . . . receive no troops into service, but such as will be subordinate to your orders and the rules of war. You will receive no troops into your command but such as will march across the Rio Grande under your orders if required by you so to do." Sam Houston to Brigadier General A. Somervell, [dated] Washington, Oct. 3, 1842, ibid., III:170–171. Again, on Oct. 19, 1842, Hamilton wrote Somervell: "You will use all expedition in the organization of the army, and in the prosecution of the campaign," ibid., III:187–188. Hamilton again instructed Somervell on Nov. 19, 1842, (ibid., III:197–199):

> Your orders were to neither *muster into service nor issue supplies of any kind to any but those who reported with a firm resolve to cross the Rio Grande if required to do so*. . . . It was expected that those who were anxious to enter the enemies territory would be prepared to march immediately upon their organization, which should have been completed the moment they reported themselves. . . . It was left to your own discretion to determine whether the strength and condition of the force, after it had been organized, would authorize you leading them into the enemies country; and if so, to act with the greatest promptitude so as to relieve the frontier of the burden of supporting them.

that would have been far from congenial with his nice sense of feeling.[15] We then elected to the command a man more to suit our notions.

The following are the reasons why we did attempt to further prosecution of the expedition:

We had been on the road so long that many horses were broken-down, leaving to many the only alternative of going home on foot or seaking the chance of a battle—this we were all willing to seak. Tharefore when the enemy on the 25th of Decem. said "come and get provisions," we acceped the chalange, and we have been fed by them a long time.

We fought them 18 hours, a little better than pleased them.

When [I] look back on time passed and acts rashly done—noticing the many misfortunes that befell us—when I bring to mind the fatigue, the misery, we endured—and *last* but not *least*—when I recount the particulars of each separation and judge of their causes, it appears evident that had we have thought—had we have judged of the future by the past, we could have formed some idea of the ill fate which awaited us! But no, we pressed onward with an unconquerable disposition to serve *Texas*. What is Texas? My *country*! We wished the enemy, as well as our countrymen, not to think so light of us, as that could be frightened by figures. But, if we had have know[n] the force against which we had to contend, we would have met them in the bushes and brush, and conquered them easily. But we were decieved; not till the 26th did we recieve the *right* impressions. We can whip them two, three, or five to one, but fifteen is rather out of o[u]r reach, not as easy as could be wished at any rate.

Further justification is useless—the Expedition justifies itself.

After we had arrived in the city of Mexico we began to look forward to a day of liberation. Our hopes were placed on the 13th of June,[16]

15. Somervell concluded that to stay longer upon the Rio Grande, especially in the vicinity of the two important Mexican military posts of San Fernando and Matamoros, would prove disastrous to the expedition, now virtually devoid of both supplies and discipline.

16. June 13, 1843, was the date the new Mexican Constitution was launched. Hubert Howe Bancroft, *History of Mexico*, V:256. Biographers of Santa Anna give his birthday as Feb. 21, 1794; yet, many of the Mier men gave his birthday as June 13. Ann Fears Crawford (ed.), *The Eagle*, p. 255; Wilfred H. Callcott, *Santa Anna*, p. 4; Thomas W. Bell, *A Narrative of the Capture and Subsequent Sufferings of the Mier Prisoners in Mexico*, p. 95; Canfield diary, June 13, 1844. Canfield mistakenly gives June 13 as the day on which the Santa Fe prisoners were released.

and the nearer came that day, the more sanguine were our hopes. But alas! when the long wished for day arrived, it brought disappointment to our expectations. Our imaginary hopes were dashed to earth by Snively's Expedition to Santa Fe. Knowing that without hope our situation would be worse than death, we set our hopes on the 11th of September,[17] but again were our hopes hurled to earth with such force as to crash for a time all animation of spirits.

Now it is the 3d of June 1844. We have again placed our hopes on the 13th of this month, and who knows but that our hopes are doomed to sink deeper than ever, if which be the case—*God* alone knows *what* may be the result. *Likely some dark deed* which will secure the *freedom* or *death* of all. *Dark* hints *darkly* given, by men in our gloomy situation, *may be darker still*! I cannot yet imagine the exact result!

Situation of Mexico

Let Mexico brag of the powerful army—her one hundred thousand regular soldiers; but she has them not—neither can she raise them, or even admiting her ability to raise, I dispute her ability to support them. Even admiting her ability to raise and support them, and supposing that she now has them at her disposal: at a moderate calculation—20 or 25,000 Texians would overrun and trample them down like reeds; 25,000 Texians would drive before them 100,000 Mexicans like wind dispells the mist.

Half the Nation are thieves in Prison and the other half are thieves uncaught. It requires the uncaught thieves to guard those who have been justly delt with. But it would be impossible for Mexico to bring all villains to justice, for the *Nation* would be to punish. Then look what a situation that country must be in!

Texas is by far more prosperous. The little Republic of Texas is in a better condition than the proud, haughty, Bombastic Mexico. The people here boast of their *liberty*—ever cursing Monarchies. But they know not the simple acceptation of the term liberty—they know not its meaning. And the government of Mexico is worse than an absolute monarchy.

The contrast between Henry the eighth and Santa Anna is but small —if any it is to the advantage of the former. The latter only lacks a

17. Sept. 11 was the anniversary of the surrender of the Spaniards under Brigadier General Isidro Barradas to Santa Anna on the banks of the Pánuco River, an act which resulted in the failure of Spain's efforts to reconquer Mexico. Bancroft, *History of Mexico*, V:74.

diadem to make him a crowned Tyrant. Such assumption of authority as Santa Anna is guilty of is before unheard of in a president elect of a Republic. But Mexico, poor country, is only Democratical in name. The people cry "vive la Republica," yet they know not the first principles requisite to constitute a Republic. For a people absolutely burried in ignorance, superstition, and trampled down by Despotic oppression to judge of *liberty* is one of the impossibilities.

The gold and silver mines of Mexico are worked mostly by English companies, and consiquently the benefit resulting to the government is but limited.

Well did Randolph[18] define that nation when he said, "A lousey—tug—and blanket nation, whare the men are all thieves, and the women, all ———" (no better).

* * * *

I have now spoken of the principle events that have transpired up to this day. I shall hereafter proceed in a different manner. It is propper to mention here that we are still somewhat scattered—Thare being in Mexico [City]—three;[19] in Puebla—one;[20] in Vera Cruz—ten;[21] in

18. John Randolph of Roanoke's definition of the Mexican nation is found in *Niles' Weekly Register*, XXX:202.
19. The three prisoners in Mexico City at the Santiago Prison early in June 1844 were Captain John G. W. Pierson, D. H. Van Vechten, and Ezekiel Smith. They had been left sick there when the main body of prisoners had been marched to Perote. Information furnished by Thomas W. Murray and reported in *National Intelligencer*, Apr. 9, 1844.
20. In April 1844 there were three Mier men sick in the hospital at Puebla. These were Jeremiah Leehan, Alexander Mathews, and Theodore Dwight Maltby. The latter suffered through the remainder of his life from a head wound received in the battle of Mier. He died Oct. 27, 1871, in New Orleans. When all of the Mier prisoners were released, he was left behind in Mexico sick at the hospital in Puebla. *National Intelligencer*, Apr. 9, 1844; *Daily Picayune*, Nov. 5, 1844; Oct. 28, 1871.

Jeremiah Leehan and Isaac Allen were released. They sailed from Vera Cruz on June 3, 1844, aboard the U.S. steamer *Poinsett* and reached Galveston on June 7. *Daily Picayune*, June 11 and 14, 1844.
21. It has been impossible to pinpoint the ten persons referred to because of the lack of precision in date and the constantly changing number of Texans held at the Castle of San Juan de Ulua because of additions, releases, deaths, and transfers to the hospital in Vera Cruz. On Mar. 3, 1844, Trueheart reported the arrival of twelve Mier prisoners at Perote Castle from Mexico

Matamoras—either two or three;[22] the last we have not heard from in some considerable time—perhaps 12 months.

The following regular narrative will lead one into the common feelings which adjutated [agitated] us at the time it was written.

* * * *

Narrative—June, 1844

1st. On this day Santa Anna entered the castle on his way to the capital. He was recieved with the ringing of bells; a national salute from the battery; and sent off under the same. He stayed in the castle but [a] fiew minutes. Thare had been a hope expressed among some of us that he would release us on his enterence, but it was unfounded. On hearing of his approach Governor Jarraro[23] of the Fortress chained

City on their way to the Castle of San Juan de Ulua, in the harbor at Vera Cruz. On the fifth of March these men continued on their way. From among them Israel Canfield was ordered to Mango del Clavo to see President Santa Anna and was subsequently released. Chabot (ed.), *The Perote Prisoners*, pp. 291–292. In a letter dated March 19 [1844], one of the prisoners in the Castle of San Juan de Ulua wrote: "Twelve of us went by Perote on our way to this place, but on the road such of the party as were English, and unfortunately there were but two of them [Major Thomas W. Murray and Donald Smith], were liberated. . . . Two of our party are in the hospital sick; consequently there are but eight of us now in the Castle. . . . P. S. Since writing the above two more of our party have been taken to the hospital sick. One of the first is dead, and his companion is hourly expected to die." *Daily Picayune*, May 2, 1844. The twelve prisoners referred to here were removed from Convent Santiago, Mexico City, to San Juan de Ulua.

22. In June 1844 there were still two Mier prisoners at Matamoros, who seem to have remained there until the release of all Mier prisoners was ordered effective Sept. 16, 1844. These two were Frank Hughes and William Y. Scott. The *Telegraph and Texas Register*, Apr. 24, 1844, reported them still in prison at Matamoros at the beginning of March 1844 and their names were not among those of the main body of prisoners arriving at New Orleans on Nov. 4, 1844, aboard the *Creole* or among those listed at that time as having been left behind in Mexico (as far as those in the main body of prisoners knew). *Daily Picayune*, Nov. 5, 1844.

23. General José María Jarero, native of Jalapa, served in 1831 as military chief in Jalapa, Córdova, and Orizaba; governor of San Juan de Ulua Castle in 1839; commandant general of Aguascalientes in 1841; governor and com-

those who happened to be loose, and locked us in our rooms, all save the carpenters, who he permitted to remain at work, and by the tyrant they were visited, so that to see them at work would satiate his thirsty vengance. But the Despot was too fearful of his life to admit all to his dark Majesty's view.

2nd. Sunday. Nothing occurs, excep[t] one of the men met with the misfortune to slip and fall into a place unsanctified and disagreeable.

3rd. More flying reports of liberty—not believed by many. But should a race so unfortunate, a crowd so harrassed as ours, be by an unbelieved or unlooked for circumstance set at liberty we will "astonish the natives." The Hurra will be so loud and long that even the devils in Hell will quake with fear and trembling! Angels will shout—Devels weep in fear—Mexicans mourn—and we will yell like Cumanchees! + + + But no! no such hopes for us! We are here and here *must* remain untill we resolve to *free ourselves*, or perish in the attempt! Fare better to perish well revenged than to linger out a life already cut short by dangers dared, death encountered, and hardships undergone! Why had we not better die, hand to hand with the foe, than to perish by lingering disease and cruelties before unthought of? If my companions will say—"Perish all in one attempt and togeather or be *free*"—so say I! This is not impossible, nor improbable!

4th. We hear that [the] Annexation of Texas to the United States will take place. If the People of Texas are willing to give up their independence, let them do so; we are prisoners and can have no influence. If I could for myself exercise influence it would be to say to the Texas and Texians hold dear those rights so dearly bought and promptly payed for in the blood and misery of your countrymen. Part not so freely with that which has cost you your best citizens at the Alimo, Goliad, and San jacinto. Remain a nation of yourselves, or Nobly Perish!

If the people of Texas think it to their interest as a nation to annex themselves, let them do so! but if they acceed to this proposition only to release us from prison—may God prevent it! Let us here perish! Let us sink in our infamous captivity rather than be the cause of our countries disgrace! Death would to me be sweet if I could die in service to Texas and revenged. Who would wish to regain their freedom—live, and remain emblematic of a nations ruin and disgrace? God grant, that Texas may not purchase our release at the distruction of her

---

mandant general of Jalisco in 1842; and governor of the fortress of Perote in 1843. Alberto M. Carreño (ed.), *Jefes del ejército mexicano en 1847*, pp. 126–127.

National honor! I had rather see the five pointed Star—the emblem of Texas, my country, soar on solitary and alone! Alone it took its rise, alone it has soared aloft, and taken its stand among the proud emblems of nations, and alone let it remain glorious and ever bright, or let it go down nobly as it has risen and with it let Texas perish! If Texians are not able to defend their bright flag, let them make it their winding sheet. Would that I had these irons off and arms in my hands that I might fall in defense of Texas, rather than live and recieve *my* liberty at the price of Texian honor! I ask not a better end than that if the Star of Texas shall sink, I may fall in its defence; that to *me* it may be my shrowd and winding sheet, and that so with it I may sink to rest! If Texian liberty falls, may I perish in its defence! So would I live; so would I die! Has Texas lost all her bravery? has heroism departed from Texas? and has this caused the United States to streach to us the arm of protection? If so, we will not recieve it! we will not accept liberty at the distruction of a nation's honor! Our liberty would be dear to us, and our life is little. When Texas has breathed her last, then have we lived long enough. *Death ever, before Dishonor*!

5th. I have today se[e]n a proclamation of the Dictator to the following effect: "All foreigners within the confines of this Republic shall have each a passport, and make monthly a report to the civil authorities, and appear before them; to prevent the corruption of Mexican morrals by coming in contact with foreign vagabonds."[24] This is with

24. This statement is another illustration of McCutchan's occasional inaccuracies. Whether intentionally or not, he has distorted the substance of several decrees and drawn his own conclusions as to their purpose.

Early in 1843 the Mexican government decreed that any person fighting under the standard of Texas should be treated as an outlaw if captured by Mexico. This decree was followed by another on July 14, 1843, ordering all American citizens out of the border states of Sonora, Sinaloa, Chihuahua, and the Californias and prohibiting any future settlement of Americans in those states. Then on Sept. 24, 1843, President Santa Anna issued an order prohibiting foreigners, six months from the date of the order, from engaging in any kind of retail business in Mexico.

All three decrees were strongly protested by the American minister to Mexico, Waddy Thompson; but, when Thompson learned of the issuance of the July 14 decree, he declared that unless it were immediately revoked, he would sever United States diplomatic relations with Mexico. When he received no reply to his note of Dec. 29, 1843, he informed José María Bocanegra, the head of the Mexican Foreign Office, of "the termination of his official relations" and requested his passports immediately. This action on the part of the American minister caused the Mexican government to limit the decree of July 14 only to "those who from their bad conduct should be

in itself is nonsense; and a noise for nothing. Santa Anna speaks of *Mexican* morrality as if such a thing did really exist. In what does the morrality of this country consist? In blackguardian murder, thieft, robbery, and cowardice. The inhabitants seem to vie with each other in [seeing] which can commit the most atrocious crimes in the most cowardly manner. Mexico can boast of one thing, and that with reason, that her inhabitants are the most corrupt and debased people who are suffered to walk the earth unpunished.

We have had the gratification of today seeing the details of the reception of the San Antonio prisoners at the city of Galveston,[25] judging from which I am induced to think that all patriotism has not departed from Texas. I see with pleasure that these unfortunate men were recieved with every apearance of joy, both on the part of the citizens and the Military. But still this might be, and s[t]ill the Texians remain careless of us, for these were men draged from their homes and thrust into dungeons, thare to undergo hardships, while we lef[t] our homes in pursuance of Houston's order; entered the enemies country; thare fought and by the fate of war were captured and made to suffer for our insolence. This may work to our disadvantage in the honest opinion of the good citizens of Texas; and if it should, I will only say by way, not of justification to our conduct, but of arousing their memory, that it was to release these same men that we first took up arms. Let the Government and people of Texas say what they will—if ever we do reach home we feel that these men, at least, will give us a heart felt wellcome.

A verry amusing incident occured this morning. The officers came to order us out to work and, having had a great trouble to get us out for the last several days, they said to us—"go to work directly, or we

---

considered as prejudicial to public order." This change satisfied Thompson and he withdrew his request for passports. Abel P. Upshur to Waddy Thompson, July 27, 1843, in National Archives Diplomatic Instructions, Mexico; and Waddy Thompson to José María de Bocanegra, Sept. 24, 1843, enclosure with Waddy Thompson to Abel P. Upshur, Sept. 28, 1843; same to same, Dec. 29, 1843, enclosure with Waddy Thompson to Abel P. Upshur, Jan. 4, 1844; José María de Bocanegra to Waddy Thompson, Jan. 4, 1844, enclosure with Waddy Thompson to Abel P. Upshur, Jan. 4, 1844; all in National Archives, Consular Despatches, Mexico City. See also, Frederick Sherwood Dunn, *The Diplomatic Protection of Americans in Mexico*, pp. 38–40.

25. The arrival of the San Antonio prisoners at Galveston was reported in the *Telegraph and Texas Register*, May 1, 1844. The prisoners reached Galveston on Wednesday, Apr. 24, aboard the *Neptune* from New Orleans.

will shut the door and keep you locked up all day"—to which we replied—lock it, and some even ad[d]ed an oath, which is often ad[d]ed to a sentence. The door was closed and we are locked up for the day. We often not only curse them with abuse of words, but not unfrequently of blows. We generally give blow for blow, and word for word, thus making a mear exchange of civilities. They can not manage us like their own low vagrant criminals.

I have seen a letter from Santa Anna to Gen. Waddy Thompson, saying that he was on the point of releasing the prisoners, when the news of the escape of sixteen reached him, which rendered us unworthy of his magnanimity.[26] Devel take such magnaminous men; he has no such feelings. *Magnanimity* of *Santa Anna*! We had as well accuse the devel of Righteousness. No he only thought it a good time to give some excuse for keeping us, and that was all he had. When *Angels* blaspheme, *devels* pray in holy candor, and all men become good, then will *Mexicans* become magnanimous.

These men mentioned by Sta. Anna, who dug out through the floor and underminded the castle of Perote, dug down 18 feet—thence horrizontal 13 feet—and thence up 6 feet—making in total 37 feet—hid all the sand and earth taken tharefrom in their room. This was a considerable and well conducted undertaking. So secreetly was it done that verry fiew of the men belonging to the other rooms knew any thing of it. I did not know that they designed anything untill the next morning after our doors were opened. This is the second time that the Castle has been broken by these Texian Devels. I am proud to think that some have made their escape. This was done on the 25th of March, the anniversary of the day on which the decimation took place. Seven[27] of the 16 have been retaken, and we are induced to believe the

26. Santa Anna informed General Waddy Thompson that he was on the verge of releasing all of the Texan prisoners when news reached him of the escape of sixteen prisoners on Mar. 25, 1844, which rendered the prisoners unworthy of his magnanimity. Extract of a letter of Antonio López de Santa Anna to Waddy Thompson, [dated] Mar. 28, 1844, *Daily Picayune*, Apr. 13, 1844.

27. The sixteen who escaped were A. B. LaForge, John Johnson, Cyrus K. Gleason, Edward Y. Keene, Richard Keene, Wiley Jones, William Moore, Thomas Smith, E. D. Wright, Francis Arthur, William Wynn, John Toops, William H. H. Frensley, William T. Runyan, Stephen Goodman, and John Tanney. The first nine of these reached Texas safely; the others were recaptured. Green, *Journal of the Texian Expedition against Mier*, p. 373. William Moore reached Texas and reported the names of those who escaped. His list of names is the same as that above, except he reported John McGinley as

remainder will reach their friends. Our guard have ever been strict with us, but since the escape of these 16, they have been doubly so.

As for indulgencies, we never recieve any.

Mr. Thompson,[28] bearer of dispatches from the United States, passed up to the capital a fiew days since and it was surmised by some of our men that thes dispatches related in some way to us; as to its foundation I am ignorant.

On the first of June he and Mr Walsh repassed on their way towards Vera Cruz. On learning here that Santa Anna had first passed up towards Mexico, Mr Walsh (said to be an officer of the British government) entered the stage and followed in his pursuit. It is probable that we are connected with Thompson's Mission, for he expressed a wish to see Santa Anna; but Old Cork Leg[29] was too smart for him, and dodged Uncle Sam's agent by taking to the bushes. Mr Thompson told one of our men, who met with him in the town, that we would not be in Perote much longer. From what he was heard to say some suppose that annexation has taken place. I do not believe it, and hope it is not the case. If this is true, we may look forward to the day of our liberation, but oh! with what feelings! I do not wish liberty at such a price! No, *death* in all its horrors would be sweet first. If annexation only will get us out, if that is all that will release us—as for others they can judge for themselves—but, *as for me*, here let me perish! let me sink alone and uncared for into oblivion. I believe this is the opinion of the majority of this neglected and illfated band.

Our health is now better than usual, but should we recieve another attack of the horrible epedimic, many of us will soon recieve our passports for another and better world. We begin to look forward to *death* as our only liberator. *Hope* has almost departed! however, the 13th[30] has not yet come.

---

escaping and being retaken instead of Francis Arthur (listed by McCutchan as "A. Arthur"). *La Grange Intelligencer*, July 25, 1844; *Northern Standard*, Dec. 12, 1844.

28. Gilbert L. Thompson, a chief engineer in the United States Navy, bore a communication from the U.S. State Department to Santa Anna in person to say that the United States and Texas had drawn a treaty of annexation and was to state that the United States was apprehensive of British influence in Texas. *Mississippian*, July 19, 1844.

29. "Old Cork Leg" was one of the titles the prisoners gave to President Santa Anna, who had lost a leg in the battle of Vera Cruz against the French on Dec. 5, 1838. Bancroft, *History of Mexico*, V:197–200.

30. See footnote 16 above.

El Escmo. Sr. Gen. de Division, D. Antonio López de Santa Anna. *From* [Ramón Alcaraz, et al. (eds.)], *Apuntes para la historia de la guerra entre México y los Estados-Unidos,* frontispiece.

Texians Paving the Street at the Archbishop's Palace. *From* Thomas J. Green, *Journal of the Texian Expedition against Mier*, p. 370.

Jalapa. *From* Brantz Mayer, *Mexico, Aztec, Spanish and Republican* II: 185.

National Bridge, Puente Nacional, formerly called Puente del Rey. *From* Fay[ette] Robinson, *Mexico and Her Military Chieftains*, p. 64.

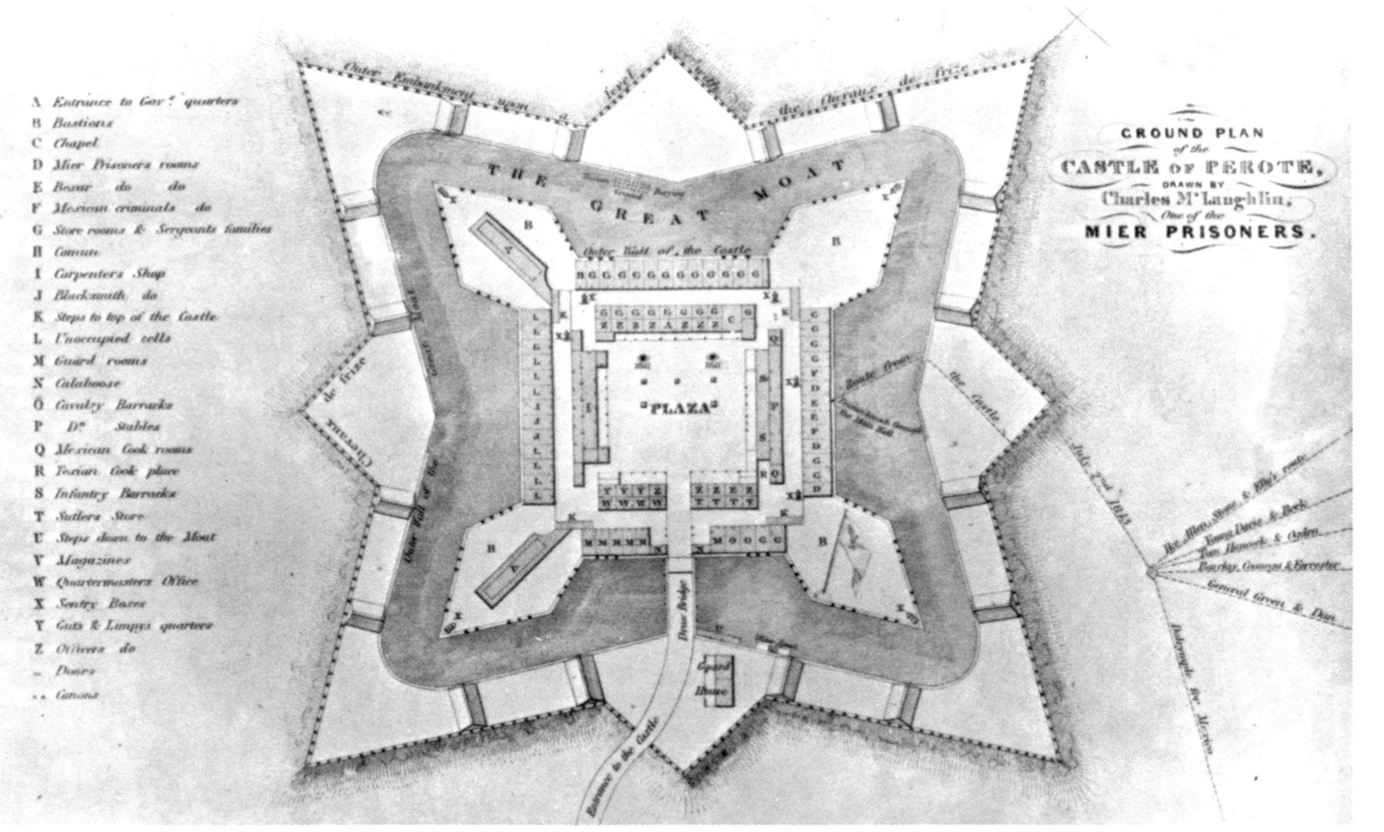

Ground Plan of the Castle of Perote. *From* Thomas J. Green, *Journal of the Texian Expedition against Mier*, p. 238.

Bridge over Moat Leading to Entrance of Perote Prison. *From* J. J. McGrath and Walace Hawkins, "Perote Fort—Where Texans Were Imprisoned," *Southwestern Historical Quarterly* XLVIII (January 1945): 342–343.

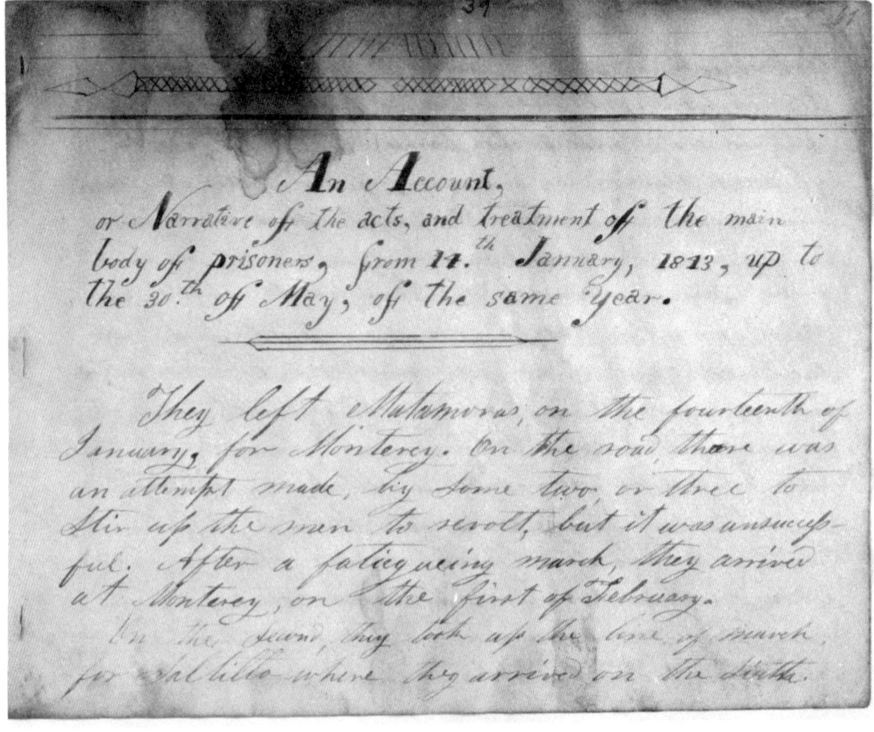

39

61

An Account,
or Narrative of the acts, and treatment of the main body of prisoners, from 14.th January, 1843, up to the 30.th of May, of the same year.

They left Matamoras, on the fourteenth of January, for Monterey. On the road, there was an attempt made, by some two, or three to stir up the men to revolt, but it was unsuccessful. After a fatiegueing march, they arrived at Monterey, on the first of February.

On the second, they took up the line of march, for Saltillo where they arrived on the sixth.

Pages from the diary. Please note that the Rosenberg Library numbered the pages of the diary's three books in continuous sequence in the middle of the top of each page. McCutchan's numbering is in the upper right- or left-hand corner of the page.

OCTOBER 1844.

Texas

Honor Truth and my Country

Mexico

Tyranny Oppression and Death

When we trust to fate,
And trust at ease,
God will come if late
Better may't please.

Friday -- 4th — All of our friends, and companions having arrived in the city, we present, to the view of these people, a subject rather of wonder and curiosity. There seems to be something in, or about us that is calculated to attract the eye, for we can pass through no street, or enter no part of the city, but what, we rivit the gaze of ever passer-by; some in pity; others with a slight degree of hatred and contempt

General Pedro de Ampudia. *From* [Ramón Alcaraz, et al. (eds.)], *Apuntes para la historia de la guerra entre México y los Estados-Unidos*, p. 62.

In a letter from F. M. Dimond[31] to Capt Ryon[32] is stated that we will not be in this place long. We wish our liberty, but not through annexation. F. M. Dimond, United States consul at Vera Cruz, has acted a most noble part by us. He has put himself to much trouble for us and is willing to do more.

We are confined now in three different rooms, averaging 36 to the room. The rooms are 60 by 18 feet, with a window looking out on the valley. On the inner side the window is 18 inches square; on the outside 8 by four inches, with double gratings. They will not do to crawl out at, that is certain. At the other end of the room is the door opening into the interior of the Castle. This door is locke[d] at night, and a sintinel placed at it, who at intervals of 15 minutes during the night cries out *Sentinela a lier-to*[33] at the top of his voice, which at first disturbed our slumbers, but we are now inexcited to all kinds of voice. About one third of the shutter to the door is open with grates across it—the opening is at the top—while lower down is a small grated window opening through which the sentinel keeps a sharp look over, or rather look in—that is when he is not sleeping, which is often the case. Upon the whole, our quarters are not as comfortable as gentlemen could wish, but we are in for it, and must stay and eat [eke] it out. I wish they would give us something to *eat* on. The nex[t] time I come to Mexico to put up at a hotell I'll look for better quarters—or rather—I wont come at all.

We have seen a statement in the News, a paper printed at Galveston, that the Bexer men on recieving money at New Orleans refused themselves many comforts thare by saving two hundred and some odd Dollars, which they placed in the hands of a Merchant to be transmitted to us.[34] We called a meeting in each respective room and voted

31. F. M. Dimond was the United States consul at Vera Cruz, whose many acts of kindness to the imprisoned Texans elicited a letter of appreciation from them. H. A. Alsbury [and thirty-four other Bexar prisoners] to Gen. Waddy Thompson, [dated] Perote, Mar. 24th, 1844, in *Daily Picayune*, Apr. 13, 1844.

32. Captain William M. Ryon.

33. *Centinela alerto*: Sentinel is alert!

34. In New Orleans a subscription of about five hundred dollars had been taken up among the local citizens for the needs of the San Antonio prisoners and other citizens in New Orleans from the western states came forward and furnished clothing, provisions, and other items. After setting aside a portion of the subscription money to relieve their most pressing wants, the San Antonio prisoners "unanimously agreed to send the ballance, amounting to

our thanks to these generous men for their noble conduct. Had it have been but one dollar—the act is the same. We are greatful to our companions and friends.

Thare is a hope among the men that liberty will be ours on the 13th inst., but I can see no foundation for such belief. Our liberty will not come untill we streatch forth our hand and draw it to us. We have been in prison 1 year, 5 month[s], and 10 days, and I see no better prospect than was ours one year since. Why should Old Peg leg take it on himself to release us now? Have we made any promises that would induce him to do that which he refused to do 12 months ago? No! neither will we promis any thing. If he wants us to acknowledge the supremacy of this copper coulered nation before he will release us, here will I die!—we had as well select a grave to suit us, for we make no such acknowledgements. No—I have it now—Sam Houston—has told Santa Cork that if he did not either shoot or distroy us in some way, he would walk over and ring his nose for him, which has frightened the latter so that he will in part comply—that is he is too *magnanimous* to kill us, but he will give us our liberty in hopes to see us kill ourselves. This is the most probable ground I can see for liberty.

Our astonishment was unlimited when we heard of that infamous letter written by Elliott at the instigation of Old Sam,[35] but not so great as the feelings of hatred and contempt excited by reading his

---

nearly $300, to their companions" who were left in the dungeons of Perote Castle. *Telegraph and Texas Register*, May 1, 1844.

35. Sam Houston in a letter dated Jan. 24, 1843 to Charles Elliot, the British chargé d'affaires to Texas, wrote:

> I am constrained to solicit the kindness of you, should it not be out of the line of your official action that you would address her Majesty's Minister to Mexico and, bad as matters, are, make this *representation*.
>
> It is true the men went without orders; and so far as that was concerned the Government of Texas was not responsible; and the men thereby placed themselves out of the protection of the rules of war. This much is granted. But the Mexican officers by proposing capitulation to the men, relieved them from the responsibility which they had incurred; and the moment that the men surrendered in accordance with the proposals of capitulation, they became prisoners of war, and are entitled to all the immunities as such. Upon this view of the subject, I base my hopes of their salvation, if it should be speedily presented through the agency of her Majesty's Minister to the Mexican Government.

This letter is found in Williams and Barker (eds.), *Writings of Sam Houston*, III:299–304; see also Ephraim D. Adams (ed.), *British Diplomatic Correspondence Concerning the Republic of Texas*, pp. 163–164, 213.

proclamation against Com. Moore,[36] who has appeared to be the only officer in the service of Texas who has taken any means or made any effort for us. Texas—all save Moore and his navy—have sunk down to sleep!—let them rest, they are weary!

Some days since Col. Fisher had a dispute with an officer, to whom he gave the *lie direct*, which has made them mad or grave toward our commandant.

Mr Dimond still sends us Newspapers and Periodicals, which serve to lighten our hours. He has exerted himself to render us as comfortable as he can. We begin to think that liberty is close at hand.

Among all the others, thare is one thing more obscure to our judgement than any thing that has happened yet. That is: since the President passed up, the guard have been more strict than usual.

It is amusing, or would be to a lookeron to see the men jump to their chains when they hear the key in the door, and then the moment the officer leaves the Room, some one will spring up commanding "chains off," no sooner said than done, off the[y] come.

6th. I had the mortification of witnessing the most disgraceful conduct in a[n] officer ever the eye of man was before bound to behold. The circumstances were these: Gilbert R. Brush, a lad of 17, had gained permission of some one of the Officers to take of[f] his chain; he did it unsuspecting any harsh treatment, and gave it to the officer, in mention, who was by confession a friend to us—by name and office Capt. Arrolla.[37] This man abused Brush with words and on his leaving the room some of the men began to laugh at some trival occurrence, he immediat[e]ly reopened the door, and falling upon Brush with his cane beet him—striking several blows. Thare was a movement made on our part but thare were some men of cool bravery among us, who judging the intention, prevented it, and thus I have no doubt saved the whole of the Texian prisoners confined in this castle—for the room in which we were was the only one open at the time, and in front of it stood 30 soldiers with cocked pieces and fixed bayonets, so it is evident that if a

36. "A Proclamation Suspending Edwin W. Moore from All Command in the Texas Navy by The President of the Republic of Texas [Sam Houston]," Mar. 23, 1843, in Proclamations of the Presidents, (Republic), Texas State Archives; also in Executive Records of the Second Term of General Sam Houston's Administration, Book No. 48, pp. 68–71 and Book No. 40, pp. 228–229, Texas State Archives; Documents under the Great Seal (Texas) Record Book No. 37, pp. 171–172, Texas State Archives; *Telegraph and Texas Register*, May 17, 1843; Williams and Barker (eds.), *Writings of Sam Houston*, III: 338–340.

37. Captain Miguel Arroyo.

struggle had have here taken place it would have soon ended in the slaughter of us. Only about thirty one in number. And our having made an attempt would have been sufficient for the death of *all.* I give these men credit who prevented the colision. It may be asked by some: How can a native son of Freedom take a blow like a man? To such men would I answer:—Go, learn a lesson in the dungeons of Mexico!

I have been creditablely informed by one of the men who has been in the castle 12 months that July and August are the two coldest months of the year in this place in consiquence of the wind seting from the snow moutains[38] at that time, but God knows it is a little to cold for me here any time. Too cold for comfort.

The officers never enter our rooms now without bringing a strong guard with them. By way of warning they had better not use their power too freely!

We are all greatly oppressed by the oppression of the infernal sons of Satan. It cannot last long. We *will not* endure it. If 20 days more *does not* bring a change of treatment *for the* better—*woe* to the soldiers of this fortress. They will *die* without a prayer. The usage is growing visibly worse every day. But we will endure it untill the 13th, and then, *a change* of treatment—*we take and demolish this* castle, or *we perish* and *sink into oblivion* in the dearing attempt. Our minds, I think, are made up, and well will we bear the test.—We will wate the event.

The troops of Mexico are good at drilling; sham fights are their greatest sport, but let the reality come, let balls begin to fall around them—they forget their descipline and are excited rather by fear than a thirst for deeds of a heroic vallor. Mexican vallor consists in massacres, such as that at Goliad and the decimation at the Salado. But one single act of herish [heroism] has never poluted their honor where as many acts of barbarity have brightened their Military Glory. Barbarity and treachery are their boasts. Well do they live up to their real belief. But we will stick to the motto and live in hope if we die in despair.

7th. The dull monotony of a Prison presents but little to direct the mind.

Our eating is bad. We get 2 pounds of Coffee p[e]r day to 110 men, 10 ozs. bread, and 4 ozs. meate, each p[e]r day; and that of the worst

38. Bound on all sides by distant mountains, the plain of Perote seemed to be as level as the proverbial ocean floor. Off to the southeast towered the Pic de Orizaba (17,373 feet), covered with perpetual snow, while closer by was the Cofre de Peroté (13,415). In the midst of the plain towered Tepiacaualca and beyond it to the north stretched the range of snow-capped mountains containing the Cerro de Pizarro.

bread and poorest Beef that can be found. To throw the meat against the wall it will Stick like glew. Some time back they gave us irish potatoes at dinner and no meat. These potatoes were mashed in water with a little salt, verry little, and a great quantity of red pepper.

We have heard that a bill passed the Congress of Texas for our relief, appropriating $15,000,[39] but it is presumable that this is only by *word*, not by deed or action, as we have never seen any *money*.

Capt. Arrolla struck another one of the prisoners for taking off his chains, but he had as well remember that a day of retribution is close at hand.

Col. Fisher has been ordered to work but he refused, saying that they had the power—might was in their hands, and that they would have to use it—this the Governor did not seem disposed to do; he therefore induced Fisher through persuasion to walk out, but not to work telling him that exercise would be beneficial to his health.

We are now locked up nearly all day.

The report is: Texas is annexed. We are not much elated with the idea of Texas salling under another nation for protection. It is true

39. The Congress of Texas passed a "Joint Resolution for the Relief of Texian Prisoners in Mexico," which was approved by the president on Feb. 5, 1844. The resolution declared that the president "is hereby authorized and required, forthwith, to employ any means in the reach of the Government, to feed and clothe our unfortunate countrymen, prisoners of war, who are, at present, starving in the prisons of Mexico; and that the amount of fifteen thousand dollars be, and the same is hereby, appropriated to carry into effect the provisions of this act, and all other acts upon this subject; and this act take effect from and after its passage." H. P. N. Gammel (ed.), *Laws of Texas*, II:1028–1029. Following the enactment of this law, President Houston made arrangements through a secret agent in New Orleans to carry out its terms, so as not to disclose that the Texas government had any connection with the relief effort. Reuben M. Potter was appointed a secret agent to go to Mexico to make arrangements to get relief to the prisoners. After many unfortunate delays, Potter reached Vera Cruz on July 22, 1844, and there faced further delays, brought on by the necessity of maintaining absolute secrecy. No wonder the Mier prisoners were upset and bitter. After Potter left Mexico, his agent in the town of Perote made contact with the prisoners and began to supply them periodically with small amounts of money, which did much to alleviate their condition during the last six weeks of their confinement. J. B. Miller to R. M. Potter, [dated] Treasury Department, Washington, June 3, 1844 (confidential), and June 15, 1844; Reuben M. Potter to James B. Miller, [dated] Velasco, Sept. 24, 1844; L. S. Hargous to Reuben M. Potter, [dated] Vera Cruz, Sept. 10, 1844; all in Comptroller's Letters (Republic) Texas State Archives.

that Mexico would pay a stricter regard to the hot lead and hard iron that Uncle Sam would visit her coast with then she does to Old Sam's bombastic and gass-pregnant proclamations; but it is also true that as for my self (and it is, I believe, the opinion of the majority)—let me die —let me perish, neglected, and obscure in prison—let my frame sink under cruelties such as never man endured,—let me go among the unnumbered dead—and, in short let my body decay in obscurity and my name sink into oblivion! but annex not Texas to *any* government. She has but recently thrown off one yoke, let her not accept another, let he[r] remain,—let her stand *free*, *independent*, and *honored*, or sink down, *down* pressed by calamities unnumbered, but still struggling to the last, untill she shall reach her grave in oblivions lonely vale—and *thart—thare let me rest with her*! If Texas falls—*may I* fall in her defence:—when none others will be found to respect it may I s[t]ill love to rear aloft the *proud banner* of Texas, and wield a sword in its defence:—when none others will be found to respect it may I s[t]ill love and serve that *star*, the proud emblem of a nations glory. And if none others honor it, may it fall to me to defend it with the last drop of my blood, and that it may be to me—"Death-pall and winding sheet." Capt. Arolla struck of [one?] of our men several times over the head with his sword—it injured him greatly. Hard thoughts against the Nation and against the Guard—but we await the 13th.

Some of the men being tradesmen get about twenty five cents per day.

8th. Nothing—but hard times and worse acoming.

I am obliged to keep calm and shy with this journal, for if it should be found and its contents ascertained by this yellow race, they would *journalize* and *poste me up* in eternity; giving five ounce balls as a credit to my account and that would not set well to a hungry man.

Sunday 9th.—Locked up as usual. 8 men have about 30 pounds each of iron, and are in a dark dungeon called the Caliboose. The man that was so severely beaten on the 7th is in the hospital with double irons on him.

We can not immagine the cause of this harsh treatment, nor when it will end, but i[t]s effect we verry well know, and we will, I think, inform Gen. Jarraro of our deliberations on the subject, about the 15th if he does not materially change his manners. Let him look to himself.

The dulness of a prison presents nothing but one series of occupations and harsh abuses. Oh! how predominates the wish to go forth into the open fields, unguarded alone, to enjoy a breath of the pure air of Heaven untainted by the breath of this perfidious people. But such reveries are only vein foolish dreams of a falicious immagination. We must turn from a contemplation of natures divine gifts seen in fancy to mourn over our fallen liberties! How dread the thought! And Oh Texas! My country! the country of my adoption! how freely would I shed the last drop of my blood in thy defence, and feel blessed in so doing! But I fear I shall ere long be doomed to lament thy fallen honor! thy tarnished glory! Arouse thyself Oh Texas! from thy apathy. Streatch forth thy gigantic arm and secure thy eternal independence!! Cast from you the phantom of annexation, and grasp the real substance of *independence*.

10th. Our hopes are not as sanguine as they were three days since. We fear to rely upon any thing untill ascertained beyond a doubt.

11th. Our treatment is changing for the better. I was of the opinion it would change. But let Mexico *remember the Salado*.

12th. Our hopes are loosing ground, but our treatment is visibly changing for the better. Not wishing new disapointment, we fear to give hope full sway. I can see no cause why Sta. Anna *should* release us, but many reasons why he *should not*. One is he knows verry well that he would have us to fight again and another is—he is deficient in magnanimity. But to morroy will tell, or as the Mexicans say mañana lo vera.[40] Will we ever gain our liberty? Sí—poco Tiempo.[41]

13th. Doors open at 8 o'clock and no work, as this is the birth day of Sta. Anna, the selfstyled Neapoleon of the South. The soldiers, poor deluded men, express great joy at the anual feast which takes place on this day.

This day is wellcomed by the roar of cannon and peal of bells. So does a nation wellcome a day that by it should be wept. So does a people wellcome the day of the nativity of the man who has trampled down their rights, seting the iron heal of despotism on the last form or vestage of their liberty. Poor deluded—ignorant men, they still cry: "long live Santa Anna," the man who has with one mighty succession of blows hurled them into the verry dust of oppression—stamping the seal of Tyranny upon their rights, thare to remain inerratic forever, I fear. They cry, "Long live Sta. Anna—long live Liberty"—thus, associating their liberty and its destroyer togeather in a manner which he does not deserve!

Our treatment is gai[ni]ng ground for the better. Our dinner—something better than common, but the rice was spoiled by a rat being cooked in it; but many eat it, notwithstanding. Had this villainous rat have kept his fingers out of the rice, we could have done *most* excel-

40. *Manaña lo vera*: Tomorrow will tell; or, Tomorrow it will be seen.
41. *Sí–poco tiempo*: Yes—a short time; or, Yes—soon.

lently today.

We are locked up early for the soldiers to go on perade. We will get our liberty some time if we should live long enough.

Miserable is the life of a prisoner—scarce worth preserving—but here we must stay no one knows how long! Dread is the thought!

About 95 or 100 of our number have died in this miserable degrading servitude.

To day the mail bring glorious news no chance for annexation. So the lone star shall shine brighter than I had hoped.

14th. The 13th has passed—*has passed*. I am of opinion that it will be some time yet before we regain our liberty. "We are in for during the war."—has become a general sentiment among us and springs from a good foundation. Sta. Anna will not release us untill exchanged, or we do the *deed* our selves. It would be an act of desperation, but I fear that it is our only alternative. Our countrymen do nothing.

Our treatment is now about like it was previous to this month.

15th. Hope has fled—we have not yet placed our thoughts upon another day. We are in low spirits.

Sunday, 16th. We are locked up untill nine or ten oclock every Sunday—as on Sundays we do not work much—but this day we are locked up untill 12 o'clock. The soldiers attend mass every Sunday, feast day, and fast day. Our officers are locked up all day, and we can have no communication with them. Our guard are very strict.

17th. All locked up, excep 25, who are at work.

Nothing but a little rice and an oz of meat for dinner.

We get three mails per week.

18th. We all feel low spirited this morning. Our situation is miserable.

When will we get out of this desolate prison? Mr Dimond in a letter to Fisher says: "keep up your spirits, the darkest hour is just before day." If this is sound philosophy, we have had one of the longest spells of darkness ever known for it has been utter darkness with us for and during the last 17 months.

19th. We are locked up 18 hours of the 24, and it is our general opinion that if this course of conduct is continued, ere long that dreadful epedemic will again be among us. But this may be the enemy's wish.

I see published in a paper that Gen. Waddy Thompson has said that he was personally acquainted with Gen. Jarraro, the Governor of this fortress; that he knows him to be an officer and a gentleman; and that we are not only treated with humanity, but with kindness. If Thompson had felt the reverse of this as often and severe as we have, he would make quite a different statement. If beating one with a hand-spike is humanity and kindness, we get it it [*sic*] by the wholesale. If this statement was made by Thompson, he has been sadly decieved relating to our condition and the character of Gen. Jarraro, or he has made a statement knowing its falsehood at the time; and it is a matter of no easy effort on our part to suppose Thompson capable of acting in a menner unbecomeing a gentleman. Tharefore, I verry much doubt that Thompson ever said any thing of the kind.[42]

Some of the men are in for a little amusement, but such amusement is but momentary while our misery is lasting.

The most debasing act was committed this evening ever I before had the mortification of witnessing in a Texian. James Young[43] (I think propper to give his name in full) fell upon his knees to a Mexican Priest, crossing himself, am [and?] making other catholic manuvers. Now had he have been sincere in his devotion, he could not have been censured so much, but his only motive was to gain favour with the Governor, who was present. To prove his insincerity, it is only needful to say that he was under the influence of intoxication at the time. But this will not excuse him for the commital of an act so debasing. For he who will commit a deed so degrading while intoxicated shame only will restrain when sober. For this debasing act of Sarvility he will recieve the well merited contempt of all his companions, inasmuch as we hold it to be beneath the dignity and honor of any one who possesses the more noble traits of character, which exalts above the common level. Young has shown himself totally void of all self respect; debased and servile to the lowest; wanting in all the principles and honor of a man; lacking all the feelings which constitute a gentleman; and worthy of the lowest wretchedness to which man can fall. Could I find words my censure should not end thus, but it is a subject hateful to me as is its origin. Tharefore I end here, as I began.

20th. *I am in prison.* Often, as did the ghost of Hamlet arise before his son, does this thought come up to me, when for a moment I at-

42. The editor of the *Daily Picayune*, Apr. 13, 1844, reported Thompson "tells us that the present Governor of the Castle of Perote, Gen. Jarero, is known to him as a man of high character as an officer and a gentleman, and that the prisoners are treated not only with humanity but kindness." A lengthy criticism of this statement by the Mier prisoners is to be found in ibid., Aug. 21, 1844.

43. *The Weekly Herald*, Jan. 1, 1853, p. 2, reported that "John Young" (actually, James Young) died at San Antonio, Texas, on Saturday, Dec. 5, 1852. He was a Mier prisoner who escaped "almost" miraculously from confinement in Mexico.

tempt to seek enjoyment. *In prison*—doomed to *death*, or for *life*. Poor fellows we are without doubt or jest.

"Home sweet home thare is no place like home."

But we seem to be cast off in our trouble with neither home nor country.

"Mid pleasures and palaces though oft we may rome"

That does not sound well—this is better

"Mid prisons and dungeons though oft we may rome

We will all turn poets—

We get a mail here tri-weekly and I wish it was more often.

21st. We are in low spirits—with good reason for it. Our friends have forgotten us—we get no letters from them. But let them forget—I for one will rouse up and cheer my sinking spirits while life shall last, and when I die, if I must die here, let me fall covered in Mexican goar.

Now rests memory on Cameron—whare is he? *that* the foe can tell who murdered him. He has gone from this world, but his memory must live while time lives; and when time itself shall have been swept from off the books of the recording angel, the aweful thunders of eternity shall peal fourth his name to ages unnumbered! But let him rest with his glory.

The officers tell us that those who will do good work shall be freed from their chains, and those who will not work well shall be chained two and two. They have previously tried several different plans to induce us to work hard, but all hitherto have failed, and I immagine that this will end in like manner.

22nd. Gen. Jarraro the governor has left here for a fiew days, and a general of cavalry[44] will act in his stead during his absence. May he have a glorious long stay. This cavalry officer is verry strict, not allowing us to leave our street.

Thare is a store in the castle kept by Don Francisco[45]—Somebody (I do not know who) where we can [get] anything we may need. He is willing to allow us credit, which is a privoliege which he will not grant to Mexicans.

Our officers have been locked up for the last six or eight days.

The castle is undergoing a therough repare.

44. General Antonio de Castro was the replacement. Pablo Max Ynsfran (ed.), *Catálogo de los manuscritos del archivo de don Valentín Gómez Farías obrantes en la universidad de texas coleccion latinamericana*, p. 164. Castro was a strong supporter of Santa Anna.

45. Don Francisco (last name not known) was a retired army lieutenant.

About this season of the year cold rains are incessent.

In a publication, I see that Houston has said in a public speech that we are better off here than we would be at home.[46] The infernal traitorous reprobate for that remark deserves death from the hand of one of this band, and, if we should ever regain our liberty, I would not like to be answerable for what might follow, for there are some among us desperate enough for any thing.

Sam Houston has been the cause of death to many of our band, and it would be justice to arreign him as a *murderer*. He must be a traitor, for his acts are not consistant with the principles of patriotism which he confesses. This is a broad sweeping assertion, but it must stand where I have placed it.

Sunday, 23d. Thare is confined in the castle Gen. Berigen,[47] who surrenderd to the Campietranos.[48]

46. I have been unable to find in the writings of Houston or in contemporary newspapers any statement made by Houston to the effect that the Mier men were better off languishing in Mexican dungeons than they would be at home. Those individuals, like McCutchan, who were highly critical of Houston might have read such thoughts into his speech of Nov. 10, 1843, at the old capitol in Houston:

> The embarrassments which have hung around my nation, have been almost unsurmountable. With a country derided abroad; discouraged at home by a disregard for law, I have had to contend with impediments almost amounting to despair. However, I have not shrunk from the arduous task imposed upon me. We have accomplished something. Peace has already shed its balmy influence upon the feelings of the people of Texas. They are quieting down from the ardent, impetuous and strange frenzy of glory to be acquired in the field. Industry is becoming the order of the day. Texas is advancing towards her glorious destiny.... And then, when all faction shall die away, and crumble into nothingness; when the nameless thousands who have been engaged in defamation and opposition, not to the man, but to the country, shall mingle with their mother earth, and be forgotten forever, then will the people of Texas arise like giants in the plentitude of their prosperity, and honor and bless the pioneers who have led them on to their destiny.

Williams and Barker (eds.), *Writings of Sam Houston*, III:455–457.

47. General Antonio Peña y Barragán surrendered the Mexican forces in Campeche, Yucatán, and agreed to leave Yucatán by May 13, 1843, and for such conduct he had been imprisoned at Perote Castle. Tom Henderson Wells, *Commodore Moore and the Texas Navy*, p. 140; Bancroft, *History of Mexico*, V:243; Bell, *A Narrative of the Capture and Subsequent Sufferings*, p. 86; *Diario del Gobierno*, May 28, 1843.

48. Campecheanos.

24th. This is a feast day, being St. John's day and on such occasions we do not work, which is a s[o]urce of some gratification.

We have one violine among us made by one of our carpenters, and we have a great dance.

We are locked up the greater part of each feast day.

25th. Our treatment is now about as it was before the first inst., but it is miserable yet.

26th. We get but little to eat—badly cooked and nothing to eat with it. 1 pound of coffee in the morning to all of us being in number 108—at noon 4 ozs. poor beef to each, with a little rice boiled in pure water—at night 1 pound of coffee to all, with about 8 or 10 ozs of co[a]rse or 4 ozs. of good bread p[e]r day. Every thing, the worst that can be got in the country.

27th. Many of the men dance at least three hours during each day and night, which bears the face of careless spirits—but these dances excite no joyful feelings—only serving to pass time away, free as practable from painful thoughts. We still try to live up to the old motto "We'll live in hope if we die in dispair."

28th. Hard times—these — a man can not form a plan for escape.

29th. This [is] a feast day. The Governor gives us permission to go into the moat and bathe in a small pool of water, unclean, but pleasant.

The Governor has opened his heart, showing his liberality so far as to give us each 6¼ cents—amounting to 6.75^{cts} which is to him an enormous sum.

Sunday, 30th. Six of our illfated band are now in the Hospital.

July [1844]

Monday, 1st. Nothing of importance.

2nd. We hear from a letter from Mr. Argus[49] of Mexico that it is believed that all United States Citizens residing in this country will be ordered out of it in a short time. By which I judge, thare will be war and bloodshed between the two countries. Verry well—go it. If they can stand it, we can. Hurra for one—and well done the other. I am like, or will be like, the Heroine of the backwoods while witnessing a bloody encounter between her husband and gentleman Bear, observed:

49. Louis S. Hargous was United States consul at Vera Cruz and a prominent merchant at that place and owner of the L. S. Hargous & Co.

"It is the only fight I ever saw in which I did not take some interest."

3d. We gain permission to cellibrate the anniversary of American independence.

4th. The great, glorious, and ever memorable day on which our ancestors, the heroes of '76 declared themselves a free and independent people—oweing allegiance to none save God. The Birthday of Liberty to a nation. On this day the dellights of a people, weak in numbers but strong against oppression, declared to the world that they were free, pledging their lives, properties and sacred honor to sustain the cause. This was done in 1776, and Texas following in the footsteps of her illusterous ancester did a simelar act in 1836—and we in supporting that independence then gained—now lay in a dungeon. Good, we'll stay here—I fear.

We were put into two rooms to night for a frolic. We dance and kick up a noise untill one o'clock in the morning.

5th. We have a visit from Mr. Stapp[50] and Mr Morgan,[51] formerly prisoners in this place—the former, one of the Mier men—the latter,

50. William Preston Stapp was born in Kentucky, Apr. 12, 1812, the son of Elijah and Nancy (Shannon) Stapp. Elijah Stapp visited Texas in 1826 with a letter of introduction to Stephen F. Austin from Green DeWitt. In 1830 he moved to Texas from Missouri with his wife and six children, settling in Green DeWitt's Colony in present Victoria County. In 1831, William Preston Stapp participated in an Indian campaign and in 1840, with his brother Oliver H. Stapp, is recorded as having title to 1,107 acres of land in Gonzales County. In the spring of 1842, he enrolled as a private in Captain Alexander Stevenson's company of "Missouri Invincibles" for a contemplated attack upon Mexico and later, in the fall, enlisted in the Somervell Expedition as a member of Captain Isaac N. Mitchell's company. Captured at Mier and imprisoned in Mexico, he was released on May 16, 1844, through the intercession of his uncle, General Milton Stapp of Madison, Indiana, with General Juan N. Almonte, Mexican minister to the United States. William Preston Stapp, *Prisoners of Perote*, p. 127; Walter P. Webb and H. Bailey Carroll (eds.), *Handbook of Texas*, II:659; Gifford White (ed.), *The 1840 Census of the Republic of Texas*, p. 59; Nance, *Attack and Counterattack*, pp. 247n.53, 605, 636–637.

51. Joseph C. Morgan was one of the San Antonio prisoners who had been released in March 1844. After being released he had visited Mexico City. Stapp reached New Orleans on July 23, 1844; but there is no report of Morgan arriving at that time. *Daily Picayune*, Apr. 13 and July 23, 1844.

one of the San Antonio men. Morgan was released with his companions in March, and Stapp since that time. After their release they went to the city of Mexico, and are now on their way home. They stay in town to night.

6th. Hard times.

Sunday, 7th. Nothing scarcely to eat.

8th. Nothing to eat with it.

9th. Badly cooked.

10th. Worse than ever.

11th. Too much to stand. We are about to start a paper among us in manuscript.

12th. We recieve 46¾ cents each of the money sent us by the Bexer men.

13th. We take it as it comes—good or bad no choice.

Sunday, 14th. We have started the Newspaper under the name of "The Perote Meataxe.[")]

15th. Sta. Anna's sister payed a visit to the castle to day on her way up to Mexico. She was saluted by the battery, both on entering and on departing.

16th. This is a feast day, but we were working untill 11 o'clock.

The Standards of all nations with whom Mexico has a treaty are flying on the ramparts, and among them is the "Star Spangled Banner" of the United States waving in haughty grandure and sheding defiance to the emblems of European Nations. Although the lone Star is not among them, far be it from me to forget it—the flag of my Country. The Bright and beautiful Star, which has taken its course through the world solitary and alone! and alone has dared to face the frowning despot of Mexico. It arose amid the Storm of war. Dark scowling and dread was the cloud of war which o're spread the Horrizon, when this lone but beautiful Star first sent forth its luminous rays. At it the darkest threats and deepest thunders of Despotic Mexico were hurled, aimend [amid] death and distruction to its defenders!

But these threats were useless—and these thunders unavailing—it yet waves in glory—and bright may be its career.

> "Saw you not the bright the glorious Star,
> Radient as the Sun of morn,
> In triump waiving o're the field of war,
> Amid smoke, death, and firey storm."

17th. This is a feast day. So by name, not by nature—that is to say —we make it a fast among us.

Not one in the Hospital at this time.

18th. We learn that the Bill for annexation was rejected in the Senate of the United States the vote standing 16 Ayes—35 Nays. Now this is joyful to me. Would *Texas* have accep[t]ed this? Would she have signed away that independence for which so much blood has been shed? I hope not. Ah, if I could believe that she would never—*no never*—would I again set foot on her soil, even though that act should give me liberty. No! before I would tread the soil of a country whos[e] people were so forgetful of their National honor! Let my hopes be blasted! let me remain in prison! let my proudest wishes be hurled to earth before annexation should coume [come].

I had forgoten—this is my birthday. *Better*—had it *never* been, for me. I spent my birthyday 1842 in Texas—1843 in the city of Mexico—1844 in Perote, and 1845—God, *only*, knows whare! Most probable in this place.

19th. We have one consolation in our trouble, that is: Our only fault is having served our country *too* well.

20th. We get permission to bathe again.

Sunday 21st. This morning I passed out with a guard—thare were about eight of us togeather. We were delayed. I threw myself down thoughtlessly upon the green sward, but had scarce touched it when my mind flew to Texas, her green prairies and deep forests. I wish *once more* to hear the merry cry of the dogs mingled with the shrill, cheering blast of the horn; and to witness the affrighted deer as he bounds away with the first scent of his foe. Oh solitude, solitude would that I could enjoy it again. Some sequestered grove, hollowed and enchanted by the merry song of birds and ripleing water—thare to mourn over the long lost happiness of childhood, and in immagination revisit the home of my youth. Thus—and thus alone, would I be once again happy. Thare could I think of days past and gone never to return, and repeat two line[s] of Tom Moore's Farewell:

> "Let fate do their worst there are relics of joy,
> Bright dreams of the past, which she can not destroy."

But *now* rests my mind upon the situation of myself and companions. So dark—so dreary, and forlorn! To dread for thought, much more so for word! A truice to such thoughts.

We have had a visit from Mr Jenkins[52] now a resident of this coun-

52. Jenkins, first name unknown, was a portrait painter by profession and an acquaintance of James A. Glasscock; he had just arrived from Yucatan on his way to Mexico City. On Monday, July 23, 1844, he "took Dr. Shep-

try, but formerly of Mobile Alabama; a portrait painter by profession. He could give us no important information.

One of our interpretors, Mr A. S. Thurmon, has been told by a cavalry officer that Sta. Anna was about to enter Texas by land and water, with the intent of reconquer or loose it. The sooner this is done, the better it will be for us. We would like to take part in the coming struggle. I think it inevitable, and let it come quickly. The cloud of war is now lowering o're our devoted country. Now the over spreading cloud, at last geathered to its most mighty and dread strength, poures down a torrent of fire upon that devoted land and we are not permited to check it in its downward distructive course. Now I hear the thunders of artillery—the roar of musquetry—and the ring of rifles mingled in one tremendous sound, as if of Hell with the shreiks of the wounded —the groans of the dieing and shouts of the victorious. Amid this dread confusion I s[t]ill see the "*lone Star*" waving in proud grandure as if in triumph. Now I see the opposing armies drawn up for a decisive engagement. Thare stand the swarthy sons of the south going to battle not for liberty—but against it—sheding their blood in an inglorious cause at the command of their despotic ruler. Opposed to them stand the proud, brave sons of Liberty. Their country calls them to her defense—and Liberty encourages them to obey—thare they stand firm as the adimantine rock of ages—asured of success. Now they engage! Now I hear the mingled roar of battle! Smoke obscures the scene! Ha[r]k! that shout! the roar has ceased! the smoke clears away—See, see—the Star of Texas waves in proud triumph—fare o're the eagle of Mexico! But *we* can take *no* part in the coming contest. *These chains —these chains*!

It is reported that Federation has bursted forth, headed by Canales. But such reports are not always to be believed.

22nd. Gen. Ampudia was in town today, but did not visit the castle.

23d. It is reported that Gen. Arista[53] has put him self at the head of

---

herds, Dr. McMaths, Judge Gibsons and Col. Wilson's likeness." Glasscock diary, July 21–23, 1844, Texas State Archives.

53. Mariano Arista was born at San Luis Potosí on July 16, 1802. He began his military career at the age of eleven as a cadet in the Spanish army, rising later to the rank of lieutenant. He served in the Spanish army until June 1821 when he joined the revolutionary cause. During General Guadalupe Victoria's administration in 1825 Arista became a captain and a distinguished member of the "Yorkino" party, which was made up of liberals, the old Hidalgoists, and revolutionaries. After 1826 he was alternately a supporter and an opponent of Santa Anna. In 1832 he was made a lieutenant colonel and when Santa Anna took office as president was promoted to the rank of

the federals, and is now in San Louis Potosí, but I fear it is like the most of such reports—false.

24th. I have trembling seen the most miserable sights. I pitying[ly] saw the warriors arm reduced to infant weakness—saw and felt the deep recking pang [?]—saw the ghostly form—the pale quivering lip—the beamless eye no more bright with ardor:—I heard the groans of the agonizing heart—saw daily layed in the cold—cold earth, the frequent corpse—while we, the still living fixed on each other a blank gaze—sad and mute, as if to ask—whom fate would next demand? All this have I beheld and even endured—yet my feelings were never more miserable than at this time! *Not one hope*!!

25th. Quite a dark gloomy morning—almost as sad as the Texian Prisoners. We are lonely and desolate, even in crowds.

26th. No Hope!

27th. Our officers have writen to Sir Charles Bankhead,[54] H. B. M.'s representative at the *Court* of Mexico, giving him a model of our treaty stipulation with General Ampudia, who pledged his honor and that of his nation that we should recieve the treatment due to prisoners of War, and informing him of the wide difference of our treatment under that capitulation from that due to us by it.

By this mail we have an account of an engagement between Maj.

---

general of division. Suffering under Santa Anna's displeasure he was forced to leave Mexico and lived at Cincinnati, Ohio, where he learned the saddler's trade. He returned to Mexico in June 1835 to accept the terms of the Amnesty Decree of May 2, 1835, and resumed his military position. He was captured by the French at Vera Cruz on Dec. 5, 1838, but was released after a short and easy captivity of two months. Toward the end of 1839 he was named commander-in-chief of the Army Corps of the North. In September 1841 President Anastacio Bustamante made him general of a division, and he opposed Santa Anna's efforts to oust Bustamante from the presidency. Upon the fall of Bustamante's government, Arista renounced his command in November 1841 but was renamed to it in 1842 shortly after being exonerated of the charge of fomenting a revolution. In March 1843 he was reported in a state of declining health (more likely political health) at his hacienda of Mamoelique. George L. Rives, *The United States and Mexico*, I:442, 448; Bancroft, *History of Mexico*, V:133–135; *Telegraph and Texas Register*, Oct. 20 and 27, 1841; *El Cosmopolita*, Mar. 25, 1843; *Diario Official*, Oct. 19, 1881; Carreño (ed.), *Jefes de ejército méxicana*, pp. 44–49.

54. Charles Bankhead was appointed British minister to Mexico, replacing Percy Doyle, acting chargé d'affaires, following Richard Pakenham. Bankhead reached Mexico City, Mar. 1, 1844. He had previously served for some years as secretary to the British legation in the United States. *United States Telegraph*, Apr. 8, 1826; *Telegraph and Texas Register*, May 15, 1844.

Hays[55] at the head of 15 men and about sixty of the Indians of Texas, supposed to be Commanchees. Hays was *victorious.*

Sunday, 28th. Eight of the men go to the mountains to day.

Saml. Mcfall[56] struck by an officer with the flat of his sword.

29th. Same old thing, no change.

30th. Our guard have been more strict than common today. I suppose they *think* "they smell a mice."

We understand that thare is an order from the general government to give us worse treatment. This we learn from Capt. Arolla, who hates us *sweetly*. I can not vouch for the truth of this as Arolla is a man who can be Depended upon under *no* circumstances.

31st. A flying report says: "The President will make soldiers of all the Texian rebells in Mexico, but I "*guess*" *He* will not try it. He had best not.

August, 1844

Thursday 1st. We have been changing rooms to day. The Governor causes us to moove occasionaly to look for holes in the floor or wall.

2nd. The carpenters are all chained two and two and put to work outside of the Castle.

3d. Nothing to eat, and nothing to eat with it—as usual.

55. While on a scout, early in June 1844, to discover the location of Indians who had recently raided the settlements, Major John C. Hays, with fifteen of his company, encountered a party of about ten Indians at Walker's Creek, about fifty miles above Seguin. The Indians fled to a clump of trees where between sixty and seventy Comanches, Wacos, and Mexicans lay in ambush. Hays' men defeated the Indians in battle, losing one of their own killed and four (three badly, but not mortally) wounded. The Indians left twenty of their number dead upon the field, including their chief, and had at least twenty or thirty wounded. J. W. Wilbarger, *Indian Depredations in Texas*, pp. 75–77; Hays' report of the battle of Walker's Creek, in June 1844, will be found in the "Annual Report of the Secretary of War and Marine to Sam Houston, President, Washington, Nov. 30, 1844," in Texas Congress, *Journals of the House of Representatives of the Ninth Congress of the Republic of Texas*, Appendix, pp. 32–33.

56. Samuel C. McFall was a member of Captain E. Sterling C. Robertson's company in Lt. Col. J. L. McCrocklin's regiment in the Somervell Expedition, and John G. W. Pierson's company on the Mier Expedition. At the beginning of the Texas Revolution he was living at Tenoxtitlán. Nance, *Attack and Counterattack*, p. 641; John Henry Brown, *Indian Wars and Pioneers of Texas*, pp. 25–26.

Sunday 4th. Our paper comes out to day under another Name—"The Perote Prisoner." H. B. Sutton entered the castle to day—stayed a short time.

5th. Hard times.

6th. We moove again.

7th. A Blank.

8th. We learn that one of our number—Daniel McDonald,[57] will be released in a fiew days.

9th. When will this come to an end?

10th. Nine of us went to the mountains after Brooms, but could not give slip for home. I sought an opportunity. About 20 of the men are engaged in drawing stone in carts the distance of 5 miles for repairing the Castle.

Sunday 11th. Mr Jenkins is still in the town of Perote. He visits us daily.

12th. Hard times, without intermission.

13th. It is said by Hannah Moore: "All is for the better;" but I beg lieve to disagree with her in that place.

14th. Nothing more has been heard of the intended release of McDonald—it must be false.

147 Mexican criminals entered the castle on their way to Vera Cruz—they stop here to night.

15th. This is a feast day among this tribe of Satanic imps, an[d] on such day[s] we do not work.

James Armstrong[58] met with the misfortunate to get his arm (or sholder, rather) thrown out of place, but it was replaced with great pain and a little difficulty.

This is mail day. Our only pleasure is that peculiar hope, arising from a desire of some news from home or the capital rellative to our friends, or our liberation, on these days which are Monday, Thursday, and Saturday.

But we are disappointed this time.

16th. This is wash day with me. I wash verry well, when I have any clothes to opperate on, but they are scarce.

My mess had a great dinner to day of my own cooking.

It is understood among us that F. M. Dimond is to leave Vera Cruz

57. Daniel McDonald was a member of Captain Ewen Cameron's company. He was released from Perote Prison on Aug. 29, 1844.

58. James C. Armstrong was a member of Captain Claudius Buster's company. He was freed from Perote Prison on Aug. 24, 1844. See James H. Calvert, Pension Papers (Republic), Texas State Archives; *Galveston Daily News*, April 23, 1882.

about the 17th, which is tomorrow, for the United States. We know that he is shortly going home, but as for his starting tomorrow that is mear conjecture raised by ourselves. With his departure we loose the best and only real friend we have found among the public men residing in Mexico.

I have to day learned that thare is a grand project under opperation in the a[d]joining room to the on[e] in which I have the *honor* to lodge. This has reference to the process of diging-out going on in No. 7. I am in no. 8.

I have written several letters home and can get no answer to them, and now I verry much wish to go and see them, and find their reasons for not writing, and then perhaps I will not return.

17th. Hard times, and worse a coming—our coffee has no more taste of the grain than if it was not of that species and not called by that name.

I came near loosing my eye by accident, but "a miss is as good as a mile."

Sunday, 18th. The governor gave the enormous amount of *six and* fourth cents to each man for us to take a *spree* upon. "Who cares for expenses."

A powder plot concieved. It is proposed by one of the men F. White[59] to blow out a stone at the end of our room, which could be done.

19th. A cool morning for this month. The project of which I spoke on the 16th will succeed. It is gowing on finely. The project is this: in room no. 7 they are cuting round the faceing of the window, which is faced with granite. They accomplish the work with tin saws made by John Tanny.[60] If that room would permit us, we could dig into them with danger of discovery, and thus both ro[o]ms having in them fifty five or six men would in one night be entirely evacuated, which would be distressing in the extreme to the dark sons of Despotic Mexico. I[n] our room we do not yet know wherther or not those in no. 7 will allow us to dig through to them.

The Powder plot was concieved in our room no. 8, but I think it will

59. Francis White was a private in the Galveston Border Guards organized under Captain William F. Wilson in September 1839 for service against the Indians. Charles W. Hayes, *Galveston*, I:394.

60. John Taney's name is not given in the rolls of the Mier men at the end of McCutchan's diary. He is listed in Israel Canfield's diary and by the other diarists and in the Public Debt Papers (Texas), Texas State Archives; also, in John Henry Brown, *History of Texas*, II:252.

not go into opperation for the report would be so loud that the whole fortress would ring with the peal and *one* man would not have time to reach the ground before thare would be *a fiew* bayonetts placed under him to ease his descent. However time will unfold all things.

We have come to the conclusion that thare is no possible chance for our liberation by peaceable means:—and tharefore, *if we risk nothing —nothing will we gain*. The first *half* chance I get—I am off—off.

The report that Daniel McDonald would soon be released must be false, for we have heard nothing more of it. It was first told to us by a Foreigner as certain.

Eight men go to the mountains; in consiquence of my eyes being verry painful, If I had have gone I would have sought an opportunity to make good my exit from this scene of Desolation.

When night comes on, to our cells we flock like sheep to their peen, for *home* we have *not*. *Home* is the resort of love, of joy, of peace and plenty, where supporting and supported, friends and relations mingle into bliss. But this we prisoners in an enemies country never feel; even desolate in crowds, and thus our days roll heavy, dreary, dark, and unenjoyed along a waste of Time! Misery and want are our inseparable companions! Desperation, ever near, presenting her motley form to the view of our distracted immagination; thus endeavoring to lead us to some dread act of her own foul—*fiendish* conception that would engulf us in the yawning abyss of distruction, on the brink of which we already waver! and one other stroke of the powerful arm of Misfortune would hurl us down *deep* into that aweful vortex! where oblivion would swallow our good deeds, and curses dark and innumerable would settle over our memory! Let me live honorable and die nobley, that infamy may settle not o're my grave. But let our fate be *what* it may, we can but wate the issue; and we find a small consolation in the following beautiful lines of Tom Moore:

> "Let fate do her worst there are relics of joy,
> Bright dreams of the past, which she can not destroy,—
> Which come in the night time of sorrow and care—
> To bring back the features, that joy used to ware."

The governor would not give us our bread to night, as is usual. "*I think he smells a rat*."

Half past six P. M. Daniel McDonald liberated at last. His release came by this mail. It had like to have killed him.

20th. The gunpowder plot is abandoned for the present. I have ever been, and am yet opposed to any such hairbrained attempts. We had better take the Castle at once. The latter we could effect, and if we fell, we would fall deeply revenged, but in the former we would have no chance, either for liberty *or* revenge.

At 12 o'clock we are locked up, for which I cannot yet account.

This is a feast day, but a part of our men wer[e] about 3 hours at work this morning.

3 o'clock P. M. They locked us up to go to town to a ball, leaving a weak guard within the castle. No chance of their shooting us yet, but they may take a foolish notion some day to help us on the road to eternity—just for their own amusement, but it will not afford much to them for some of their number will suffer while we are under the operation. They should either shoot us at once, or set us at liberty. McDonald takes his leave of these gloomy walls at half past one o'clock P.M.

21st. We recieve 75 cents each of the money sent us by the San Antonio prisoners from New Orleans.

22nd. Gen. Ampudia is in the Castle. He entered at four o'clock P.M. On his enterance the governor caused the flag to be hoisted and a salute royal to be fired.

By the battle of Mier, fought on the 25 and 26th of December, 1842, Ampudia raised himself to the topmost spire of the temple of *Mexican* fame. This is Mexican glory capturing 260 men with 3,000 soldiers, two pieces of cannon, and several hundred citizens to aid. Ampudia is a heroe, and we are prisoners. He built his temple of glory upon the ruins of ours. He arose with our downfall. He came to see us all while in the castle. He expressed joy at seeing us, and made some enquiry about some of those who fell at the Salado on the 25 of March 1843.

23d. The Hon. F. M. Dimond left Vera Cruz on the 17th inst.

This morning 15 men went to the mountains about five miles off after rock. (They have been holling stone in a cart for some time). While loading the cart two of them taking advantage of a slight negligence of the guard ran off. The guard could not fire, for but a [few] of their guns were loaded, and those who's guns were not empty forgot their duty in the hurry of the moment. G. W. Bush[61] and A. S. Thurmon[62]—the latter was run down and brought back in about two hours—the former we have not yet heard from. Thurmon states that he was fired at by a soldier who came near him, but the ball passed

61. George W. Bush was a private in Captain William S. Fisher's company on the Somervell Expedition. Nance, *Attack and Counterattack*, p. 632.

62. Alfred S. Thurmond was an interpreter on the Mier Expedition and a witness to the execution of Captain Ewen Cameron. He was from Victoria, Texas. Brown, *History of Texas*, II:216 and 252.

over his head harmless. After runing for some time—as long as he could, he fainted and fell. He does not know how long he thus remained senseless—but on recovery he arose scarcely able to walk—but managed to pull himself along by some bushes in the bed of a ravine in which he had fainted. In a short time—while thus working his way—he was overtaken by two mountain Indians, these he kept at bey with a pocket knife, but at length casting his eye up the mountain, over which he had just passed, as a person would naturally do under such circumstances—he saw advancing on him an officer of cavalry and a little further back two or three soldiers of infantry:—he at once saw that in his present situation he could not escape—he tharefore gave the Indians one Dollar each to say nothing of the knife and his resistance, and thus calmly wated the advance of the soldiers. He was taken and is now laying in a damp, dark cell, alone double ironed and verry sick. He says that a taste of blood is perceptable within. I fear it will end seriously. He was in advance of Bush and does not know when he seperated from him.

The Major of this post now says that we shall not recieve any more money from our friends—nor cook any more food in our own way—in short—that we shall live as do the criminales on weak coffee in the morning, poor meat and broth at Noon, and boiled beans at night; and that we shall not even make strong coffee when we have the coffee to make it of. He is greatly enraged. Let him look out for Squalls, and we will do the same.

24th. Thurmon was taken out of the lone confinement this morning and chained to another man. He tells me that the soldiers who overtook him would have shot him immediately had it not have been prevented by the two Indians to whom he had given money. Such is the effect which money will produce on these people. Bush is not yet heard from and I suppose he is now doing "*tall walking*."

The Governor has ordered *all* to work—the well—the maimed and lamed.

Six o'clock P. M. An order has come for the release of six of our men, but one has been dead for some time, which name is marked dead giving no chance to "*ring in*." The names are as follows: Capt. Wm. Ryon, Wm. F. Willson,[63] Thomas S. Tatum,[64] James Armstrong,

63. William F. Wilson was elected the first sheriff of Galveston County in 1838 and in September 1839 he was captain of the Galveston Border Guards organized to defend the frontier against the Indians. Hayes, *Galveston*, I:279–300, 304, 350, 394, 398, 417, 421; William F. Wilson, Public Debt Papers (Texas); *Daily Picayune*, Sept. 19, 1844.

64. Thomas S. Tatum served in the James Davis command under Captain

W. D. Wallace[65] and J. A. Cruz[66]—the latter is dead, and so marked on the list. Thus making 5 liberated—who will leave in a day or two.

Seven o'clock P. M. The U. States minister[67] came in to see us—he is on his way up to the city of Mexico. He tells us that he will apply for the release of all, and thinks he will obtain it. These were his last words to us. "Wate with patience, and any thing that I can do for you, you may rely upon me for its accomplishment."

Thus Hope seems again spreading her protecting wings o're our heads.

Sunday, 25th. The *Liberated* depart at 4 o'clock P. M. Thare are now in the Castle of Perote *one hundred and four Texians.*

Thare seems to be a strange coincidence in all the most notable oc-

---

Ewen Cameron, from Apr. 12 to Aug. 12, 1842, and in the campaign against General Adrián Woll. Thomas S. Tatum, Public Debt Papers (Texas).

65. The name is William A. A. ("Bigfoot") Wallace. Wallace was a descendant of the great Scotch Highland fighters William Wallace and Robert Bruce. He was born in Lexington, Virginia, on Apr. 3, 1817, the third son in a family of nine children. He came to Texas with his uncle Blair and cousin James Paxton, arriving on Oct. 5, 1837, at Galveston on the *Diadem*, seeking adventure and an opportunity to kill Mexicans to avenge the massacre of his eldest brother Samuel, his cousin William, and a distant relative Major B. C. Wallace, all of whom had been members of Fannin's ill-fated command. Wallace was a magnificent physical specimen. In the prime of life he stood six feet two inches "in his moccasions" and weighed 240 pounds without surplus fat. "His giant stature and childlike heart, his drollery and whimsicalness endeared him to the frontier people. His inexhaustible fund of anecdotes and a quaint style of narrative, unspoiled by courses in English composition, made him welcome by every fireside." Walter Prescott Webb, *The Texas Rangers*, p. 87; [Doris] Shannon Garst, *Big Foot Wallace of the Texas Rangers*, pp. 3, 5, 23; Webb and Carroll (eds.), *Handbook of Texas*, II:856.

66. See footnote 9 above, for José A. Cruz.

67. Wilson Shannon of St. Clausville, Ohio, was a former governor of that state and had been appointed envoy extraordinary and minister plenipotentiary to Mexico to succeed General Waddy Thompson, resigned. Shannon arrived in Mexico City on the evening of Aug. 26, 1844. He had been "robed and plundered on the road" from Vera Cruz to Mexico City "by an armed banditti of all the property I had about my person. This outrage was committed in broad daylight, on the public highway and within two miles of the City of Puebla, and while traveling not only under the implied but express promise of the public authorities that I should receive ample protection on my way to this city [Mexico City]." Wilson Shannon to J. C. Calhoun, [dated] St. Clausville, Ohio, Apr. 17, 1844, and Legation of the U. S. of A., Mexico, Aug. 28, 1844; both in National Archives, Despatches from United States Ministers to Mexico; see also *Daily Picayune*, July 11, 1844.

currences which have transpired with us: As thus: We entered Mier on the 25th of December—after the insurrection of the Salado, the Men were retaken on the 25th of February, the decimation occured on the 25th of March 1843, Capt. Cameron was *basely* shot on the 25th of Aprile following—sixteen of the Mier men escaped from perote on the 25th of March 1844, and now five men leave the Castle on the 25th of August. We surrendered on the 26th of December 1842, and entered the City of Mexico on the 26th of Aprile.

The Bexar men were liberated on the 24th of March 1844—and five men recieved their liberty on the 24th August. Now judging from the grand conincidence, hether to existant in our most noted acts and calamities, I form the conclusion that if we are *ever released* or shot, it will be the 24th, 25th, or 26th of some month. No other day will do.

26th. James Willson[68] and Wm. H. H. Friendely[69] have been chained together and put to the cart. We are all wearing single chains now except those who displease the governor in some way. Governor Shannon was robbed between Puebla and the city of Mexico, which will likely be condusive to our release because Santa Anna will wish to return some great favor to him on account of this accident.

Santa Anna's wife[70] is dead, we learn by this days news.

Capt. Arolla *struck* one of the men while out at work.

27th. A verry cold day—after winter of the North.

28th. We are generally of the belief that Shannon will be able to effect our liberation, but this belief may only arise from an earnest hope.

29th. Hope now spreads her downy wings over us—when sleeping or walking. God grant that she may not again decieve us.

30th. Eight of us went to the mountains after brush to make brooms.

31st. The last day of August.

68. James Wilson was a private in Captain William M. Barrett's company of the First Regiment of the South Western Army under Colonel Joseph L. Bennett from Oct. 1, 1842, until the return of Bennett, when he joined Captain William M. Eastland's company. He mustered into service at the town of Montgomery. He served as a Minute Man in John R. Austin's company during the Vasquez campaign. James Wilson, Public Debt Papers (Texas), James Wilson; Nance, *Attack and Counterattack*, pp. 624–626.

69. William H. H. Frensley served as third sergeant in William Ryon's company on the Mier Expedition. He was among those who escaped in March 1844; but he was recaptured. Brown, *History of Texas*, II:252; William H. H. Frensley, Pension Papers (Republic), and Public Debt Papers (Texas).

70. Santa Anna married Doña Inés García, age fourteen and a half, August 1825. She died at Puebla, Aug. 23, 1844, at the age of thirty-three. Callcott, *Santa Anna*, pp. 56–57, 200–201, 203–204.

We have some hope of Liberation on the 11th of the coming month —if not then, we look to the 16th.

September, 1844

Sunday, 1st. Prospects brighten.

2nd. The corpse of the late wife of Sta. Anna was taken by this place to day on the way to Mango del Clavo,[71] his residence, when in the lower country. The flag is half mast, guns are fireing four to the hour through the day. A Nation in mourning for a woman.

One of the men recieved a letter from Shannon saying that on Sund[ay] next he would see the President and make his request. This letter was dated 30th ultimo. Last Sunday was the day specified—tharefore our fate is *sealed* ere this.

3rd. The officers of the fort are in mourning for Señora Sta. Anna.

4th. Henry Miller[72]—a dutchman, has been informed by the German consul that he would shortly be liberated.

5th. This mail day, and we may look with some probability for a letter of Fate from Wilson Shannon.

Sir Charles Bankhead, the English minister, has been writen to by the subjects now in prison here, but their letters have yet produced no visible effect.

A letter from Sir C. Bankhead desiring immediately a list of all the English born subjects among us.

6th. A Dull day.

7th. 8 of us go after brooms.

Sunday, 8th. We learn that several petitions have been presented to Sta. Anna for our release. One from 220 members of the United States Congress.[73] One from Adams[74]; one from Waddy Thomson[75]; and one

71. Mango del Clavo (Clove Spike), located along the road from Jalapa to Vera Cruz, was the center of Santa Anna's vast landholdings. It was only one of Santa Anna's several holdings and extended from within a few miles of Vera Cruz to the edge of the plateau. In 1845 he said it contained fifty *sitios* (nearly 220,000 acres altogether). Ibid., pp. 56, 153, 217.

72. Henry Miller was a private in Captain Clark L. Owen's company of the First Regiment of Volunteers in the Somervell Expedition. He served in Ewen Cameron's company on the Mier Expedition. Muster Roll, Nov. 23, 1842, of Captain Clark L. Owen's company, First Regiment Volunteers, Col. James R. Cook, in Sam S. Smith Collection, Archives, University of Texas; Henry Miller, Public Debt Papers (Texas).

73. In his *Journal of the Texian Expedition Against Mier*, p. 477, Green says

from Almonte,[76] the Mexican Minister at Washington City. Taking every thing cooly in view, these petitions with the influence of Shannon combined, we may now begin to look forward to a time when we will again breathe the free air of Heaven, untainted by the foul, infectious breath of this abandoned, degraded race.

9th. This is mail day, and we look for news from Shannon. Our fate I suppose ere this is sealed. I feel as though my life was staked upon the turn of a die. I hope it will fall *right side up*.

6 o'clock P. M. True we get some news but such that a bolt of death could not have struck greater consternation to our hearts. Col. Fisher recieved a letter from His Excellency Wilson Shannon saying that he had lost *all* hope of being able to effect any thing in our behalf, but that he will continue to do all he can in an honorable way. Enclosed

---

that James C. Armstrong, Captain William Ryon, Thomas Tatum, William A. A. Wallace, and William F. Wilson were released by a petition "from many members of the United States Congress." The editor of the *Daily Picayune*, Oct. 1, 1844, who reported the arrival at New Orleans on September 30 aboard the *Anax* of these men (except Wallace), commented: "The release of these gentlemen we deem in a great measure due to the active exertions of Gen. Thompson, but that of Capt. Ryon more particularly to the exertions of Hon. William French, of Kentucky, who obtained the signatures of upwards of two hundred members of Congress in a petition in his behalf."

74. John Quincy Adams and Mahlon Dickerson, secretary of the navy during the Jackson administration, requested and obtained the release of Israel Canfield who was from Dickerson's home state of New Jersey, *Daily Picayune*, Mar. 31, 1844; but when Adams was asked to intercede in behalf of P. M. Maxwell, he wrote on Apr. 25, 1844, to Sidney Breese: "Sir—Conformity to your request, I return herewith the letter of Mr. Maxwell, for whose liberation it would give me pleasure to contribute by any suitable means in my power. But the present state of the relations between Mexico and my own country, forbid any communication from me to the President of that Republic, interceding for any personal favor" *Daily Picayune*, Aug. 22, 1844.

75. General Waddy Thompson is credited with effecting the release both of a number of Mier prisoners, including James C. Armstrong, William Reese, William Ryon, Dr. J. J. Sinnickson, Thomas Tatum, William A. A. Wallace, Robert Waters, and William F. Wilson, and of a number of San Antonio prisoners–Anderson Hutchinson, William E. Jones, Samuel A. Maverick, and, finally, all of the remaining thirty-five Bexar prisoners on Mar. 24, 1844.

76. Juan N. Almonte sent a petition to Santa Anna requesting the release of William P. Stapp. Stapp, *Prisoners of Perote*, p. 163; see also footnote 49 above.

within the letter to Fisher is a copy of the reply of Sta. Anna on hearing Shannon's request. I give it in length as follows:

"National Palace 5th Sept. 1844

To His Excellency Wilson Shannon
Envoy etcetra. of the U. S.
Much esteemed Sir

I have received the friendly and attentive letter which you addressed to me under date of the 30th ultimo, requesting the liberty of the Texian Prisoners confined in the fortress of Perote. In reply, I have the honor to inform you, that, as well for the efforts made on various occasions, by members of the Congress of the United States as through respect for Messrs. Jackson[77] Clay,[78] Thomson,[79] and others of respectability, I have liberated many of the Texian Prisoners, who were captured in various actions and encounters between the Mexican army and the adventurers, and now only those are retained in prison, who, abusing the kindness extended them have attempted to escape, assassinating the Mexican soldiers who guarded them. These criminales deserve death, and nothing but the mildness and benignity natural to the Mexican character has prevented its application. Justice, however, demands that they should be treated with greater severity

77. Andrew Jackson, who as president had befriended Santa Anna in the United States, requested and obtained the release of John Bradley, uncle to Mrs. Samuel A. Maverick, who had brought his family to San Antonio on Jan. 29, 1841. He had been captured by General Woll in that city in September 1842. Andrew Jackson to Waddy Thompson, July 12, 1843, in John Spencer Bassett (ed.), *Correspondence of Andrew Jackson*, VI:224; *Niles' Register*, LXV:338; Rena Maverick Green (ed.), *Memoirs of Mary A. Maverick*, pp. 54, 84; idem, *Samuel Maverick, Texan, 1803–1870*, p. 138.

Jackson also interceded in behalf of George B. Crittenden, son of John J. Crittenden, and helped to effect his release. Francis P. Blair to Andrew Jackson, [dated] Washington, Feb. 12, 1843; Andrew Jackson to Francis P. Blair, [dated] Hermitage, Feb. 27, 1843; Andrew Jackson to General Antonio López de Santa Anna, [dated] Hermitage, Feb. 27, 1843; all in Bassett (ed.), *Correspondence of Andrew Jackson*, VI:205–206, 211, 212.

He is also reported to have obtained the release of Patrick H. Lusk, whose mother was a sister of General John Coffee, one of Jackson's favorite officers. Jonnie Lockhart Wallis and Laurance L. Hill, *Sixty Years on the Brazos*, p. 116; *Daily Picayune*, May 9, 1844.

78. Henry Clay, an early exponent of Latin American independence, was influential in obtaining the release of several of the prisoners.

79. Waddy Thompson, United States minister to Mexico.

than those who have not agrivated—slaying the innocent soldiers who guarded them.

This is all I ought to reply to your esteemed communication, and in having the honor to do so, I have the satisfaction of subscribing myself for the first time, your most affectionate, attentive, and constant Servant

A. L. Sta. Anna"

This cuts off all hope. Thus does hope elude us, or, rather, reality. But yesterday, and our prospects were bright, and we looked forward with spirits boyent as air to a time not distant when we should again grasp the hands of friends, that vision has flown. To day—and all is dark. Not *one* lighted fire of hope to which we may look. All, *all* dreary and desolate. When oh! when will this cease? Destiny seems to answer

"*with* our lives!" It would be better—
Death—death alone will release us—

10th. All dark and dismal, as Nightly Horrors;
Great God above is this our doom,
Must we, in dread prison lie!
Through years unnumbered, yet to come
And in destitution die!
If *this* alone, must be our end,
And no one will interpose!
Cursed by *all*, and on none depend—
Abuse, and insults from those,
Who hold us with in their power!
Then let it come, *quickly* come!
And see, World, in that aweful hour,
Freemen bravely meet their doom
With fearless heart, and dimless eye!

11th. A letter from Benjamin E. Green,[80] Secretary of legation of the United States at Mexico, stating that Shannon would again see the

80. Benjamin E. Green of Madison, Indiana, son of General Duff Green, was appointed by President John Tyler in June 1843 secretary to the United States legation in Mexico, succeeding Brantz Mayer, who resigned Apr. 24, 1843. Green acted as chargé d'affaires at Mexico in the interval between the leaving of Waddy Thompson on Mar. 9 or 10, 1844, and the arrival of Wilson Shannon at Mexico City on Aug. 26, 1844. Green landed at Vera Cruz on Sept. 25, 1843, and left that evening for Mexico City, which he expected to reach on Sept. 28. Ben E. Green to H. S. Legaré, [dated] Madi-

President, and that he thought he would at least get off a part of the Mier men. But can we allow such hopes, as are raised by this statement, to give us any deep, or firm sensation of pleasure?

This is the anniversary of the evacuation of Tampico by the Spaniards. Cannon have been firing all day.

12th. Eight of us go to the mountains after brooms, which is fatiguing.

A letter from Sir Charles Bankhead stating that he has sent the list of the bonefide English (14 in number) to the President. He thinks that he will be successful.

13th. We learn that Sta. Peg Leg will reach or pass this place to morrow on his way down to Jalapa, for what purpose I can not tell.

14th. The flag is "half mast" for Sta. Anna's wife. It is strange to see a nation mourning for a woman of nothing more than ordinary tallents.

But such is Sta. Anna['s] power that if his horse was to die his *Subjects* would mourn for him. I do not by this intend to insinuate any thing derogatory to the dignity of Woman. Yet thare is nothing military due them. They elicit respect, but not of a martial nature. Loved and even reverenced they should be, but war and blood, they are not connected with in their common course of life—tharefore Military respect is not theirs under any circumstances in a republican government. In possessing the heart of a woman I am told, you possess an inestimable prize, but they are totally disconnected with war and governmental concerns.

This is mail day, but be [we] dare not look for any thing advantagious to us. We cannot allow our hopes to retake flight in the azure vault of Heaven fearful least they should thence be hurled into the deepest darkest pitts of Hell! It has often been the case, and would be again. But I cannot deny but that I have a slight hope, not at all, but of a fiew—myself not among the number—for when I am released all will go. We will wate the event. I do not think that we will stay in prison much longer, for life is worthless to men in our situation. And if we knew we were here for life, it would soon end with death to this body of soldiers.

6 o'clock P. M. *Great* and *glorious News*. *We* are *all* to be released

---

son, Indiana, June 16, 1843; Ben E. Green to A. P. Upshur, [dated] Vera Cruz, Sept. 25, 1843; both in National Archives, Despatches from United States Ministers to Mexico. Brantz Mayer's letter of resignation is in National Archives, United States Resignations and Declinations File.

on the 16th of this month. Mr Benjamin E. Green in a letter to Thomas H. [or K?] Nellson[81] says: "At the earnest desire of my sister I wated upon Gen. Santa Anna, in company of Shannon, and asked for your release. Sta. Anna replied that he could not release one without *all*. Which reply led to a conversation between Shannon and Sta. Anna—the result of which was that the President sent for the Secretary of War and in my presence told him to make out an order on the 16th for the release of all the Texian prisoners confined in the republic."

This is the first happiness I have experienced for many months, but I cannot comment on it. Thare are still aweful fears!

Santa Anna passed this place at half past six P. M. on his way down to Mango del Clavo.

Sunday 15th. This morning breaks with unusual brightness. I hope now with some prospect.

Forty of us walk four miles to an old powder mill after furnature—we were more strongly guarded than we have ever yet been.

3 o'clock P. M. Our chains are all taken off. I had worn mine without intermission on the same foot for better than six months. I could hardly walk when it was taken off. This look[s] like something unusual would happen shortly.

Four o'clock P. M. The order for our release is *in* the Castle.[82] It has been read to us by Col. Fisher. It says that they release all Texians confined within the limits of the Republic taken in war between the Republic of Mexico and the rebellious province of Texas. This most undoubtedly includes Jose Antonio Navarro,[83] in as much as he has been

81. Thomas K. Nelson was third sergeant to Captain William M. Eastland's company on the Mier Expedition. Muster Rolls (Republic), Texas State Archives; Canfield diary, muster rolls; John Henry Brown, *History of Texas*, II:252. The letter to Thomas K. Nelson has not been located.

82. Santa Anna's order for the release of all the Mier prisoners was issued on Sept. 12, 1844, to be effective on the sixteenth, that being the day of Mexican independence. "There were one hundred and four [prisoners] confined in the Castle of Perote, ten in Vera Cruz, three in Mexico [City], one in Puebla, and two in Matamoros, making in all one hundred and twenty, who had formerly been residents of the U. S.," reported Wilson Shannon to John C. Calhoun, Sept. 21, 1844, in National Archives, Despatches from United States Ministers to Mexico. The order for the release of the Mier prisoners did not include José Antonio Navarro, a Santa Fe prisoner still being held at San Juan de Ulua.

83. On Dec. 18, 1844, José Antonio Navarro was released on parole to the vicinity of Vera Cruz, from where he escaped aboard a British vessel bound for Cuba. He reached New Orleans on Jan. 18, 1845, and eventually his

tried by two courtmartials and by each declared to be a Texian Prisoner of war, justly demanding treatment as such. But I do not believe that he will be considered under it for it is the avowed intention on the part of Sta. Anna *never* to release him.

Thare is great and lively preparations going on amon[g] the men in geting what necessaries they can for the road.

We are in debt here to a merchant about $80.00 for which he is well satisfied to wate till we reach Vera Cruz or our homes. The fact is he *must* wate, this he is well aware of, and takes it easy. One of the men offered to give him an officer as security, but he refused saying "that he had rather have the *word* of a Texian than the *note* of a Mexican officer." I mearly mention this to show the extent of distrust reigning amon[g] the Mexican people. This is *conclusive* evidence that they have no confidence in the honor of each other. And if the people forming a Nation can not trust themselves—if they can not trust each other *individually*, who can or *will* trust them *Nationally*? And from *whom* do they deserve trust?

16th. Immense exertions are being used in order to get ready for the road. Some of us have not a cent of money and badly dressed, others have tolerable good clothes, that is, for this place, while others again have pretty good clothes and a little money but not enough to divide. I have better clothes (verry little better) than some others but am behind hand in the money line—but I think we will make out—of Mexico.

Some of the Mexicans, both officers and soldiers seem to be verry much elated with our coming liberty, and it is with a good right too, for the room of No. 7 has a hole through its wall; or thare is nothing to doo but knock out a stone which is already loosened. We will let them know nothing of the hole; then, if any of us should get back by some freak of fortune, we will know where to get out. But speaking free for myself, when I once get clear of this country,—*never* no *never* will I again enter it as a prisoner.

3 o'clock P. M. We are formed in the square of the Castle to awate our passports.[84] The most of us have not felt like eating any thing today. I myself have had [nothing] all day, and still have something of a sickly sensation at heart, and a feeling like something sweling in the throat and breast, at times almost to chokeing.

A little before or about five o'clock we were called up to the Gov-

---

ranch on the San Geronimo Creek, in that area of Texas that later became northwestern Guadalupe County. Webb and Carroll (eds.), *Handbook of Texas*, II:263; Joseph Milton Nance, *After San Jacinto*, p. 125.

84. "Passports" were letters of safe-conduct or identification.

ernors room. We were called up to take an oath, solumn and decisive that we would never again raise arms against Mexico. When called upon to take the oath, some raised their right hand, some their left, and some neither raised a hand or responded to it in any way, but I believe *all*, or nearly so, were scinscere in vowing *revenge* (even while the oathe was being administered to them) for the fall of our companions in arms and countrymen, and for the ha[r]sh treatment which we as a body had received while in the power of the brutal foe. I made no response to the oathe, but was inwardly vowing *never* to grant mercy to a Mexican foe. I felt that I had been deeply injured—*injured* beyond reparation, and that I could never forgive the inflictors of this injustice. After we were sworne, we then signed our death warrent, if ever taken in arms against the power of Mexico. This we *all* signed, and I did so earnestly hoping and praying that *death* might be my irretrivable doom if ever retaken with the firm determination also of again defending Texas with my life, if necessary. When I die, let it be amid the thunder of cannon and the grand, sublime scen[e] of a glorious field of battle where Texian Liberty is to be defended. Let the last shout I hear be that of victory to the lone star. The conditions inserted in this document which we signed were: that if every retaken, we should die, to which we showed our willing acquiescence by placing our respective signatures with our own hands at the conclusion. Now, I contend that these conditions instituted and inserted in that article over our signatures releases us in toto from the oathe previously taken. It leaves us free to use our own pleasure, whether we shall risk our lives thus in the service of Texas with the certain knowledge that if taken we die; or retire to live in some country at peace with Mexico (for I would live in no country that I could not defend). As for me, I go to Texas and let come what may, I will, if requisite, die in its defence against *any* nation that may encroach on its rights. I except *none*. But I must acknowledge that even had these conditions not have been inserted—and had I have taken an oathe, solumn, replying to the whole, I *would not* have ever thought of paying any regard to an oathe thus extorted! No under no circumstances would I refuse to raise arms in the defence of Texian liberty whenever *she* may call for her sons to shed their last drop of blood in her service! The moment when I set my foot on the soil of Texas that moment will I be ready and willing to give her my idolized country the poor remains of this life. And had I the power of body possessed by Sampson and the combined powers of mind possessed by *all* the learned of the age—*all*, *all* would I give to the service of my adopted country! How much more then should I be ready to give, the service of a weak body, aided by a shallow mind—to the honor and wellfare of a young, but glorious Republic!

In the governors room one dollar was given to each to bear our expenses to Vera Cruz a distance of near fifty leagues, or one hundred and fifty miles. This was a pittance insufficient for its object, which we were well aware of, but we thought but of the unexpressable bliss which would accrue from the idea of liberty possessed.

We then descended into the square where our passports were handed to us in the presence of the troops of the garrison, who were drawn up in front of our line, and thus we stood a short time. We had often stood thus while prisoners to them and I did not think of thus standing in battle but now, when I held in my hand that instrument of writing which gave us freedom while in the Country, I thought how happy will I be when I meet these troops face to face, and *hand* to *hand* on a bloody field of death where liberty and *revenge* may be wone and life is often lost. While thus standing Gove. Jarraro delivered a short address to the soldiers and closed his remarks to them by saying—"Shout for your country" and immediately the walls of the castle revibrated with their cry of—"*Viva la Republica* Mexicana." Thrice did they repeat their cry. The governor then turned to us for an approving shout—he recieved something of an half moaned yell from some, but even that was forced by those who uttered it—and but scattering along our line, and *Mexico* not once mentioned. But the most of our little band stood motionless and silent as the grave absorbed in our own reflections in the prospect of future *revenge*. What were my feelings individually? I can only speak for my self on points of such immense weight. I felt all the [w]rongs which had been heaped upon me at different times by that ignoble enemy, returning as it were, enmass—and a swelling heart borne down by repeated insults and unresented oppressions, was like to burst with its emotions. O that I could at that moment have been placed with a fiew men of our own little band among thrice our number of the dastardly sons of Mexico, thare to *live* victorious or *die*, *deeply* revenged.

At six o'clock we marched out of the Castle. It was raining as we left it. A salute was fired to *us*, and one to the nation. The rain, the report of Cannon, the smell of gunpowder, with the shouts of our men as we emerged from the Castle, all combined, reminded me of *Mier on the 25th day of December 1842*. In less than thirty minutes we were scattered over the valley like sheep without a sheppherd, or rather wild horses, without a leader. Perfectly wild in appearance. Some three went to Mexico [City], five or six to Tampico, and the rest of us to Veracruz. Some even started then, late as it was, and walked three leagues that evening. About fifty (myself among the number) went into the town, one mile from the Castle. I had determined that I had taken my last look at the interior of the Castle of Perote.

Here let me pause to mak[e], if possible, the feelings of a man on emerging from a confinement dreadful to the preception, after having endured all that man could endure for twenty months and twenty one days. But no! language is inadequate to the task. My pen refuses, my mind and tongue will not obey. Were I to live while time *is*—language sufficient would never be mine to express the ecstacy of my feelings when I set foot on earth a *reinstated freeman*. Nor can I now after some hours of thought realize my situation. Thare seems to be something wanting around me. But the want of that verry thing renders me happy beyond immagination. Is this *Reality*?—or is it but a transient, a visionary illusion of a feavered mind? Am I again *free*? What a sudden transit of feelings from utter dark dispair to incomparable bliss! A sensation is created partaking of the feelings of an *innocent* man condemned to death, when reprieved under the Gallows! One, which for a time destroys both mind and body. Should I live ages on ages, never could I define my feelings at that *memorable* time. An attempt could be presumption of the highest order.

When leaving the Castle the Old governor stood by to embrace those with whom he was a little acquainted personally. He gave me the embrace of a friend, as he had once excused me from work when I was unable to do any thing.

We, about forty in number (the others having scattered over the valley and on their way homeward), went into the town, where we got lodgings for the night.

17th. I left the town of Perote a little after daylight. I left alone, though thare were some in sight, both in advance and in the rear, and in the course of three hours walk I had overtaken two or three, and others had overtaken us. About twelve at noon we stoped to *dine* at a little town the name I did not learn. Here, others caught up with us, and we made a fire under a shed in the center of the town where we served to draw the attention of many of the dark sons of pusilanimous Mexico. We took a dinner as much after Texas camp fashion as the nature of the case would admit of. When ready to take up the line of march, we mustered about eighteen or twenty strong, but we had not proceded far ere we were again scattered in groups of two or three togeather. Thus we proceded. Towards night I found myself in a "Mess" with five others. Rain falling, or rather a mountain mist all day. During this days travel we were more freaquently above the clouds than we were under them, and we stop tonight in the midst of them at the Town of San Meguile. Here our mess (6 in number) rent a small room or shanty, which was built by men, who, I presume, disdained to tread on *wood*—prefering earth, in as much as it has an earthen floore, or rather no floore save that which nature gave it. Judge man by his works—in accordance with this saying, we may suppose the builder of our temporary mansion to have been a devout worshiper of Nature and her works, in as much as the workmanship of his hands is not atall embellished by any of the inventions of art. Thare is one other "mess" (five in number) in this town. They encamp about 150 yards from our "Stately Mansion," or Cow House, as the latter is the most appropriate appellation. Thare are still many in our advance and rear. I think we occupy about the center of the "Texian army of opperations" in Mexico. Through the march today, I frequently on reaching a place of more ellivation than other adjoining parts of the road would stop and look in front, then in the rear, and could see the road dotted by little parties of Texians, two and three togeather for miles—as far as the eye could reach, but thare are 11 now in this place. We have marched nine leagues to day over a paved road—paved with round rock, for which we feel exhausted and soar in every limb. We do not stir about much, but after supper "our" mess set down round a comfortable fire built in the center of our stately Cow House, where we amuse ourselves with anecdotes told by each in succession.

18th. According to a resolution entered into last evening, we awoke this morning as we at the time supposed, one hour before day light, but owing to the excitement under which we were still labouring in mind, we found on waking that it was three hours before day. It was still dark with thick clouds above us, but we were midway in the main, and apparently most dense portion. The prospect was fine for rain above and beneath. We bid adiew to San Maguile and our lovely Cow Hous about half an hour before the light of Morn made its appearence. We left the other "mess" fast asleep. One of "Our mess" (Mess no. 1) "was bad off to do for himself," being soar from the preceding day's walk. He walked verry slow, but we had made a solemn promis to "*stick* to each other," untill we should reach Vera Cruz, or untill this compact should be mutually *dissolved*; and we all remained—taking it leasurely alon[g] in a body—one of the Divisions of the Texian Army of Opperations in Mexico. This march, like that of yesterday, is "*in the clouds*." After walking four leagues we reached Jalapa—thirteen leagues from Perote. We entered this place about half past nine A. M. Shortly after we arrived, and while standing in the Square, our eares wer[e] saluted by the ring of many little bells, and upon directing our eyes to the direction from whence came the sounds, we perceived a procession emerging from the portal of a church and slowly winding its way towards the place occupied by us, headed by children fantastically dressed, bearing banners and crosses—then Priests, monks, and friars bearing miters and immages, and among them, borne upon the sholders of four men, was a large immage of the Virgin Mary. These were followed by a body of armed soldiers. The Citizens were falling on their knees around us and drawing their hats. This did not suit us, and one of "our mess" observed "let us take our lieve of this place," and we did so, but not quick enough to escape the curses and maledictions heaped on us or thrown at us rather by many of the citizens. But after threatening to "dress" two or three of them, the[y] let us pass, and so we escaped. This was the procession of the Host, or consecrated wafer, representing the body of Christ. They did not catch us that time; but we *walked* briskly. We had seen enough of this place, and were determined to abandon it as we would a thing unholy; but while marching down the side walk leading towards Vera Cruz, we met with some of the men who had reached thare before us, and we concluded to stop and spend the day. So we went to a Merchant, who was a verry Gentlemanly Spaniard, and of him rented a room, verry comfortable and having a good fire place in it. During the day we learned that thare was some money in the place for us sent up by Hargus, the United States vice consul at Vera Cruz, who also rote that he wished us to stay at Jalapa untill he procured a vessel and wrote to us of it, as the Yellow Feaver was verry bad in Vera Cruz. We will tharefore stay here untill we hear something definite from Mr. Hargus.

But this *money* is the most lucky bit of fortune that has befallen us for years. But yesterday, and we did not know where, our next dollar (for we had but *one* when released) was to come from, nor how we could manage to get out of the country! *Now*, we have money furnished us by the magnanimous heart of Hargus, and a proffer on his part to furnish or charter a vessel for our transportation to our country. Our prospects are still brightening.

As soon as Fisher shall have arrived here the money will be drawn. To day we add another to our mess, making seven.

This evening we conclude to rent another room in the same House. Now we are comfortably situated with a cook house and a parlor. Our parlor serves as dining room, sleeping room, and reception room, and seting room; while, also, our cook house answers many purposes.

Six or eight more arrive today, and three left for Vera Cruz. Thare are fifteen or twenty Texians in town.

I have not yet had sufficient time to examine this city.

19th. We contemplate staying here for several days.

I am quite fatigued and sore with the walk from Perote to this place, consiquently I have not yet taken a sufficient view of this city to give any satisfactory description of it.

We get along finely with our family. We take it by turns in succession, cooking, marketing, etcetra. We live like *lords* on a small scale, but our money is nearly all gone, and under this calamity we have one consolation; that is, when Fisher arrives we will get more.

Fisher came into town this evening, and we were verry much conserned on learning that he had been verry sick; but we now have the satisfaction to know that he is recovering perceptibly.

The other men have arrived to day and taken quarters in different parts of the town, wherever they can rent rooms to suit them.

We have created quite a sensation in this City.

It is not definitely known yet when we will leave this city.

20th. I find that this City is built like Rome on hills; but how many I do not really know. It ranks as about the third city of the Republic. First Mexico—second Puebla—and third Jalapa (pronounced Halapa). I am verry much pleased with the appearance of this place. The buildings are lake all other Spanish built town or city which I have ever seen: of stone and ciment, with flat rooves and generally two or two and a half stories in hight. The streets here are of greater breadth than other cities, which I have *visited* in this promising country. This is a place of about 75,000 inhabitants, and several foreigners among the number. The streets are paved with rock of coblular form with narrow side walks. If I did wish to live any where in this country here would it be, but I could not be induced to live any longer than till I could get away in a country rendered obnoxious and hateful to me by the combined abuses of two years of continued and harsh imprisonment. No, I could not look at one of the hateful inflictors of wors than death upon my unfortunate companions and my self without a thirst for revenge; consiquently I would be miserable, *even* from that alone; but I have also other causes;—causes which I shall not here mention.

I have seen the coffee tree growing in this place and many other growths of the Torrid Zone.

It rains this evening, as if Old Ocean had yielded up to heaven her mighty waters that they might be hurled on earth with crushing force. It rained yesterday, but not so hard. We recieved $4.50 cents each to day of money sent up by Hargus. "*Now we'er in funds.*"

21st. I do not often lieve my room before ten o'clock A. M. for I wish the Host to pass before I am seen in the Street.

Sunday, 22nd. This evening I go to the Bull fight. Thare were five Bulls killed but none of them made much show of fight. They were worked down. I would like to see them go into a pen where thare were two or three wild bulls from the Texas Prairaries.

23d. Some of the men left today for Vera Cruz.

We recieved $4.50 each today making nine Dollars in *all*, since we arrived at this place.

24th. A fiew of the men leave today for Vera Cru[z].

25th. We do not yet know when we can leave this place.

26th. Thare was an earth quake in town last night. But it did but little damage.

27th. Nothing interesting to us.

28th. Our mess was split, and some have gone to Vera Cruz.

Sunday 29th. At a Bull fight.

We will, I think, leave tomorrow. We have organized another mess in which four of the old mess are concerned. We pay 25 cents p[e]r day Room rent.

Some of the men leave town to day for Vera Cruz.

30th. We leave Jalapa and travel nine leagues to Plan, which is situated on a small but romantic river over which there is a bridge, made as is their custom of ciment. This town is verry small—neither more nor less than an Indian village in appearance, it being principally built of a reed similar to the Bamboo (perhaps its propper appelation) and clay. Thare are but two or three stone buildings in it. To the right of the town on the opposite side of the river, and situated mid-way on a hill stands an antique building, which is I am informed, a fort; and if so, it is well situated to command the whole valley and pass; but I must confess that to me it has more the appearance of and [an] old barn than a puissent fortification.

October, 1844

Tuesday, 1st. About one hour after the God of day makes his appearance in the east, we take our leave of Plan and its swarthy inhabitants, and persue our march *Homeward*! *Homeward*! Oh what music thare is in that expression! But, alas! May we not find many of our friends in the grave. We are on our march toward home, but such a home! Great God, our Country men, and our country have placed their signature to our death warrent from which we were only reprived by foreign influence! But down with such thoughts now.

Our march lays through a delightful country, but the scarcity of water renders it quite distressing. The road in some places is so stright that we can see for miles in advance, which, by the by, is rather objectionable on a warm day. We halt a short time to refresh ourselves at a little town, but it is so insignificant in appearance that I have not even asked its name; and if I should do so, most likely it will be so folded and twisted out of shape that I would brake a dozen pens in writing it, and I have them not to spare. But this place, pittiable as it appears, is sacred to my memory, for here have I quenched a most horrid thirst.

Six o'clock, P. M. finds us "hard, and fast a ground" at "Puente National" (National Bridge) and as much fatigued as one can suppose. I came in with four others, and we found ten or twelve here, making about sixteen soldiers of the Texian army of opperations now quartered in this place. In as much as we will spend the night here, I will take an observation of the place and its localities; and for the sake of variety (for variety is the spice of life) I will take a peep into some of the houses and make an effort at drawing the general character of the inhabitants, as they are some what civil in their conduct. I may converse with some of them.

This place is situated on a river, which is said to be impassabe at all other points, and even here it is only passable by means of a bridge. Thare is one verry fine mansion in the Suburbs of the city (or village) which is the residence of a German Colonel in the Mexican Army. The principal part of the remainder of the buildings seem to be in congeniality with all other Indian huts of the country; that is, built of the Bamboo and mud. That which adds most rudeness to its general appearance is the irregularity with which the streets are layed off; or, rather, their not having been planned atall, for every man has placed his "Shanty" where the location best suited his notions of Elligant taste. Thare is one Hotelle here, which is kept by a *Dutchman*. I find that these enterprising Europeians are nearly a match for the "*Johnethans*" of Yankee Land in forming modes and planing Schemes to "raise the wind." Place an enterprising Dutchman, or a Nutmeg making Yankee, where you will, and you need have no fear of Starvation ever gaining possession of him.

Thare is no fortification here, save that which Nature presents, which is ample for its defense. But I am of the opinion that this would have been the propper site for Perote's Castle. The Bridge here, which is so cellibrated as the key to interior Mexico, has nothing remarkable in its appearance save that it is built to last with Time. The materials are stone and ciment, which to substances are so concreted that they form a mass, the appearance and durability of which is equivalent to solid stone. It was built in the first place near a century ago by the Spaniards, and its construction is such that it will remain to future generations as a memento of their conquest.

The inhabitants so far from being gentle are surly, insulting, and rogueish, and regard us with rather a suspicious eye. But that last is reasonable for even among Americans one rogue or a mean man will allways suspect the honor of his neighbour.

Col. Fisher leaves this evening in the Stage for Vera Cruz.

2nd. Three of us arose two Hours before daylight, and find that some have already gone. Whilst making preparations for our march, we heard the noise of a troop advancing and to our astonishment found them to be Texians. From their own accou[n]t they had halted to pass the night about four leagues back at a small village, but about eleven of clock at night, they razed a "row" with the Alcalde, and were forced to put for it. They were not as clear headed as men should be to transact business in a foreign land,—or, in other words, they were some what under the influence of liquor.

We took our leave of Puenta National as soon as we were allright for the road and bid adieu to the remainder, who thought it expedient to awate the dawn of day. We did good duty to our "*mother*" of footmen on that day. About 1 of clock, or half past, we halted for rest at a small village or rather a farm, where we were so fortunate as to find pulque of the best quality in abundance; and here, being well situated, we took a Siesta; and resumed our joourneay about 3 P. M.

A short time previous to our arrival at this resting place we came up with a Negro who reported to have came from New York. He was Driving a fine team of mules with a respectable waggon at their heels. He spoke quite contemtiously of the Swarthy sunbur[n]t white men—or rather the Devils of Mexico.

We arrived at a small village and halted for lodging at a Hotell kept by an outbreaking [overbearing] insulting African Negro.

We could not endure the situation, so we left them to their ease; leaving, however, seven or eight Texians who we had found thare to their miserable quarters. We were our own men and were determined to show that *we* would not endure the misery attending a nights sleep in a Negroes hotell. We decamped reaching Sta. Fe about Sundown, having walked 13 leagues during the oppressive heat which reigns thare at that season of the year. Here we found those who had left before us in the morning—or rather—the over [?] night, to wit, Daves,[85] Gumlat,[86] Van Dyke,[87] and Clark.[88] And Here, We are three

85. Three "Davises" were released on Sept. 16, 1844—Thomas Davis, Wil-

leagues from Vera Cruz—in fine spirits and apparently among those who are at least half civilized.

3rd. After a night of refreshing sleep, we rose, and, preparing well our appearances took the road to Vera Cruz, full of a new life and animated joy at again nearing our homes; for once we believed that, if once on board a vessel and out at sea, we should ere many days should elapse again meet our friends and feel the green turf of our own dear *adopted* country plyantly yielding to the pressure of our long estranged feet. Having arose some time before daylight, we reached the gates of Vera Cruz just as they were thrown open, which service is done between the dawning of day—at the gilding of the Eastern horrizon by the luminous God of light. Here near the South-Eastern gate we found those of our companions who had displayed more activity, or avidity to enter that City. But, oh! Horror of horrors! Such a sight as did they present! Their features so swolen and mis-shaped that it was with the greatest difficulty that we could even reognize our most intimate friends. This distortion of feature was the production of the Mosquito's bite, which in this climate is almost venomous, and the insect itself is abundant. These men tell us that the only way whareby they can gain rest is to go to the beach and thare, even it is with great difficulty and inconvenience, for the sand fly, which abounds here in great numbers, is nearly equal to the Mosquito for its annoyance, but not so painful. On first beholding the almost closed eyes, disfigured countenances, and distorted features, swollen to an enormous size, I could scarcely forbear commiserating them, but their jocund expressions and loud laughfs soon informed me that commiseration was useless; and farther, my feeling for the sufferings of my

---

liam Kinchen Davis, and William Davis. It is impossible to determine from available evidence which Davis is referred to here.

86. Isaac Zumwalt was a private in Charles K. Reese's company in the battle of Mier. Canfield diary, muster rolls; and *Northern Standard*, Dec. 12, 1844.

87. William N. Van Dyke served in Captain Charles K. Reese's company on the Mier Expedition. *Northern Standard*, Dec. 12, 1844; Brown, *History of Texas*, II:252; Wilson N. Van Dyke, Public Debt Papers (Texas).

88. George Wilson Clark saw service in the Vasquez and Woll campaigns of 1842, where he served under Colonel Edward Burleson, and in the Somervell Expedition as a private in Captain Isaac N. Mitchell's company; and on the Mier Expedition in Captain Charles K. Reese's company. Muster Roll, Nov. 11, 1842, of Capt. Isaac N. Mitchell's company, First Regiment of South Western Army, in Sam S. Smith Collection; Brown, *History of Texas*, II:251; George Wilson Clark, Public Debt Papers (Texas).

companions were soon checked by the thought that the next morning would place me upon an equality with them.

Feeling somewat fatigued and hungry, I soon questioned those who had proceded me as to the time, quantity, and quality of our meals; and was informed in reply that we took breakfast at nine A. M. and dined at Three P. M., which constituted the number and the time; and as for the quantity the single monosyllable, "Scarce," which was returned as an answer was sufficient to convince me that we would not hurt ourselves by garmandizing. But when it came time that my informant should answer as to the quality, the simple words "*worse than perote*," delivered as it was with a most horrid oath and imprecations on the heads of all Mexico, accompanied by a grimace and dark scowl of future retribution, gave me but a light hope for comfort, and was rather an inducement for me to seek the quarters which were hard by, and thare examine them and thus forget, if possible, that eating was necessary. On turning to view my temporary abode, I was something better pleased with its appearance than I had anticipated. It was large and had seen the day when it was rather comely in its structure, but it was many years since; and it had been in time prehaps the abode of pomp, wealth, and power, but it is now converted into a home for those who will pay rent for it. It has advanced a great length towards the state of dilapidation. The enterance (as is usual in old Spanish Buildings) is through a hall. The lower story in front is occupied by a dealer in intoxicating spirits, who also keeps a small room for gambling, while the rear is used as a residence for quadrupeds, such as Horses, cows &c. We enter the inner court, from which leads a stair case to a corridor, which extends entirely around the interior fronting of the upper chambers. The Rear apartments in the upper Story are occupied by Mexicans and we are stowed in front. We have a long corridor and four rooms for our especial accommodation, and we are pretty well crowded. Thare is nothing within to ease the eye; the rooms present one dull, monotinous aspect, thare being nought but cold bearen walls, blackened and disfigured by the ravages of Time, who is no respector of persons or property, treating all with equal severity.

We found that verry near all the Texians had reached the City; and also we have met ten of the men who have been some months confined in the Castle "*San Juan de Ulier*"[89] (I am not sure that this is rightly

89. In his explorations in the Gulf of Mexico in 1518 Juan de Grijalva discovered on an island before Vera Cruz the people of Culhua, whose name he pronounced "Ulua." The time of year being the feast of St. John the

spelled), which is situated about one and a half, or two miles, out in the Gulf founded on a reef. We were much rejoiced to meet with them, more so that we could extend *and grasp* the hand of a *freeman*! What music thare is in the sound of *Freeman* and *Liberty*! But alas Near *one hundred* Texians, our companions in *arms and chains*, now lay low under the sod of base Mexico, and a base, cowardly, servile foe treads ore their sacred resting place without e're yielding one tribute of respect. Oh! that I, or that *Texas* could but for one day hold the avenging power of supernatural beings and that she might with one stroke hurl this debased Nation into the vortex of Oblivion! But what—oh what! will Texas do?—or what would she do, even if the power was hers? *Deny another band of her unfortunate citizens*, and place them at the mercy of Sta. Anna; then form *another armistice*, which should be concluded without noticing those who had lost *their liberty* in *defending* hers! Oh *Texians*—can we *ever* forgive you for what you have done? Nay but you ask not our forgiveness, but boast of your generous acts! *Generous*, indeed! Yes generous you were Texas, if it was thus that you would relieve your imprisoned defenders—*by death*! Base ingratitude! But this will not do. I cannot morralize—*my blood boils* within me as if *heated by the demons* from the *infernal pitt of Hell*!

Would to heaven! that I had power to avenge the sufferings of this band and the death of my fallen countrymen. *Then deep—dark and dread should be* the sweet revenge which I would take. *Long—long* should Mexico remember the name of her bloody butcherer. Aye, *butchery* it *should be*! But lo I am not savage—I am not a murderer! No, but I *am almost* mad.

The hour for breakfast arrived, and on entering the room of our temporary hotell, what horror I felt at beholding a mat spread on the floor covered with dirt and filth, upon which were plates and spoons and one small cup half full of pale sickly looking coffe. Our breakfast consisted wholely in a verry small piece of sour bread, about one dozen mouthfuls of spoiled beef (badly boiled) and broth, with the aforementioned Coffee. I felt sick and could not eat, yet I was wolfish in my appetite.

Baptist, he called the island San Juan de Ulua. Upon this island, at a distance of less than a mile from the mainland the Spaniards started the construction of a fort sometime between 1582 and 1625. This fort was probably the strongest in the new world. It had seven large cisterns, containing nearly 100,000 cubic feet of water; and below the cisterns were damp, narrow dungeons, where Spain and Mexico kept their most notorious criminals. Few ever came out alive. Bancroft, *History of Mexico*, I:27, 93, 116–142; III:213, 214–216, 217, 489.

The dinner hour came on, and upon entering the room—Great God—dinner was the exact immage of breakfast. Save the coffee, which was "*falto*."[90] Breakfast, I could not eat, Dinner worse—Great God, will I starve? No, no, not so bad as that I will soon regain all my former appetite.

And for this board Mr. Hargus pays fifty cents per day for each, whith which we live worse than any dogs in Christendom; while I have lived like a prince on twenty five cents per diem when I had the privolige of expending it at my will.

90. *Falto*: lacking or missing.

[Chapter VIII]

[On the Way Home]

BOOK THIRD

October 1844

Texas	Mexico
Honor Trouth and My Country	Tyrranny Oppression and Death

When we trust to fate,
And trust at ease;
Good will come, if late,
Better may it please.

Friday, 4th. All of our friends and companions having arrived in the city, we present to the view of these people a subject rather of wonder and curiosity. Thare seems to be something in or about us that is calculated to attract the eye, for we can pass through no street or enter no part of the city but what we revit the gaze of ever[y] passer-by; some in pity; others with a slight degree of hatred and contempt and many in fear. The pitty, or love which is shown for us is not much, but I think that thare are some who do commiserate our desolate appearence.

Col. Fisher, by special invitation from the Capt., went on board the vessel which is to bear us to our *home, the land of our birth*. The capt. informed him that we would sail on the tenth. Fisher promised to return on the morrow with a list of provisions necessary, and then took lieve of the vessel and returned to shoar to communicate the joyful intelligence to his companions. This vessel is chartered by Hargus,[1] the

1. Louis S. Hargous, the American merchant and vice consul at Vera Cruz, made arrangements for the Mexican schooner *Rosita* to take the released prisoners to New Orleans, since the Mexican government would not grant permission for the vessel to land them in Texas. No Mexican ship captain, however, could be found to command the *Rosita* loaded with the Texan "devils." Consequently, an arrangement was worked out whereby the Mexican schooner would be sold and converted to the *Creole* under United States registry, and a Captain Dessechi was obtained to command her, rather than

American vice consul, to transport *one hundred* and *eight* men to New Orleans at the enormous price of *three thousand two hundred dollars*, or about *thirty dollars* each! This vessel, too, is nothing more than an old Topsail Schooner not worth (going to its real value) *fifteen hundred.*

Thare are fourteen who claim to be good and loyal subjects of Great Britain and are boarded at an English house at the expense of the British consul. Their living is good. Those who have money are boarding at their own expense with a Negro Woman (or *lady of coulor*) who is keeping a first rate Hotell well furnished and supplied with good eatables, or as good as the market affords. These fellows live high and do not feel so sharp twitches of a keen cuting and unsatiated appetite. Among them are Col. Fisher, Judge Gibson,[2] Dr. McMath, Joe Smith,[3] John McMullen,[4] T. K. Nellson,[5] F. W. T. Harrison,[6] and some others

---

Captain Lapetique who had commanded the vessel late in August 1844. *Telegraph and Texas Register*, No. 13, 1844; *Daily Picayune*, Aug. 21, 1844; L. S. Hargous to Reuben M. Potter, [dated] Vera Cruz, Oct. 5, 1844, in Comptroller's Letters (Republic), Texas State Archives.

2. Fenton M. Gibson of Fort Bend County, later editor of the *Texas Sentinel*, was a native of Tennessee. In February 1837 he opened a law office at Brazoria and on May 24, 1838, was elected by the Congress of the Republic of Texas chief justice of Galveston County. He later moved to Fort Bend County and practiced law at Richmond and in Houston. Charles W. Hayes reports, in *Galveston*, I:306, "Gibson was erratic and revolutionary. . . . Possessing good abilities, and well versed in law, the routine of life of his profession was irksome to his restless soul, that reveled in scenes of danger and excitement. During the early days of the Republic no enterprise or expedition, no difference how hazardous, but found a ready volunteer in Fenton M. Gibson." See also ibid., pp. 279, 294, 301, 304–306; Joseph Milton Nance, *Attack and Counterattack*, p. 415; Walter P. Webb and H. Bailey Carroll (eds.), *Handbook of Texas*, I:686.

3. Joseph F. Smith was born in Fulton County, Kentucky, in 1808. He moved to Arkansas at an early age and there accumulated considerable property in land and slaves. Arriving in Texas in the late 1820s or early 1830s, he entered into a partnership with his uncle, Henry Smith, later provisional governor of Texas (1835 to 1836), in the purchase of large quantities of land scrip which they located in Refugio and San Patricio counties upon land allegedly previously illegally located. John Henry Brown, *Indian Wars and Pioneers of Texas*, p. 549.

4. John McMullen was chosen to represent the municipality of San Patricio in the General Consultation in 1835 but did not attend. William C. Binkley (ed.), *Official Correspondence of the Texas Revolution*, I:40.

5. For information on Thomas K. Nelson see footnote 81, Chap. VII.

6. F. W. T. Harrison, of Washington County, served in William M. East-

—all living among and through each other in some way; some with money and some without it. The Main body are boarding with an old filthy, trifling, thieving Mexican at the expense of Hargus, who will look to Texas for his remuneration.

Our living is so despicable that we are trying to prevail on Hargus to consent to a change of quarters.

Not withstanding the annoyance of musquitoes by the thousand on last night, I slept admirably well, but my face is some what larger than usual.

Night is again approaching and I dread the consiquences attending for our inveterate foe (the race of musquitoville) is again humming his hated note through our apartments.

> But he who'd face a steel and fire clad foe,
> And with pointed sword, make the hearts blood his choice;
> Should not quake in fear of base musquito,
> Or start at the sweet hum of his low voice.

5th. Old man Smith,[7] Capt. Pierson,[8] an Vanracton [Van Vacton?][9] arrived to day from the city of Mexico.

They are a portion of those left thare in September 1843, in consiquence of being ill, and in the present hurry I had almost forgotten them untill their presence reminded me verry forcibly of *where I had last seen them*; and of the misery which we were then enduring; and then contrasting our condition at that time withith our present, it really gives new life and hope for a better day yet to come.

---

land's company on the Mier Expedition. F. W. T. Harrison, Public Debt Papers (Texas), Texas State Archives.

7. Ezekiel Smith was known among the prisoners as "Old Man Smith." He was for some time sick at Convent Santiago, Mexico City, and was left behind when the main body of prisoners was moved to Perote Castle. He had been a member of Edward Burleson's command in the Vasquez campaign of 1842. *Telegraph and Texas Register*, Nov. 8, 1843; Ezekiel Smith, Public Debt Papers (Texas).

8. Captain John G. W. Pierson was freed on Sept. 16, 1844.

9. The proper spelling of this name seems to be D. H. Van Vechten, Israel Canfield diary, muster rolls, Texas State Archives; Lorenzo Rice, Miscellaneous Claims Papers (Texas), Texas State Archives; *Northern Standard*, Dec. 12, 1844; John Henry Brown, *History of Texas*, II:252. Other sources give the name as D. H. Van Vacton, Muster Rolls (Republic); Joseph D. McCutchan diary, muster rolls, Company B. The *Galveston Daily News*, Apr. 23, 1888, reported him to be still living at that time and gave the name as D. H. Van Vecton.

All of those who are going home are now in the city. In saying "*all who are going home*,["] I would say all who go with us, for it is presumeable that those who remain now will at length return home.

The wind, which has been blowing from the North for the last ten days, has now changed to the Southward, and our prospect for good weather is promising, but we can depend with certainty upon nothing in this country.

Thirty of the men have at length moved to better quarters to board, having left the Mexican Hotell and gone to a French establishment. Fisher does all that man *can do* to render every [one] comfortable, but even his best efforts are treated with indifferent contempt by some of the more rude and heartless.

Sunday, 6th. A schooner entered this port to day from Havana, via New Orleans, but unfortunately she brings us no news.

We here have a pleasure (and one of the necessaries of clenliness) of which we have been for many long months deprived, that of bathing, and by way of remunerating my self for the great length of time during which I have been deprived of that refreshing gratification, I now enjoy it at least twice in each successive day. Thare is nothing more cooling, refreshing, and enlivening (to say nothing of its cleansing powers) than a sea bath; more especially if it be taken on the free and open beach with no enclosure to exclude the bracing air, or check foam crested wave in its course, untill it bursts upon you, yielding a peculiar censation as pleasing and beneficial in its effect as it is incomparable in its nature.

Having availed myself of a short strole through the city to examine somewhat minutely its situation for defence and general advantages, or disadvantages, both as a port and as a depot for the inland productions, I am induced to believe that its advantages for either are nothing of which they can boast with any verry great degree of propriety. But in order that all may judge for themselves I will give its situation as near as my pen can perform the Task.

The City is surrounded entirely by a stone wall about two and a half feet in breadth, or thickness, by ten or twelve in highth. Through this wall there are something like eight gates with ports between at intervals or from three to four feet. At the two corners of the wall fronting the Gulf thare stands two Fortifications (one at each) mounting about thirty two guns each, and built of good materials. On the land side there are three or four smaller forts, varying from twenty to twenty five guns each, and in this consists their land defences. But to the seaward stands the Castle of *San Juan de Ulloa*, whoes Dark frowning walls scowl forth a deathly defiance to all who may be so maddened as to attempt its capture, and thus wake up its now sleeping thunder to a Terrific scene equal in grandure to the craters of *five hundred* volcanic Mountains. Thare it stands like an ancient, but invincible warrior, upon whoes crest has fallen the ravages of Time and War si[n]ce ages long since past and whoes armour yet bears the sign and seal of deadly fight on its unpolished front. *Invincible* scenes imprinted on its venerable blackened sides and defiance seems pearing forth from every port. It bears on its walls upon the north and east sides and upon its Northeast corners the marks of balls and bombs as if they had been hurled by the powerful arm of—who?—*by the powerful arm of the* FRENCH *Nation*! Yes, the arms of France have left that old castle covered with scares and marks which it shall bear to its obliteration. Well did the french do their work, and manfully did they contend for Verra Cruze, but most shameful was the defence. If that place had have been garrisoned by English, Texians, or United States soldiers, the french might have thundered to this day without effecting any thing to their advantage; that is, if we take the distant or external view as a true representation of its strength; but if we do this, I think upon closer examination we will find that we have recieved a wrong impression. I have not been in it, but I am told the materials are rather bad. Taking all in all, it is a good and strong fortress when assaulted only by the common sized guns, but bring paxian[10] shot and such guns as they are now making for the United States, and its strength will vanish like a shadow. It mounts near two hundred guns and will soon mount three hundred with the outworks and improvements which they

10. Paixhan cannon were newly invented guns that fired explosive shells. The Washington, D.C., correspondent of the *Boston Atlas* described the paixhan cannon as follows:

> The Paixhan gun differs from a common 44, in having a very wide chamber; the metal is also very thick at the chamber. The bore at the muzzle is also larger than the bore of a 44 pounder, but this depends of course upon the size of the ball. The hollow shot range from 64 to 120 pounds, to fire which latter ball, 10 lbs. of powder are necessary. A pound of powder is placed inside of the ball—a fuse is attached, which will burn about ten seconds—the ball is then placed in the gun with the fuse turned from the powder. When it is fired, the flames enveloping the ball sets fire to the fuse, which is intended to explode the ball, after it is buried in the object. Of the devastating effects of these missiles everyone has heard.

Quoted in *Telegraph and Texas Register*, June 8, 1842; Tom Henderson Wells, *Commodore Moore and the Texas Navy*, p. 118.

are making. The most of these guns are small; some, however, are *sixty eights*, which, by the way, are no infants at the work of death and distruction. I cannot say w[h]at may be the exact thickness of the walls, but it is presumable that they are from twelve to sixteen feet at the base, and from six to eight at top; nor can I tell its form, but it seems to be admirably shaped for defence, both from sea and land.

Taking all in all, it is well constructed and has the appearance of great strength, but lacks *soldiers* without which a fortress is as nothing. And thare it stands, alone, gloomy, and difying as if the giant arm of Freedom rested within. But oh! vain thought! Tyrranny and Oppression hold thare their gloomy reveles, regardless of the cries from earth of those upon whom they trample.

Rising from its sea encompassed base, it seems formed to the defence of Freedom, but alas, it is but the strong hold of Tyrranny.

Let it thare stand and *frown* defiance to the world; but better for it that it should not *dare* the grim tiers [fire?] of American batteries, for their distructive vengance would soon annihilate the verry *Name* of "*San Juan de Ulloa*," and level the proud city in ruins, even to oblivion's deepest recess.

The city of Verra Cruz is not as large as I had anticipated, not being *more* than one mile square, and I doubt its being that large.

The Houses are stone and Cement, with square interior courts and generally flat roofs; and many of them are verry handsome, and some elligant in their appearance.

Thare are also many verry handsome public edifices; churches, &c. with an elligant Theatre. All built on the old Spanish style, and the most, or all of the public edifices, and many of the dwellings were built by the Spaniards.

Thare are a great ma[n]y foreigners here from all parts of the world, even to the Ethiopean, but the american, english, French, and spanish are most aboundent. The port or Harbor is bad, thare being no protection from the Northward. The vessels ride at anchor Near the Castle San Juan de Ulloa, about two miles from shore, and discharge and take in their cargo by mea[n]s of lighters or small boats which circumstance render[s] great inconvenience to vessels. And during a gail from the northward if their anchorage should give way, they would drift right on shore and certain *distruction*.

With regard to the advantage to the inland country, it of course affords an opportunity to all (who possess it) to ship their produce, but in bring[ing] their produce into the city a heavy tole is required by the Guard at the gate, thus making the tax on their own productions something considerable; but I suppose as they are content, I should not grumble.

I am told that each man, if he wishes to kill a hog, a chicken, a beef, or any other such animal property, must pay *one dollar* to get permission to do so. And this is not only once each year or month, but it must be done at each and every time when he kills any one of such animals as above mentioned. A[l]so if a man wishes to use a barrel of Flower, he must pay two dollars for his license. Now that is a government for freemen to inhabit!—but they care not, and I am content.

Thare is one wharf extending out from the custom house, which is the only one to the city. It is built of large hewn stones on each side filled in between with peebles and cement, thus rendered perminent as time itself. It is now about fifty feet in breadth and thirty yards in lendth, extending out to sea, and they contemplate extending it to the channel, but it will be centuries ere they accomplish this, if *ever*.

7th. To day, at the earnest request of Fisher, Mr. Hargus has procured a New bording house for thirty more, and I have the good fortune to be included in that number. We remove to the house, which is kept by an Englishman, and so far are well pleased with the change. We take breakfast at 8 A. M. or half past, and Dinner (which serves for supper too, as we get but two meals) at three P. M.—and the eating is verry good considering our situation.

8th. I find that the citizens generally are verry fond of gambling, and Monte is their favorite game. There are several gambling establishments in the city of different grades. Some houses a man cannot enter unless he wear a coat and bears the front of a Gentleman. These are the better orders of Monte banks at which no small beting is countenanced. Then thare are others in class descending to the lowest order, where bets of any size (unless it be large) are taken, and all who choose are privaliged to enter; consiquently the crowd assemb[l]ed at such houses are generaly of the most depraved and debased class of Mexicans, who are *low* indeed.

The reason why the rules of some of the houses prohibit the enterance of the Coatless is that among the poor and most numerous class in that country, you rarely find a coat, for they supercede the necessity of both coat and bed by keeping constantly about them "jerga,"[11] or what we term a Mexican blanket; consiquently if a man wears a coat,

11. *Jerga*: a heavy napped wool cloth for coats; also applied to coarse, hairy cloth. Its use often gave the Mexicans the name of being "the blanket nation."

he fills their ideas with regard to the principles of gentility, and they pass him in as a *gentleman.*

Thare seems to be a doubt concerning our departure on the 10th; I believe the case hopeless for that day, but *Time* will prove.

9th. Our doubts are pretty well satisfied with regard to our anticipated departure, for the Capt. has not even procured his provisions or water, and that alone will take three days at least.

10th. The day has arrived and brought with it as I had surmised a doleful disappointment. But with our present quarters, we can endure a fiew days longer with a small degree of patience.

Thare are twenty five living with the old Jack a naps of a Mexican with whom we all lived at one time, and they say that he does verry well now. I suppose he thought it better to mend his ways, than loose all his chance for swindling boarders.

11th. Thare is a current report that we will go on board the vessel on the morrow but I doubt it, for I know that the Captain has not yet procured either provisions or water.

About twenty five of the men who were living at [the] house of a Frenchman have fallen out with their land lord and cut his acquaintance, and are now safely "anchored" in the house of a "*Coulored* Gentleman," with whom they are much pleased.

12th. Oh horror! No prospect of sailing in less than—I cannot say *how* long.

Sunday, 13th. I have been, I think, correctly informed by Col. Fisher that the captain has taken nearly all his Necessaries on board, excepting the water, and that he will get [it] in the course of two or three days.

Our land lord whiped an Irishman, for which he payed five dollars to the State Treasury, or the City Governor, and I am not certain which.

14th. The water is all on board at last, and now seems to draw near the time for our departure. Oh, joyful will be the hour when I shall tak foot off this putrid soil and bid adieu to Mexico and its swarthy, villainous, theving sons. But softly, perhaps, this language will be discovered, and if so—if this writing is found in my hands, my chance for liberty and home will be but slim. The nearer approaches the time for my lieve taking of this people, the more fearful do I feel that some mischance, some terrible misfortune may prevent our departure, *perhaps* FOREVER! Or, until relieved by *death*, the leveler of mankind. Tharefore it is better that I be a little more cautious and discrete in my remarks for the future; *so let it be.*

15th. It is said that we will go on board on the morrow. I hope it may be true, for if I could leave here on a raft without a bite to eat, or one drop of water, I would almost dare the terrors of the deep, in that frail rep[r]esentative of hope; or *any* thing that I might clear this country of my presence.

16th. Dull dull! Will these dull hours never roll round, and present an opportunity for us to leive this place?

17th. *At last*! We bid adieu to land and try our fortune at sea.

Some went on board at 10 o'clock A.M. Others at 12 M. Others, with myself at 2 P. M. and the last (with the exception of Fisher, Gibson, and Lyons) at 4 P. M. At sunset this evening, with the exception of the three before mentioned, we are all on board and as merry as men could be who expect soon to see their home, country, and friends. And I asshure you that our merryment was unbounded.

I think that I have set foot on the soil of Mexico for the *last* time, untill an opoortunity may offer for me to again raise an arm in defence of the rights of Texas, and for my own *deep* vengance and retribution on their heads for the unparalleled murders which they have left as monuments to their shame. Oh, that I had it in my power to avenge my fallen countrymen and the insults which the living have endured!—dread and dire should be that revenge—whitch I would feel satisfied. The Tortures of the stake; the wheel; and the block and axe would be but light punishment compared to that which *they* should endure, the whole Nation, *to a man*! All the Horrible racking engines and all the *hell* invented machines for torture that ever were invented, could they be combined in one mighty Helldivised plan, would not excede in severity that torture which I *believe* I could inflict upon this people, with a calm soul and clear conscience!

18th. The vessel upon which we find ourselves is an *old* Topsail Schooner,[12] or Brigantine, of one hundred and twenty tons burthen, and every timber seems to be decayed save her masts, and they appear sound; but she has lately been coppered with new mettal, and has reasonably good riging. She has a perfect "*tub*" bottom—is said to be 17 years old, but looks to be twenty five, at least; and to all appearencies will not sail more than seven "knotts an hour." Upon the whole she is a crazy, rotten old craft, not worth saving from a gale; but, perhaps, by the aid and protection of Divine providence we may reach New Orleans in her, but the case is exceedingly doubtful. However, any thing,

12. Passage to New Orleans for the released prisoners was arranged on the American schooner *Creole* (formerly the Mexican schooner *Rosita*), Captain Dessechi, *Telegraph and Texas Register*, Nov. 13, 1844.

the botom of the gulf—or, any thing that may come in preference to this City of Perdition and iniquity.

About 6 of clock P. M. a heavy gale arose, ore came *down* from the North; and thus it is that our worst enemy, Miss Fortune, continues to bear us company, regardless of the many plain hints which we have given her to leave us. But we *should* be thankful! with no great reason to complain.

19th. During the whole of last night we experienced great inconvenience from the rolling of the vessel, but nothing serious occured. At five this morning the wind lulled, and at least it again arose, but not so high as it was in the outset. At ten P. M. the wind calms down to a gentle breeze from the southward.

20th. We have fair weather and a prospect of sailing in two or three days. We are induced to hope that Fisher will come on board to day.

21st. Oh, how this dull delay does effect the mind! The mind being wholely engroced and the feelings entirely absorbed in the one grand wish to depart, and that wish being partially satiated by a faint hope, disappointment is rendered doubly accute, and the mind doubly pevish and fretful. But it is, I think, a virtue in a man to accommodate his will and desire to conflicting circumstances. For an instance, if a man should have his feelings highly excited with the expectation of some great benefit or hapiness and that expectation is dashed to earth, the lighter that disappointment is borne, the more hapiness will fall to the lot of the disappointed. The man who bears reverse or advancement lightly alike is a happy man. I have learned to bear things patiently, perhaps more so than many others with whom it is our lot to meet; but yet I have not *more* patience than a saint should possess.

Tuesday, the 22nd. *All hail, most glorious morn*! The danger is past, the work is done, and we sail to day. O what an expression of joy is thare contained in that word. It is *True* this time, and no mistake. We Sail to day. Fisher, Gibson, Lyons, and the Captain of the vessel came on board at half past six, and we sailed a little after seven, A. M. Up goes the fore and main sails, while the anchor is drawn from its bed to the sailors merry not[e] of Ho, he ho! and, like the light winged birds of heaven, lightly our boat gives way to the wind. Fare well! Fare Well thou base and oppressed people—if ever I press thy putrid soil again with my foot, *may it* be to reak a terrible vengance for wrongs inflicted and to free thousands of you from your galling yoke, *only* to *hurl* you into *eternity*.

We stand to the eastward to clear the breakers and shoals, running with all canvass spread and a light wind at the rate of only six miles an hour. Rather slow for we who are so gifted with impatience as this little band seems to be; but we can but awate our time; and come when it will, I will feel thankful for mercies thus bestowed.

I think that it is time that I had made some enquiry abo[u]t the commander of this craft, the crew, and the strange[r]s, of which latter I find several on our decks. I will enquiry about the matter.

To begin then with the captain of the vessel, which is my duty. He is a Native of France, speaks English verry well, has been in the gulf trade for a long time between Vera Cruz, New Orleans, and Havana, is about thirty three or four years of age, and that is all I know of him, except that he is a good looking fellow.

The crew, which is next in order, is a complete mixture of various countries. In addition to our rightful and necessary crew, we have three shipwrecked sailors who were formerly on board an English Barque, which being lost off the Isle of Cuba during the prevalence of the late September gales, they (supposed to be the only living of her whole crew) made their safety in an open boat, with which they dared and endured all the fury of the conflicting eliments for six days, which time was passed all most without food or fresh water, and were at last picked up by an english merchantman bound for Vera Cruz, and were put on board of us for a conveyance to New Orleans. Two of them are english and the other is a Scotchman. Our rightful crew are—First and second mates—cook and three seamen. The first mate is a Havana Spaniard, or perhaps a Mexican; the second mate is either a creole Frenchman or a Spaniard; the cook is a Frenchman; two American sailors; and one Maltese; so we have a complete assortment.

The strangers come next in order. There is a Irishman and his family (three children and a wife) who have been residing in Mexico for some time and are now going to try the United States. He is not much or he would not put his family on board with such piratical looking fellows as we are. Then thare are four others, who I do not know any thing about.

Then comes, last but not least, the Texians, who, to judge from their appearance have been raised on the Deck of a pirate ship and tutored amid scenes of *Dirt, smoke, Fire, blood and Death*! Some (or in fact all who can raise them) have an overgrown pa[i]r of whiskers and mustachios, with long, kinked, and sunburnt hair, and for the want of hats, we generally wear a handkerchief on the head tied to a turban. *Really an interesting group*. And if this vessel does not sink before we reach our Destined port, then I will acknowledge the falacy in judging from appearances. Thare are cords of Sin and eniquity on board of us.

2 o'clock P. M. We tack and lay an Northwesterly course. Breeze verry light. At nine P. M. We can still plainly distinguish the light

hous[e] on the Castle of San Juan de Ulloa close in on land north west of Vera Cruz.

23d. We had a light wind all night.

The Mountain of Orazabo[13] is in sight all day. Calm from 12 M to 2 P. M.—then a light breeze.

At sunset the wind arose, and we now have a good breeze. Seven knotts per hour at sunset.

24th. We had a stiff breeze all night, and under all the canvass she could bear and all the wind she could stand our vessel only ran about 8 knotts per hour. Plague on the old wash Tub bottomed thing.

We can see no land.

> "We are on the sea, the wild the free
> 'Tis where I would not forever be."

A verry light breeze from the east.

25th. A calm from Nine A. M. to one P. M.—then a light breeze from the South East, or east south east, with which we make headway of about five knotts an hour. Owing to the peculiar roundness of the keel of our vessel and its awkward-luberly shape, we make great leaway, in consiquence of which we lay nearly north-East to make the North point; that is, if the wind be near ahead.

26. Runing as usual—slow, and not *verry* sure. The wind howls towards the north east, and we give to it—still runing on the northwest tack.

Thare is great anxiety among the men with regard to the water, as we are now drinking sour water, which was put up in wine casks, and its quite pungent in its taste.

Sunday, 27th. Still light winds, and occasionally a calm.

There are a great ma[n]y of us sea sick, though I am not yet, nor do I fear it.

We have had a row to day, and I will now state the particulars. In looking around, some one found two or three ship's casks filled with water, which was to us (who have been using sour water for some time) really splendid—excellent to the taste, so we took a notion to drink a little of it, which notion we carried into effect by drawing it with a vial belonging to some one of our number. But about one o'clock P. M. when the mate (1st mate, the Mexican) wanted some water on deck, he asked some of the Texians to help him, to which several assented their willingness by immediately jumping down the hatch and fastening onto a barrel, but lo! and behold! it was a barrel

13. Mountain of Orizaba.

of the good water! When the mate discovered this he requested that it should be replaced in the hold of the vessel, and the men acted according to his request, taking instead a barrel of sour water; but we determined that the sick should have good water at all hazerds as long as thare should be any on board. In about one hour, or less from this, one of the sick, an Englishman by birth and George Lord[14] by name, drew a pint of fresh water from a barrell, and was drinking it when the mate mistrusting somthing went below and on seeing Lord he snatched the cup from him and threw its contents in his face, for which Lord knocked him down without a word of cerimony, and would have thrashed him well, but was kept off of him by our own men. As soon as the Mate could recover his standing position, he went to the cabin and got a pare of Pistoles, which I, myself seeing, communicated to Lord that he should be on his guard. Fisher told the Captain not to allow him to go below with the pistoles, but the capt. thinking a useless warning, payed not attention to it; and as the Mate jumped down the hatch, several voices exclaimed at once "*Throw him overboard*! *kill the Mexican*! *if he dares attempt to draw a weapon*." But he was either too smart to attempt it, or his courage was not sufficient. When the captain heard these hurried exclamations, mingled with the most horried imprecations, he could no longer doubt as to the probable fate of his Mate, if he should draw a weapon and wisely judging it best to stop his mate, just at the moment when several were preparing to lay violent hands on the body of the Mexican; but he came in time to save him and his only remedy was to order the mate aft and command him not to interfear with us. The capt. was the most livid featured living man I have ever seen. He supposed that we were destitute of every think like Conscience, and feared, least in our rage,

14. George Lord, son of Fetsled and Anna (Siggs) Lord, was born Apr. 21, 1816, in Essex County, England. From there he went to Canada in 1834 and, later, to New Orleans, where he worked for a brief spell on steamboats on the Mississippi. He landed at Galveston in February 1837 and joined Captain John J. Holliday's company, Texas army at Camp Independence on the Lavaca River. In the late winter of 1838 and 1839, along with Alfred A. Lee, John R. Baker, Henry Whalen, Ewen Cameron and other men who were to join the Mier Expedition, he participated in the Federalist attack upon Monterey in northern Mexico. In March 1839 he was in the fight against Vicente Córdova, the east Texas conspirator, near the present Seguin, Texas. In the fall of 1842 he participated in the Somervell Expedition as a member of Ewen Cameron's company. Joseph Milton Nance, *After San Jacinto*, p. 152; idem, *Attack and Counterattack*, pp. 629–630; Maude Wallis Traylor, "Benjamin Franklin Highsmith," *Frontier Times* XV (April 1938):257–265.

we should murder the whole crew. But he knew us not, for a man of any nation but Mexico could have had a fair fight, but the moment a Mexican or Spaniard should attempt a row, he met the whole force. Thus ended the affair with the First Mate.

Gale from the North. Oh, it is perfect scissors. We roll and pitch like a dieing whale. We were some what surprised at this storm, for about day break we were becalmed and laying to, when upon a suden all sails were ordered in and before the time could expire, which was necssary for reafing, we were going under bare poles at a tremenous rate directly before the wind. This continued but for a moment, when up went the fore and main sail, close scafed [reafed?], then the gib with the bonnet off and we were brought up to the wind, as near as could be, then we lent away to the eastward with a vengance. The Billows rolling mountains high, the vessel reals to the blast, and on and on we spring like a thing of life.

As the vessel reals to the terific blast
And the waves, tumultuous, higher rise,
And as the sharp crack of the low bending mast
Gives warning that it may never rise,
We think of home, perhaps, to us forever lost
But mourn not by words or even sighs.

A fine time we have.

29th. Calm, or nearly so, at 3 of clock, this morning, though the sea still runs high. The wind is South East. We run on the same tack.

Wind rised at 10 o'clock A. M.—heavy gale from the north—sea rolls mountains high—we begin to look for a long leap into Eternity.

30th. The wind subsided at 12 oclock at night, and left a smart sea on which became nearly smooth at daylight.

Calmed untill 12 oclock M when we have a fine breeze from the north East, and we tack to the northward.

31st. The north East wind still continues and we keep the northward cource.

November, 1844

Now Homewhard my lads   Home, Home, Sweete Home

We are homeward bound
Let the joyful sound
Ease our hearts, and cheer us,

And our foes still fear us,
And we can sing "*Homeward bound*."

Friday 1st. We came in sight of land this morning, but the Capt. fearing a squall and wanting sea room, tacked to the southward. And thus we fare, expect such men to act in all such vessels as this. We saw lights on shore a little after dark, which gave our timid captain such a fright that he gave the order, "*About Ship*"—and obedient to the voice, around we swung and made way to the Southward.

Saturday, 2nd. About 8 o'clock A. M. we put about again—now stearing north east—east north East for the Balize. At 10 P. M. the animating shout of "*The Light House*! *The light House*!" was heard from the lookout at the Mast head, striking through our organs of hearing with the effect of electricity, and upon close investigation or examination the report was confirmed, and in the course of three hours we were "laying to," under "bare Poles," awaiting the dawn of day. And oh, what comfort was that, with which we reposed within view of the coast of our Native land. Sweet and calm was the sleep which that night stole over our illfated band. And yet it was not unmingled with sensations of unfeigned fear least a gale should sweep us off, even when so near our long desired homes. Although a cessation of our troubles was desired and anxiously prayed for (that is if we prayed for any thing), Yet, looking back on the fatality which seemed to have been our attendant from the first, we could but tremble still between hope and fear; and amid all our joyous clamor and hurra, thare was the sign of dread anticipation.

Sunday, 3d. This morning the joyful sight of land met our first gaze with the dawn. And oh, happy pleasing sensation, *it is* "the Land of the Free, the home of the brave." The Land of Washington, and the land of my nativity.

"What need I care so I but take my last long rest, Dear Native land upon thy breast." We hoist a signal for a pilot and tow. The pilot comes, but the Tow Boats pay no attention. However, about 8 o'clock A. M. one of the Tow Boats came down within speaking distance, and then holding on steam, made the foll[ow]ing enquiries, to which the following answers were returned by the pilot. "What vessel is that, and where is she from?" "The Creole from Vera Cruz." "What are all those men doing on board?" "They are Texians released from Mexican prisons." But this even did not seem to have satisfied his curiosity; and I am under the impression that he thought us rather a suspicious looking set, which we were. He approached with caution, and at length, having become convinced of our good designs, or that we held no ill ones, he fastened on to us and off we went like an arrow. After conveying us a short distance above the separation of the three passes, he droped us, giving orders to let go our anchor and await his return which instructions, averse as they were to our wishes, we could but obey, while the Tow passed down to the mouth again after another vessel. Here we felt almost over powered by the emotions which you may well suppose would animate men on again viewing the land of their people, after an incarceration of *twenty months and twenty one days* with most *wreatched* treatment. But we had not long for reflections of this kind ere the Tow hove in sight, and Taking a Barque on one side and a Brig on the other, with two topsail scho[o]ners astern of her she started up the river with us. We were delayed, from one fault or another, on our passage up, and night closed upon us without hope of reaching the city before the following day.

4th. At daylight we are a long distance still below the City. I have not been on this master piece of Nature since December, 1840, and it was then night when I passed where we now are, consiquently I can amuse myself by taking a view of the scenery of the Banks on each hand, which consists principally of large sugar plantations. But, by far the most amusing acts or objects to me are the movements of our nearest neighbours—the occupants of our vessels mate in size—a topsail schooner—who are negroes from Baltimore it seems on their way to Louisianna, and who interest themselves in viewing and commiserating our destitute condition. Some of them (among the rest a large Buck Negro) threw some tobacco over to some of the boys. I was aloft at the time and it was sufficient to excite the sympathies of an adamantive heart to see the voracious and haisty struggles which ensued to gain the small bits of tobacco thus donated by the generosity of *Slaves*. Oh, how can man find it within his heart to abuse and maltreat his servant! I am no abolitionist, nor do I advocate one single principle of abolition, for I am a *Southern man*, with *Southern* principles, advocating strongly the actual necessity of the continuance of slavery to support the existence of our Republic. For on the existance of slavery is founded the safety of our country as a free Republican and Independent Nation; but I *am* opposed to the abuse of slaves. No man has any right to kill or otherwise injure his slave, even though he *is* his property, for he is also his fellow creature endowed with like capacities. I do not say that a man shall not chastise his servant for bad conduct, for in thus doing, he only does his duty toward that over which God has given him controle. But he should feed and clothe well, and chastise them more to correct and reform their conduct, than for the pittiful purpose of revenge. Do it to *reform*, and the act is good; do it to *revenge*, and you are wrong. Now in the case of these negroes, they actually possessed sympathetic feeling for the whites when they saw them in distress, and were more liberal in accordance with their means than the whites generally are.

We reached the City of New Orleans at 4 o'clock P. M., and found the good citizens of that City all turned heals upward with the election, as it was the day on which was held an election for President—we were an utter blank—having no friends, *no* home, and not much country. We could do nothing, nor did we know what we should do for something to sustain life. . . . . . . [*sic*] I will pass over this Painful part without farther notice than this. Had thare have been any vessel then leaving the dock for any port whatever, so it was off—entirely away from my country (or that which was once my country) I felt so wreatched and so disgusted, almost with life itself—that vessel I would have taken to at once, biding "adieu" to Home, country, and Friends, perhaps Forever!

5th. After sleeping all night by permission on board the vessel, I arose feeling quite hungry from having eat [or] drand [drank] nothing, nothing save water, except I cup of coffee, since the morning of the 4th. But I knew not where or how to satisfy my hunger. Hard and Pittiable is the wreatched fate of him with whom fortune is severe, and casts upon a land distant from friends, among strangers, without food—without money—without clothes, and too ill, both in body and mind, to work.

Not content with having recieved us *so well*, the Citizens of New Orleans have raised—raised *what?*—Raised a *report* that these *Texians* have had the presumption to go to the polls and vote for Polk and Dallas. May Heaven forgive all such unprincipled Lyars, and make honest men know Texians better. But let their conduct pass—let the scoundrel who raised the report find his punishment in his own abused conscience, if any thare yet remains to curb his passion. I pitty that poor—puny—insignificant scamp, void of every principle pertaining to a gentleman, who can find nothing more interesting to his ignoble mind than telling base, unfounded, and uncalled for lyes upon a body of poor ragged—yet noble prisoners—one of whom he dare not face.

About 10 of clock A. M. I met with an old acquaintance and friend J. M. Brown and was immediately provided for. But alas! there are numbers of my companions yet in destitution and want. Great God! When will our misery end? Can we never find peace or rest from this loathesome way of living?

I met with Mr. Richardson—with whom I had had some slight acquaintance, and felt verry grateful to him also.

Thare are other matters incident to myself alone which I might mention but I forbare.

6th. We have nothing to avert the attention. I have engaged a passage on board the New York[15] bound for Texas. *Texas*! Oh, the bare mention—the *thought* of that Country calles up before me recollections too painful—also too pleasin for a notice in this place! *Texas* the country of my adoption—my *devotion*! The Steamer "New York," Capt. Wright[16] was to have sailed to day, but Sea Captains will not comply at *all* times with their promises. I do not aim this at *all* sea captains, but it will strike the majority.

7th. We had the pleasing knowledge this morning that we should assuredly "cut cables" this day. But about 10 of clock A. M. we recieved intelligence to the effect that the steam ship Republic[17] had entered the river, which has induced Capt. Wright to lay untill she shall have entered port. This is far from pleasing or desireable to us, as our only wish, it seems, is to land on Texian soil. Although that country did forget us in adverse circumstances, we now, when enjoying the divine gift of sweet liberty, have a deep and lasting reverential affection for her—we feel with the poet that "thare is no place like home!"

15. The *New York*, a steamer of 150 tons burden, was placed in operation between New Orleans and Galveston in the fall of 1838 by Charles Morgan of the New York and Charleston Steamship Line. Morgan lived in New Orleans, where in 1836 he had become the owner of the Morgan Iron Works. The *New York*'s deck was 180 feet long and 22 feet in breadth. She had accommodations for 200 passengers and was advertised to make the run between the mouth of the Mississippi and Galveston in thirty hours. Hayes, *Galveston*, I:323.

16. Captain John T. ("Bully") Wright, formerly commanded the *Columbia*, a steamer that was similar to the *New York* but older. Ibid.

17. The steamship *Republic*, owned by Williams, Whitman & Co. of New Orleans, was commanded by Captain John R. Crane. It plied the waters between New Orleans and Galveston and left New Orleans on Saturday, Aug. 3, 1844, to make its first run to Galveston. It was described by the *Daily Picayune* as "having handsome accommodations, with staterooms," and as having been built especially for the Texas trade; it was equipped to sail under canvas as well as steam. The *Republic* arrived at Galveston from New Orleans on Oct. 20, 1844, bearing four Mier prisoners (James C. Armstrong, Captain William Ryon, William A. A. Wallace, and William F. Wilson) who had been liberated on Aug. 24, 1844. It then returned to New Orleans on Nov. 7. *Daily Picayune*, July 24, 1844; *Telegraph and Texas Register*, Oct. 30, 1844.

At the hour of 1 of clock P. M. the Republic touched the Wharf, and at 2 of P. M. the New York pushed off into the stream with a full head of steam, and we were soon under good headway, with hearts as light as the air.

Here, for the sake of Justice and satisfaction to all, I will mention that thare were many of the men who were anxious to come on board, promising to pay their passage as soon as they *could*, but Capt. Wright was misanthropic enough to refuse a passage to the poor fellows, untill John M. Brown, actuated by that same noble generosity that has characterised his career since first I k[n]ew him, kindly steped fo[r]ward and offered his name to Wright as responsible for the whole amount. This was sufficient to satisfy the *Noble Captain Wright*, and all who wished it soon obtained passage on board the vessel. I make these fiew remarks in justice to Mr. Brown, than whom no man is *better* or more generous, and who is not excelled as one of the most noble works of God. A noble an[d] honest man.

We lay all night at a wood yard. Some 25 miles below New Orleans.

We have quite a merry time. Thare are seventy six of us on board and all (two excepted) of that number take Deck passage.

8th. By dawn of day we were under weigh and making a line towards Texas. Ah, that name again awikens recollections. . . . . . [*sic*] But still, amid our hopes of soon meeting friends—amid our high anticipations of future enjoyment, thare is a sting to dull our brightness of spirit, turn our joy to bitterness of soul, and darken our features, already made gloomy by endurances more than the soul of man can long bear. We think of our homes, and joy beams forth from our eyes; we think of friends dear to us, and a smile plays about our faces; but alas! we think of the conduct of *some* of our *countrymen*. And gloom settles over us.

I can occasionally notice one who is naturally gay and frolicsome standing apart, leaning against the mast, or gunwalls, his arms folded, head bent and eyes sternly fixed, as if gaizing upon some enemy—and often as he gazes, his lip will curl in scorn, as if the eye rested upon some hated and contemptable object! And I am so well schooled in the disposition of each individual member of this body that I can take up the train of his thoughts and pursue them as though they were my own! Well do I know what calles forth that contemptious smile that scornful glance! Now he thinks of the vain endeavors of the Mexican people to break the spirits of a freeman by all manner of inhuman barbarities —and now that scorn is produced by a glance at the ignoble conduct of *Sam Houston*! In truth, so well can I geather from his looks what his thoughts must be that I resign my pen for one moment that I may pursue them.

. . . . [*sic*]

We passed out at the mouth of the River about noon, and now the Dark blue gulf opens before and fast we leave the land of Washington behind us; Peace be with its people, and may they protect those rights for which their fathers fought, and for which we struggle. *Farewell* to the land of my birth, the land of my sires. *Farewell* to the sons of those whose blood now flows in the veins of those unfortunate Texians. *Farewell* to the ashes of the departed heroes of the American Revolution; we return to our adopted home, but that country—week as it is, and that home new as it is is not void of memories of the heroic defenders of Liberty. No! Where is Crockett—where is Fanin, where is Bowie and Travis? The soil of Texas has drank their blood, and their bones now whiten her plains, but their spirits are enjoying that sweet repose due to the martyrs in the cause of Liberty. And where is *Sam Houston*? buried in the hearts of his countrymen? *No*! I hope not. What will they, or do they still cling to the vile reprobate, the monster? It cannot be—they will not lend the hearts devotion to a murderer. . . . . . . [*sic*] How beautiful and calm is the sea. Oh, that my thoughts were so . . . . [*sic*] But not [no], that will not be—sorrowful gloom seems to have mastered me. So let it do.

9th. High are those hopes that animate the soul of man when about to lay eyes upon a long loved and hardly won object. Such were the hopes that now enlived our whole sould, mind and body. Sweet and enviable is the feeling of that man who has been torn from home and friends and subject for months and years to an incarceration, when he is nearing the goal of his desires, the haven of his heart—the home of his friends. Such, or similar were our feelings at this time, but alas, one thought would still darken the Brow. *We were denounced by our countrymen, and outlawed by our countries President*. But let *that* pass and rest with the forgotten.

Sunday the 10th. Ah! Great and eventful day! ever to be remembered by me as my second enterance into the land of *Texas*.

At Daylight, we found ourselves in sight of land, and bouyant were our feelings on that account. About sunrise a wind was apparent, and we feared for a moment that we should be baffeled and miss our landing. However that thought was soon crushed, and we hastily neared the land. Crossing the bar, we lay for the pass between Bolliver point and that of Galveston Island. As approaching nearer, and yet nearer to the Isle, oh, what joy was thare depicted in each countinance! As they stood gazing, as if entranced, you could see happiness on every face.

With proud anticipations we reach the Wharf—not a shout—not a hurra—not a sound of wellcome, went up towards Heaven, evincing the joy of our countrymen at our return! No friendly hand was stretched out to congratulate us, save those who had, perhaps, a personal friend, or rellative among! How, then were our proud anticipations of an honorable wellcome dashed to earth! No—Oh, no—even though no glad sound wellcomed our return to home and Liberty—we yet had one proud—grand satisfaction of which the coldness of our countrymen could not deprive us! *We would soon be on the soil of that country for which we suffered, many bled, and many died*! Grand —consoling thoughts to a soldiers heart.

Now we touch and leeping on shoar soon seem mad with joy! While the concourse of people, naturally drawn togeather by the arrival of the Steamer, stand around with various remarks—some make the cold —half enquiry and half assertion, "These are the Perote prisoners," and being affirmatively answered, proced to make enquiry about Mexico—Perote—how we got off—were we released—or did we escape—and how we arrived at New Orleans? with a thousand other curioisities to satisfy—and upon being totally satisfied—some would retire, perhaps, to speculate in their minds upon what our situation might have been while confined in the dungeons of Mexico:—while others perhaps, a little more humane *in words*, would procede to an investigation of our situation in prison, right in our presence, and with their expressed pitty and grief at our misfortunes, would render us almost as unhappy as we were in prison. Yet it seemed that all were studiously careful to avoid an enquiry into our present condition. I, however, was provided for, for thare I had a brother, and thare I was at home! But, Great God! what was the condition of many of my companions? Without a home thare, and without a friend save among those who were as destitute as they themselves;—they were forced to stand on the wharf or wander out to seek for what they had no hope then of finding.

As for myself, upon reaching the wharf, I stood on board the steamer for the space of three or five minutes seriously contemplating the scene around me and contrasting our brilliant anticipations with our cold reception. Little had I thought that Texians would thus recieve their friends. After thus standing for a short time I steped on the wharf, sullen, and despondent; not a smile to wellcome me back. On the wharf I met my Brother,[18] who had just been informed of our arrival. Then I was *at home*, in the complete sense of the word; but, oh, how different was the situation of others! Many of them, perhaps, possessing the acquaintance of not one single individual in the city, apart from our own men, and without the means of procuring a days sustinance! What, I ask, must have been the feelings of those men thus thrown upon the *Charity* of that people for whom they had fought, bled, and suffered indignities beyound conception without a murmer, and from whom had orriginated to us the base epithets of *Coward*, *traitor*, and *Outlaw*!—and above all, knowing as they did by experience that, that people held within their bosom but verry little of Heavens Gift—called Charity. I thank God that I am indebted to the people of Texas for naught, save the base epithet of *Outlaw*! Orriginating from a source still more degenerate—*Sam Houston*! He it was, who, when sorrow and trouble stood over us, at the verry time when a word from him would have procured us the protection of the Civilized World, with that natural baseness of his life, deserted us! Not content with our misfortune, he boldly declared that the expedition was *unauthorized*, thareby bring[ing] death to many—and a protracted incarceration to others! That is one *Lie* for which Sam Houston will answer to his maker, and I doubt not but that in Eternity he will remember it. And even now could remorse reach a heart so guilty and a conscience so smothered in crime, he would feel the weight of his errors.

God forgive him, for I fear I never can. I doubt not but that Sam Houston will die the death of a guilty man before God and the world, condemed not by *Law*, but by *Justice*. I am well convinced that thare are those who condemn that expedition, and those concerned in its raising or execution, without ever once enquiring into the causes which conduced it. Now, in justice to those poor, illfated, but brave soldiers of an oppressed country, who had the misfortune to fall among enemies, I say, in *justice* to their memory, *condemn* them not untill you give them a hearing! Those of us who yet live, ask nothing of you either in words or deeds, for *we are able* to defend ourselves, our honor, and our fame from the attacks of all such ill minded men, *but* we also feel in duty bound by the sufferings we have endured togeather to defend the good name of each other, and above all to protect the memory of our companions who fell in battle at our sides, or sunk by disease, expired in our view!

Will you then censure us for this? Would you blame that man who

18. William H. McCutchan.

would protect his *honor* with his life? Assuredly not! Then I say, sooner would I stand and hear a man or set of men impeach my *own* honor than that of my fallen companions! He who would come to my face with an impeachment of my honor, places me on equal ground with himself, and if he have a cause, he is justifiable, but He, who tramples under his unhallowed foot the fame, the pure memory of those brave men, I pronounce before the world, *a coward*, a VILLIAN—unworthy the smile of High Heaven, and fit alone for the Society of the infernal friends of *Hell itself*! Then where stands *Sam Houston*? or where *should* he stand? *I answer*—condemned before *God* and *man*, a traitor to Friendship, a villain, deeply dyed in crime and a *Coward* before the World! Yes he *is* void of every principle that should actuate a gentleman, a soldier, and a patriot! The inveterate hatred which he has for every act of honor, and the avidity with which he swallowes all that can be said against him, with his knowledge of right and wrong, is enough to convince all that he knows, he deserves the *curses* of his own countrymen. He can plot the everlasting distruction of his companions or friends honor, and at the same time, hypocritically smile and say, "*My friend*, *I much* regret the cause which has forced me to do this," when in reality thare is *no* cause, but his *vanity*, his *pride* of the laurels he won on the field of *San Jacinto*, which prompts him to commit any act that can conduce to the speady downfall of any man (*friend* though he be) who is likely to eclipse the glory he thare gained, and destroy his *self-importance*. But, if we are to judge from *cause*—to *effect*, we must believe that his faiding laurels will soon drop from that ignoble brow, for I do not believe but that Texians have too much love of honor to uphold such a *villain*—such a murderer, in his perfidious career. His acts prove him unworthy the fellowship of *Honest men*. With regard to him in private life, he *may* be honest, and even that is doubtful; but in public—Politically, he *is a villain*!

No one need accuse me of letting my prejudice run too far, because the act of *Sam Houston* which produced this prejudice, if such it can be called, was one sufficient to damn him, not alone in *our* estimation, but that of our friends, if any we have.

If thare are those who did sympathise with us during our incarceration, he must have lost his influence with *them*; if thare are those who had friends in Mexico, he must have lost their respect; and if thare are those who had relatives in that illfated expedition, he must have gained their enmity; inshort he could but have made ma[n]y enemies and lost many friends by that unparalelled act of inhumanity. I allude to the Letter which he is said and proved to have writen—or, rather, the letter which Capt. Elliott is said to have writen by his instruction to Mr.

Packingham, then Minister of England to Mexico, in which it was staited (or said to be, and never denied with any appearance of truth) that although we had gone out without authority from the Government, yet, as we were countrymen of his—treat us with as much lenity as could be extended to us. This, if written by Houstons instructions was an assertion of his that we were *Out Laws*, which took away all power of Foreign ministers to interfear in our behalf. *And yet*, Notwithstanding the many proofs of his villainy, the people still *adore* and many pay him a tribute in worship, which should be given to their maker alone, that Great—"I AM" to whom alone it is due.

Let no one accuse me of exaggeration in this matter, for only those are competent Judges who have noticed well the effect which the policy of this man has taken on Texian interests, and marked well, withall, the submissive manner in which this distructive policy has ever been received by the majority of the citizens of Texas; and from those I fear not condemnation or contradiction, for they are well aware of the fact that there are those in Texas who are not only acquiescent to his will, but submissive to his slightest thought, and who would readily grant him dictatorial power did it lay within the bounds of their ability to procure it for him. Even since I reached my home, I have heard it said that the best deed Texians could perform would be to grant Sam Houston unlimited authority untill he could bring the critical position of our country to a final issue. And can it, I ask, be for one moment doubted by a descerning mind what *that Final Issue* would prove? If we look at cause and effect, judging the future by the past, which is the only safe meanes whereby we can judge, it *cannot* be mistaken. If placed under *those* circumstances, at the disposal of *that* Man, judging from what has been performed, it can not be doubted but that our people would be reduced to poverty by the continued incursions of the enemy, emmigration checked, our credit lost, and *that final issue* could only be the *Ruin of Texas* and Death of a Republic.

If I am thought severe in my remarks upon the character and acts of Gen'l. Houston—if his friends think me too cruel, or unjust, let them not think me vindictive. If my friends think him wronged by me, they will not, I hope, believe it to eminate from a wish to scandalize, or heap calumny upon him on my part; but I believe it will be attributed to the propper cause; an *honest*, but false opinion. These facts, which I have mention[ed] are beyound a doubt, FACTS INCONTRAVERTABLE, but many of the deductions drawn tharefrom may be the effect of false conclusions, but still, *they are honest ones*, and *he* alone can prove to me that my belief is erronious; and this can only be done by proof *conclusive—direct* and *plain* which alone will satisfy myself and many others, and this can only be performed by the production of letters, which *undoubtedly* Gen'l Houston holds in his possession. I allude to Letters addressed to Mr. Packingham by Capt. Elliott under the connizance of Sam Houston, and it is to be supposed—Nay, *believed*—under his instructions. Houston assuredly kept copies of all such Letters, and if so it is within his power to *clear* or *condemn* himself in the Eyes of the World. He alone can make this point clear; and if the ballance would be in his favor, it is but natural to suppose that he would avail himself of the first opportunity to show to the world that he was not culpable of this offense and teach us how [by?] incontravertable proof that he had acted no part in procuring the Decimation. A sad and lamentable tragedy performed by order of the Mexican Government on the 25th of March, 1843, whareby seventeen Good, Loyal, and brave Citizen soldiers of Texas were sent to the Grave! *Yes, murdered*! If it lay in Houstons power to clear himself of a charge so darkly criminal as this, we must believe that he would make use of the means. It is useless for men to say that he regards not the opinion of those who oppose him, and any man, a friend to Houston who says this, and justifies him in thus sitting at defiance the opinion of his countrymen, and siting at naught their belief, I hold as one blindly submissive to the will of a man who he cares not to know; and the assertions of such men in Political or private matters are not of value sufficient to merit confutation. For any one disposed to act with justice to all and enhance the interest of their country, are ever anxious to learn all they can regarding the acts and the pollicy from which eminate these acts of their Ruler so that they may rightly judge of his Character and disposition, and when found unworthy of the trust reposed in him, that they may discard or continue him in office, when safety may demand or judgement require, and that they may justify or condemn his acts according as they may merit. For, if we do not learn something of the cause which has actuated a man to the commital of a deed, we are not prepared to form a correct estimate of his conduct. Thare are acts performed with certain views to the glory and enhancement of the general interest, which by a mischance, prove fatal to those interests; and all such acts are undoubtedly praiseworthy; and again, thare are acts which openly bear this front but when traced out are found to orriginate as a wish to injure, and yet bear the semblance of these mistaken judgements. That is, men may often appear anxious for the conclusion of certain things, when secretly they are doing all in their power to thwart their good effect. We can not judge of a mans intentions by his bare conduct, and his *assertions*, unsupported by any coroberating testimony; hence, I conceive it to be necessary for a man to explain his conduct when it is thought intricate (particularly, a *President*) and not only to *explain*, but to produce *evidence*, and also to bring ample proof of the validity of this evidence. Then we can correctily estimate his character, and *justify* or *condemn* his conduct as its merit may deem fit.

There is one thing which I will say, that if Sam Houston did aim at the Wellfare of the "Mier Prisoners," he can establish the fact, and he has not done this. I believe he holds himself culpable and fears the hazard of the attempt; nay—did it lay in his power to clear his name, he would have done so long since, even before we reached home; and I again say that he holds in his hands his own *justification* or total *condemnation*. And if he finds that he can only settle the evidence of his guilt more firmly with the people, he will give satisfaction by future promises and never fulfill them; *nor even attempt* it; but if he can prove that his aim was for the *best*, but a short time will elapse ere he cleares himself entirely of this stigma. His silence on this subject, or his attemt to avoid any explanation or proof, *can* sittle guilt upon him *where no doubt it propperly belongs.*

Now after a series of repeated trials and misfortunes, the majority of us are here in Galveston. We left some in Mexico, a fiew in New Orleanes, and the remainder, seventy six in number, are about to sepperate, perhaps, forever. It is a sad thought, for misery has made us the family of her patronage and our feelings are those of a family; but we *must* part and many of us will *Never again meet!*

Let those who would accuse us of being precipitate in our attack on the town of Mier, remember well the circumstances under which we did it. It was not for gain, for that we could not expect, but it was for the interest of Texas, and to retrieve our fallen honor, which had received a terrible blow from the disgraceful conduct of Genl. Somervilles Troops at Loredo. *Let it be remembered that it was not Col. Fishers Troops who were guilty of Plunder and Robbery at that Town, but those of Genl. Sommerville.* AND BE IT REMEMBERED TO THE FORMERS CREDIT AND THE LATTERS CONSTERNATION.

Following will be found a complete Muster Role of the Companies comprising Col. William S. Fishers Command, after Genl. Somerville had left us to our fate, and carried through untill our release, giving remarks &c &c.

[Chapter IX]

List of men comprising the command of Col. Wm. S. Fisher, In 1842 '43 & 44, In the Campaign Known as "The Mier Expedition."

STAFF & COMMAND

NAMES	REMARKS
Col. Wm. S. Fisher	Col. commander in chief
T. J. Green	Aid. Escaped, Perote 1843
F. [T?] W. Murray	Adjt. Liberated—1844
F. M. Gibson	2 Q. Master
Wm. M. Shepherd	Surgeon
Wm. F. McMath	Assist. Do
J. J. Senixon	Do Do Liberated, Mexico 1843

(LETTER A)
Capt. Camerons Company

NAMES	REMARKS
Ewing Cameron	Captain. A Scotchman by birth, shot by order of the Mexican Government at Huehuetoco, Aprl 25th 1843
J. D. Cock[e]	Shot by order of the Mexican Government at The Salado March 25th 1843
John Cash	Shot by the same order, at the same time
Patrick Mahon	Met the same fate
James Turnbull	Do " " Do
Henry Whaling	Do " " Do
Thos. Colville	Died, Mexico, June 20th 1843
Lynn Bobo	Died, In Matamoras 1843
Saml. McLelland	Died, on the march to Mexico 1843
James McMichen	Died, Mexico Nov 20th 1843

John McLindel [McKindel?]	Died, of wounds, at Mier 1843
P. Rockefellow	Died, at San Luis Potosí
Joseph Simon	Died, Perote, Decem. 3d 1843
Patrick Usher	Died, Mexico, Aug 23d 1843
Wm. H. Vanhorn	Died, Perote, Oct 6th 1843
Wm. Martin	Died, on the march to Mexico
Doct. Towers	Killed in Battle at Mier, Decem. 26th 1842
A. White	Do " " " " Do " Do
I. Canfield	Liberated, March 5th 1844—1st Srgt.
P. H. Lusk	Do April 23d 1844
Jerry [*sic*?] Leighorn	Do to the English Minister 1844
George Anderson	Left in the Mountains, 1843
F. Bray	Do " " Do Do
Wm. Morehead	Do " " Do Do
A. B. Laforge	Escaped from Perote, March 25th, 1844
Wm. Thompson	Do " Mexico 1843
Samuel H. Walker	Do " Mexico Do
[blurred] Wright	Do " Perote March 25, 1844
C. K. Gleason	Escaped from Perote, March 25th, 1844
Henry Weeks	Do " Mier 1843
Nat. Mellon	Do " " 1843
Wm. Ripley	Do " " "
John R. Baker	1[st] Lieut. Wounded at Salado in the rescue
A. A. Lee	2d Lieut.
P. A. Ackerman	
A. Arthur	
Alexander Mathews	
John Brenam	Interpretor
G. N. Downs	
George Lord	
G. K. Lewis	
John McMullen	
John Mills	
Lawson Mills	
Daniel McDonald	Liberated, Perote Aug. 29th 1844
A. Mosier	
John Hoffer	
Jam[e]s Glasscock	
James Nealy	
James Peacock	

Wm. T. Parker	
John Sweesy	
A. S. Thurmon	Interpretor
Thos. Tatum	Liberated Perote Aug. 24th 1844
G. W. Trahern	
R. Willoughby	
R. W. Turner	
H. Miller	
T [F?] White	
J. T. Dillon	
William Wynn	
Total 61	In The Battle of Mier
A. J. Yates	Left on guard, East Bank Riogrande
——— Donelly	Do " " " " Do
——— Earnest	Do " " " " Do
Wm. Ward	Do " " " " Do
John Canty	Do " " " " Do
Total 66 men	Rank & File in Company A

LETTER B

Capt. Eas[t]lands Company

NAMES	REMARKS
Wm. M. Eastland	Capt. Shot, Salado 25th March 1843
Robt. H. Denham	Do " " " "
J. L. Shepherd	Do " " " "
M. C. Wing	Do " " " "
T. J. Cox	1[st] Lieut. Escaped from Mountains 1843
J. D. Blackburn	Do " " Do
Lewis Hays	Escaped from Mier 1843
J. D. Morgan	Do " Mexico Aug. 1843
Wm. A. Clopton	2nd Lieutenant
P. F. Bowman	
Thos. W. Bell	
Richard Brown	
Wm. Davies	
Wm. Dunbar	
Wm. Gibson	
Friendly Grubbs	
A. D. Headenburg	

Mathew Alexander	
D. H. Vanvacton	
A. B. Hanna	
F. W. T. Harrison	
E. B. Jackson	
[?] B. King	
John McGinley	Shoemaker, In the Castle
Wm. Middleton	〃 〃 〃 Do
Thos. K. Nelson	
H. H. Oats	
M. M. Rodgers	
Wm. Sargent	
Wm. H. Sellers	
Levi Williams	
James Willson	Tailor In the Castle of Perote
J. T. Blanton	Died in Mexico 1843
Benjamin Middleton	Do in D[o] May 3rd 1843
E. J. Cofman	Died, San Louis Potosí April 8th 1843
Allen L. Holderman	Do 〃 〃 〃 1843
Wm. McLeyea	Do Mier 1843 of wounds
Perry Randolph	Died in the Mountains
Carter Sargent	Do Mexico Aug. 3d 1843
Robt. Smith	Died Mexico June 18th 1843
L. Saunders	Died of Perote epedemic, Jan[ry] 12th 1844
James Ury	Died of Wounds at Mier, 1843
Z. Willson	Died of Perote Epedemic Dec. 6th 1843
Charles Hill	Died, San Louis Potosí 1843
John P. Wyatte	Died of Perote Epedemic Oct. 21st 1843
James Barker	Died of Wound at Matamoras 1843
Asee Hill	Liberated Mexico 1843
J. C. Hill	Liberated Do 1843
Jeffery B. Hill	Liberated Perote 1843
Donald Smith	Liberated Vera Cruz 1844
John Nealy	Left in the Mountains Feb. 18th 1843—Suposed to Die
Total 51	In the Battle of Mier
G. W. Alley	Lef[t] on Guard on the Rio Grande
M. Ambrose	Do 〃 〃 〃 〃 Do
Oliver Buckman	Do 〃 〃 〃 〃 Do
Theadore Bissell	Do 〃 〃 〃 〃 Do
——— Clark	Do 〃 〃 〃 〃 Do
David Hudson	Left on Guard, on the Rio Grande

Wm. S. Holton	Do "	"	"	"	Do
Edward Martin	Do "	"	"	"	Do
E. A. Vincent	Do "	"	"	"	Do

Total 60 Rank & file Company B

LETTER C
Capt. Piersons Company

NAMES	REMARKS
J. G. W. Pierson	Capt.
P. M. Maxwell	
A. W. Alexander	
R. P. Boswell	
Jacob Humphries	
Wm. H. Moore	
Saml. McFall	
A. D. Runyan	
Daniel Sulivan	
Thos. A. Thompson	
John Bidler	Escaped from the Hospital, Mier
James Rice	Do " " Do Do
Charles Chalk[1]	Do " Mier, by concealing themselves, before the surrender
Wm. St. Clare[2]	Do from Mier by concealing themselves, before the surrender
Wm. Oldham	Escaped from the Mountains
Wiley Jones	Do from Perote, March 25th 1844
Robt. Harris	Shot at the Salado 25th March 1843
Christopher Roberts	Shot " " " " " "
J. P. McThomson	Shot " " " " " "
Frank Hughs[3] } Wm Scott[3] }	Left at Matamoras, wounded, and released with the main Body, Sept. 16th 1844

1. John Henry Brown has written in the margin after the word "surrender": "Not so. The name is Whitfield Chalk = John Henry Brown April 24, 1886."
2. John Henry Brown has written on the page of the diary: "(Clair). Not so. The name is Wm. St. Clair = John Henry Brown April 24, 1886."
3. By his bracketing of John Hughs and Wm. Scott, John Henry Brown indicates that William Scott, too, was "left at Matamoras, wounded, and released with the main Body, Sept. 16th 1844."

Eliza Porter		Died, Mexico Aug. 24th 1843
John Lyons		Killed in charge on the guard at Salado
Total 23	In Battle of Mier	
Jessee Yocum		Killed, accidentally Decem 23d 1842
Thos Oldham		Lef[t] on guard, on the Riogrande
George Arith		Do " " " " "
——— Owens		Do " " " " "
Total 27	Rank and file comprising Company C	

LETTER D

Capt. Buster's Company

NAMES		REMARKS
Claudius Buster		Capt.
D. F. Barney		
James Calvert		
L. D. F. Edwards		
Charles Hensley		
Wm. Kaigler		
Wm. Millan		
Joseph D. McCutchan		
David Overton		
John Toops		
Joseph Watkins		
James Young		
James C. Armstrong		Liberated 24th Aug 1844
G. W. Bush		Escaped Aug. 23d 1844 from near Perote
E. Y. Keene	1st Sgt	Do Perote March 25th 1844
Thos. Smith	2nd "	Do " " " Do
Richard Keene		Do " " " Do
K. M. Crawford		Do Mexico Aug. 25th 1843
Campbell Davis		Died Perote Feb. 16th 1844
D. R. Hallowell		Do " Decem. 11th 1843
Wm. Mitchell		Do In the Mountains 1843
R. F. Brenham		Killed in Charge on guard, Salado
Lorenzo Rice		Do " " " " Do
Stanley Lockerman		Killed In "*Battle of Mier*"
——— Bassett		Killed In "*Battle of Mier*"
——— Dixon		Do " Do
——— Hobson		Do " Do

A. Jackson	Do 〃 Do
John E. Jones	Do 〃 D[o]
James M. Ogden	Shot at the Salado
Total 31[4]	In the Battle of Mier
Lieut. W. Wilkinson	Left on guard, on the Rio Grande
Wm. Hensley	Do 〃 〃 〃 〃 Do
Thos. Ransom	Do 〃 〃 〃 〃 Do
Maj. McQuine	Do 〃 〃 〃 〃 Do
——— Furman	Do 〃 〃 〃 〃 Do
J. Vaughan	Do 〃 〃 〃 〃 Do
——— Hicks	Do 〃 〃 〃 〃 Do
Gabriel Smith	Do 〃 〃 〃 〃 Do
A. C. Hide	Do 〃 〃 〃 〃 Do
G. W. Bonnell Doct. Robt. Watson ——— Hackstaff	These three were lost from the advancing Collumn, by attempting to descend the river in a Boat, consiquently, returned to camp missing the engagement to their great regret.
Total 43	Rank & file in Company D

LETTER E
Capt. Ryon's Company

NAMES	REMARKS
Wm. Ryon	Capt. Liberated Aug. 24th, 1844
A. J. Roark 2nd Sgt.	
Wm. H. H. Friendsly 3d Do	
Steven Barney 4th 〃	
Alexander Armstrong	
David Allen	
Gilbert R. Brush	
John E. Dusenbury	
Wm. K. Davis	

4. John Henry Brown has added the number "30" adjacent to the number 31 to indicate that McCutchan miscounted the number of men who were in Captain Buster's company (Company D) in the battle of Mier.

Fenton M. Gibson	
Charles S. Kelly	
John Lacy	
M. R. Pilley	
E. H. Pitts	
Wm. M. Shepherd	
Ezek^{l} Smith	
John Sansbury	
Willis Copeland	
Theodore Maltby	
F. Whitehurst	
H. Woodland	
Wm F. Willson	Liberated Aug. 24th 1844, Perote
Francis Rily	
H. V. Morell	
Stephen Goodman	
H. H. Roberts	
John M. Shipman 1st Lut.	Died Mexico 1843
James Burk	Do Perote Feb. 20th 1844
Barney Bryant	Do Saltillo 1843
Robt. Beard	Do San Louis Potosí Do
Wm. Beard	Do Mexico Do
A. F. Burass	Do Perote 1844
Saml. Bennett	Do Do Do
John C. Grocejean	Do Do Do
Z. Iceland	Do Do Do
Wm. Morris	Do Mexico 1843
C. R. Willis	Do Do Do
Saml. McDade	Do Rio Noso Do
J. S. White	Do Perote 1844
Hanks Kerkendall	Killed in "*Battle of Mier*"
George B. Crittendan 2d Lt	Liberated, Mexico, 1843
Robt. G. Watters 1st Sgt.	Do Do 1843
Robt. Beal	Escaped from Mier, 1843
P. H. Daugherty	Do " Mexico 1843
John Fitzjerald	Do Do Do Do
B. H. Gattis	Do Do Do Do
Malcolm McCanly	Le[f]t wounded in Matamoras, Supposed to be Dead

G. B. Piland	Escaped from Mier 1843
Wm. D. Cody	Left in the Mountains, supposed to be Dead
Sanford Rice	Do Do Do Do Do Do Do Do
W. E. Estee	Shot, Salado 25th March 1843
Thos. L. Jones	Do Do " Do Do
Wm. Rowan	Do Do " Do Do
James Torry	Do Do " Do Do
Total 54	Rank & file In Battle of Mier
Moses Kerkendall	Lef[t] on guard on the Rio Grande
Ralph Gilpin	Left on guard on the Rio Grande
Edward Brown	Do " Do " " Do
Z. Lucas	Do " Do " " Do
J. Buckhannon	Do " Do " " Do
Wm. E. Dressler	Do " Do " " Do
Schneider or Snider	Do " Do " " Do
Total 61	Rank & file, In Company E.

LETTER F

Capt. Reece's Company

NAMES		REMARKS
C. K. Reece	Capt.	Escaped from Perote 1843
John R. Johnson	1st Sgt.	Do " Do 25th March 1844
Daniel Henry[5]		Do " Do 1843
Wm. Moor		Do " Do 25th March 1844
James [C.] Willson		Do " Mexico 1843
C. Clark	1st Lut.	Liberated Perote 1843
O. C. Phelps		Do Mexico Do
Wm. Reece		Do Do Do
J. J. Senixon		Do Do Do
Wm. P. Stapp		Do Perote 1844
Fre[e]man Douglass		
Wm. Atwood		
D. H. E. Beasley		
J. B. Berry		

5. The name is Daniel Drake Henrie. Muster Roll of Captain John P. Gill's company of mounted volunteers, March 20, 1842, Militia Rolls (Texas), Texas State Archives.

B. Z. Boon
Henry Bridger
G. Willson Clark
Thos. Davis
John Harvy [*sic*]
Henry Journey
L. C. Lyons
J. H. Livergood
Joseph F. Smith
Charles McLaughlin
T. J. Sensebaugh
W. Vandike
Isaac Zumwalt
Daniel Davis

W. D. Wallace	Liberated Aug. 24th 1844 at Perote
John Alexander & Lewis[6]	Left in the mountains, supposed Dead
James Austin	Killed at Mier in Battle
Joseph Berry	Do " Do " Do
John Ervin	Died, Mexico 1843
John Owen	Do Do Do
W. Miller	Do Perote 1844

Total 36 At the Battle of Mier

Sidney Colder, or Callender	Lef[t] on guard, on the Rio Grande
F. Hancock	Do " Do " " Do
Virgel Phelps	Do " Do " " Do
[Jame]s Warren	Do " Do " " Do
George Walton	Left on Guard on the Rio Grande
——— West	Do " Do " " Do
Michiel Cronigan	Belonging to the Company, and started with it into the town, by [but] by some accident, or mistake, or perhaps intentionally, he returned to camp before the fight commenced. We supposed him to have been killed in Battle untill we re-

6. It is not clear whether McCutchan intended an ampersand here or started to make an "L," then drew a line through it, and wrote the word "Lewis." There is no known Mier prisoner by the name of John Alexander Lewis or John Alexander. There was a John Rufus Alexander. Unless Lewis is counted here as a separate name, the list of names given by McCutchan as members of Reese's company participating in the battle of Mier adds only to 35, rather than 36 as shown.

turned home, where we found him enjoying good health, &c &c.

Total 43 Rank & file, In Company F.

When Reviewing the scenes which we have passed through, it strikes forcably the minds of all that it was through the interposition of Divine providence which held us and encouraged us to bear up against and support manfully the severe trials through which the vindictiveness of a murderous people compelled us to pass. Yes—Deity must have exercised his power there, or under such treatment not one would have again reached his home! Yet look at our Muster Roll, and there see how terror engendering and fearful was the distruction which raged among us! how *many* poor fellows, but Brave Devoted Soldiers, were hurled frome time to Eternity! brought thus to an untimely end, far—far from home, friends, and Country! Their Country was as nothing to them, for in the midst of their distress, where Death & Destitution reigned, perminent; *She* had forgotten and neglected the duty which, in *honor*, was due them. Alas! How many of our number droped off, one by one, untill our number was fearfully reduced. Yet, *Be* it said and with truth, to honor the memory of those Devoted fellows, that amid their suffering when death became inevitable, they would calmly exclame, while expiring: "*We suffer, and die for Texas, what more could we wish*," and is it possible that this Country had so far forgotten her duty as to show neglect or carelessness for the fate of brave men, who were thus devoted to her wellfare?

Let those who are disposed to condemn us for that surrender, which proved so fatal to many of our brave Companions, remember that man can not always do as he would think best;—that, had we have been supported by our Government, as justice could demand, the surrender would never have been—that had Genl. Sommerville remained with us and prossicuted the war as prudence and energy required, we would have held the Valley of the Rio Grande, even to the Mountains, against any force that could have been sent against us, until reenforcements should have arrived from our country—which would undoubtedly have been the final termination of Mexican war upon the Texian frontier—last, but not least, that, to the fortune of war we had been committed, and to its fate we could but yield.

I know full well that there are those who would boast that "*had they have been in the Battle of Mier, they would have surrendered their arms but with their lives*!" *Had* THEY *have been*, aye, there is point, HAD they have been there, the fate of our band would have been better, for it *was assistance* we were in need of! But, why *were* they not thare? Was it because they lacked the authority of Government, or was it because they had not hope of good resulting from an attemp[t] upon the Mexican Frontier? *No*, we may safely say; but we, being well convinced, firmly assirt that it was rather a *fear*, or a carelessness for the Texian wellfare that caused their backwardness. Indeed it was true that no good could result from a measure, if that measure was left untried. Men will say that energy was wanted, yet those same individuals made no timely effort to aid our distressed country. Are we to believe the assertions of that man who proclaims abroad that the men of Texas have not guarded strictly as they should the interests of the nation, and openly asserts that he did all within his power to aid her soldiers, when it is known that he not only refused himself to fight, but likewise would not grant aid to others who were willing but unable to go and fight the battles of their country? If this is to be believed, then I freely confess that Texas *is a* HUMBUG! I know some who have thus acted and thus asserted, and still assert, and yet, strange to say, still more strange believe, are listened to with credence by many who have been and are still "Good soldiers of the Republic." But this is the world, one man becomes the Dupe of another, and a Nation is sometimes dragged to ruin by the effort of a sing[l]e arm—her bright star dimed—her destiny planed, and her fate irrevocably sealed by the plans devised in the head of a single man whose tongue in the mientime pleads for her advance in the onward and upward [tra]ck [?], which seems to have been designed for her step. Yes, a bright, brilliant and glorious career has been that of Texas, seen through the smoke of her enemy's Cannon besprinkled with the blood of her sons, who have nobly fallen in desperate strife, for the ascendancy of the dazlingly beautiful "*Lone Star*"! Proud and noble emblem of a youthful and glorious Republic! Proud now, and prouder may it yet be, ere its destiny shall be united to its Mother Republic! Go ye Cowards, who fear to face a foe—go humble yourselves in the Dust before a Despots feet; tell him that, of all who have raised arms against his "*noble*" race—self styled generous but thrice damnable in their perfidy, when theroughly studied, you were not those who would have commited such an act. Go tell that perfidious race of cowards and midnight assassins that you fear them, that you lament the cause of rupture between Texas and Mexico, that you detest the Revolutionists who would tare asunder these two countries, and that you willingly submit to any punishment that can be by them devised—Go you who would ask protection of others, tell them that you have proved your inability to defend that liberty which has been so nobly wone amid strife, blood, and Danger; and that you now yield your birthright to those who can defend it. Indeed it would seem that Texians are not able to defend their rights; or, at least, they think themselves incapable of self protection and thus give way to dispondency. By what reasoning this opinion has possessed them it is hard to determine. Why they should become thus dispondent can only be supposed. But perhaps after having endured many years of hardships and privations, without a single comfort, they are willing to give up the idea of self government, abandon their long cherished and proud hope of becoming a mighty Nation of themselves, and return to that country's protecting arm from whence they Came, bearing with them a broad extent of territory, the fruit of their labour and Blood, that they rest the remainder of their days in peace and Security. This desire is *reasonable* but not all togeather laudable the kindred of in in [*sic*] those who have suffered, Fought and fell in a bloody strife for the Nationality of *Independent* Texas. Yet all may be for the best—as we are a people of their own Blood, speaking the same language with them and many of them are of that Country. But, yet again, would it not have been of greater advantage to Texas in future generations to have stood an independent *Republic*, Constituted within *her self*? This is a question that can only be left to the Future for a Decision. All that can now be said is drawn from supposition. We may guess and surmise for the probable termination of the consiquences of this act with regard to its future bearing upon the interests of this People when it shall have been consumated; but we can not assert with any degree of safety either that it will be better, or that it will be worse. We yield the trial to Time and Fate. That the Expedition of 1842, ending in the Capture of Col. Fisher and his Command has prove[d] a small advantage to Our country will not be disputed; That it was effected at great loss of life, has proved itself; That it will be long remembered by the Conquerors is beyound a doubt; That its ill fated termination, at the defeat of Mier, was owing to Genl. Houston's wish to thwart it is certain; That *Texas* and *Texians* will remember us with a small shear of thanks and gratitude, we believe; And, that we feell compensated for our trials in the thought that we have served our country is but a natural consiquence to those who love their country—for their c[one or two words illegible] its honor, glory, and aggrandisement. We feel as ready to serve as ever, and look forward with the joy of others to the time when Texas shall be freed from the incursions of a base and treacherous Foe. The will of Texas is ours, her fate is ours, and her soil is our home.

I feel confident that those who served in that ill Fated Expedition will all eventually make "The Land for which they Fought" their home. As for me Texas is my home, and on earth *I ask no Other.*

Jos. D. McCutchan

Appendix 1

The following seems to be an earlier version of pages 43 to 69, by the Rosenberg Library's pagination, of the diary. Page 78 of the diary is blank, and page 79 is only partially filled with what appears to have been an "intended" introduction. The original draft is reproduced here with the library page numbering of the manuscript being shown in brackets.

[79] . . . [*sic*] McCutchan's . . . . [*sic*] Campaign of 1842—which was begun under the command of Genl. Summerville, and ended under Col. W. S. Fisher. Battle of Mier, and the subsequent imprisonment of that band, known as the "Mier Men"—with an account of their sufferings, while confined in Mexico during the space of *Twenty months and twenty one Days.*

Also their release; Journey towards and arrival at Galveston, Texas. Commenced in the Castle of *San Carlos De Perote*, thence onward. Written as things transpired; and concluded in Galveston, Texas, shortly after the writers arrival.

What may not man endure?

[80] [. . .] all mingled in one mass of confusion nor was there anything so full of grandure, so full of excitement and sublimity, as this, amid the darkness and would be stillness of the night. It was by much the most exciting and interesting Christmas night that ever I had passed or ever expect to pass, again were I to live five hundred years. And also more powder burnt, and a thicker and more weighty shower of iron and lead than I will ever again witness on the night of the twenty fifth of December.

On the morning of the 26th we began the fire in a more lively style, yet I am bound to believe that thare were men among us *Cowards* by nature who did not fire a gun, but I would dislike to be called upon to name them, for I could not do so, as I was but little acquainted with those who formed the army, almost an entire stranger among them, but I think thare were men who were connected with that illfated expedition who will bare me out in the ascertion which I have made. The mingled roar of rifles, musquetry, and Artillery is the sweetest music man ever heard, that is, if he be a man of spirit and admiration, for the sublime. After two hours hard fighting, the Mexicans would but seldom show their heads above the parripet. We had cleared their cannon, by nine o'clock A. M., killing two entire Artillery companies, with the exception of five men, three of whome were wounded, leaving only two fit for duty. Then might we have taken the piece, which was situated within sixty yards of our position, but in so doing we could not have but lost many men, and we had not them to spare, as our numbers were small, and it was already apparent that we were contending with an overwhelming force. [81]

But their Artillery was of no use to them, for during the whole action they neither killed nor wounded a man with it and the fire was incessant.

Between the hours of ten and twelve they made either two or three separate and distinct charges (I disremember which, I think though three) with the intent to drive us from our position, but to no purpose; we met and drove them back with great slaughter. The fight continued —blood flowed freely—death and firey distruction swept around us—our rifles belched fourth death to the foe at every ring of their clear tones—and the angel of death sat clothed in bright glory over the town of Mier.

> Where firey distruction swept around,
> To geather were death and glory found!
> Amid death shots falling thick and fast,
> Many great and brave men breathed their last!

Thus proceeded the battle, untill between the hours of one and two P. M., when thare was seen advancing towards us a flag of truce, and about this time two of the men who we had left with Joseph Berry came in reporting that the others were killed or taken, the former most likely. Some wished to shoot down the bearer of the flag, but Col. Fisher would not consent, alledging as a reason for his not doing so that "*his name should not be sulled by such an act of barbarity*." As well as I can recollect, this was his remark, at least the purport of it. The Flag advanced. Fisher demanded the occasion of it—the answer he received was that Gen. Ampudia *demanded* our surrender, and in case of a refusal "*every Texian would be put to the sword*." Fisher requested an hours consideration, which they granted. [82] Here did he show himself unfit to command. Admiting that we were unable to hold the contest it should have been his endeavor to force upon them the belief that we were. But no, he tamely and quietly *requested* one hour to consider on it!—one hour to think whether he would be a slave or a freeman. One hour to study whether or not he would deliver up his men to *chains* and *slavery*, in the dark dungeons of Mexico. Had he peremtorily have ordered the flag back to whence it came, the face of affairs would have materially changed! That day, which ended in our misery and desolation, would have given peace to Texas, and honor and glory to Col. Fisher and his command. Yet Fisher is not as much to blame as many think. It is my belief that the blame should be equally divided between the *Officers* and the *men*, the latter merit an equal share with the former. Again I contend that we had an indisputable right to shoot the bearer of the flag, and I go to the rules and regulations of warfare between civalized Nations, by which it is agreed that when a Flag of Truce is hoisted, all hostile movements shall be suspended by both parties;—that this was strictly adhered to by us, but with them it was not. We had driven them (in a manner) from their main position, and when the flag of truce started to us, and we had ceased our fire, the enemy commenced regaining their position, which was a direct violation of the rights of civilized warfare.

During the trice [time] Fisher visited the Mexican officers at their quarters; what he said or done, I do not pretend to say; but it is known that a solumn treaty [83] was entered into between them. At the end of the hour or rather about three o'clock we surrendered, in parties of from one to ten, as *prisoners of war*, with every assurance from the enemy that we should recieve the treatment due such. We laid down our arms in the Square in the presence of the whole Mexican force. Then did we find ourselves prisoners to the most barbarous people who disgrace the name of civilization. Then did I, for the first time in my life, see the light of Heaven through prison windows. *Honor* and *Glory* to every Texian who will lay down his *life* rather than part with his arms. Let the battle cry of Texas be "victory or death." And let her sons go to battle with the determination to *conquer* or *die*, and then we need fear *no* enemy. I cannot here avoid giving thanks to Summerville for our imprisonment. For it is to his weak heart, and old woman's Soul, that is to be attributed, the unfortunate termination of that illfated Expedition. For had he have taken the proper course on reaching the rio Grande, had he have pushed forward, regardless of circumstances (a course which any commander would have pursued) the disgraceful conduct of some men at Loredo never would have occured, and consiquently then men would not have become dissatisfied; the separation at Loredo, nor that at Gurarro, would not have taken place. We would have swept the whole valley of the Rio Grande before us of every one who dared raise an arm against Texas. After the disgraceful conduct of many, hitherto respectable men, I had sooner have found my grave in the desolate wilds of a western prairarie

[than] to have returned without meeting the foe. Though many good men returned home disgusted with Texian vallor, [84] they returned even with the Robers, rather than remain to witness another act so base. I applaud their motive. But I for one was determined to wipe out the stain cast upon Texian character by base men, even though I did it with my own blood. I love my life much, but I love my honor better. Give me death, in preference to dishonor.

About nine o'clock on the morning of the 26th the enemy ascertained that a small party of our men was stationed near half a mile from our main position. (The party left with Joseph Berry.) Three hundred of their cavalry immediately undertook to dislodge them, in which they could not succeed untill the Cannon had been planted against the house. Our party than saw that it was worse than madness to attempt its defence; tharefore they determined to retreat towards us, leaving Berry and Doctor Sinixion (the latter being a cripple was unable to follow, naturally so I suppose) thinking that the enemy would not injure cripples, but how widely were they mistaken. It is true, that Sinixon they did not injure, only capturing him, while Berry, a noble fellow and a good soldier, they mangled most horribly, fourteen or fifteen lance thrusts through his body, and butchered up with a sword. This base and dastardly act was perpetrated by Captain Elduret, formerly a resident of Texas on the Guadaloupe, near Victoria, and the villain had the heart to boast of it afterwards, in a Newspaper. Doctor Sinixion bore to us the flag of truce, and I think had a promis[e] of his liberty for so doing, as it is known by most of the men connected with that expedition that he was expecting his liberty from the verry moment we surrendered; and further-[85]more it is known that he was placed on his parole but a few days after the capitulation. This alone is sufficient to rest on him a *dark* and *deep* suspicion inasmuch as he was the one to whome that kindness was extended. Far better would it have been had we have shot him while bearing the flag. Many of the "Mier men" will support me in this statement.

It is a remarkable supposition that Gen. Ampudia, in sending the flag, intended in the first place to demand a surrender, and, if a refusal was given, which he had ample right to expect, then to make a treaty stipulation, to save the town, as he could only conclude that if we gained the place, that we would destroy it as near as practical, as we had entered the town on the 23d and behaved peaceably, paying for all we had received of the Citizens, and only demanding a sufficiency of provisions for our consumation. When the flag was advancing I once or twice heard the cry from the Mexican Soldiery "*Vive la Federac-*

tion," which was proof conclusive that they expected to surrender the place. But It was otherwise ordained.

Our loss was, killed, eleven—wounded twenty three, that of the enemy we could not correctly learn, but the supposition is, killed six hundred and fifty; wounded, two hundred, that is at least a reasonable supposition, though many think there were more.

Our poor fellows fell bravely in defence of their rights, and they have escaped the misery to which their survivors were doomed. I know not, that they were allowed a grave, but

> Their spirits are now with the glorious dead,
> And their bodies lie among the enemy
> Where base and villanious reptiles o're them tread;
> Unwept, unloved lie the sons of liberty!

Yes, unwept, save by the remnant of the *abused*, *cursed*, *uncared for*, and *unfortunate* soldiers of Texas, styled "*Mier Men.*" We remember them with animation and pride; and long as thare is one of us living, will their names live but I think their country cares but little for them, or us.

The force of the enemy was two thousand infantry, eleven hundred cavalry, and the citizens of the town, making about thirty five hundred men, to oppose which we had about two hundred and fifty. Gen. Canales was in command of their cavalry, and Ampudia commander in chief of the whole force. *The fight lasted 18 hours.*

An account of this engagement going to the world will show good reason why the troops of Mexico fear a contest with Texians.

We are blamed, but when we were enduring hardships and suffering from an inclement skye—when we were exposed to privations of every kind, and doing all we could for Texas, little did we thi[n]k that the reward which we would recieve would be "*you are robbers.*" When we stood face, to face with the foe, recieving and returning death, for death, never once did we think that, for it our countrymen would call us *cowards*, and blame us for the part we were acting—that we would be cursed for doing our duty. But such is the case.

We may be blamed for entering on the expedition, but to such as censure its rashness, I will only say that we had Gen. Houston['s] order for leaving our homes; and farthermore that the love of country and humanity induced it. Gen. Houston never intended that the expedition [87] should result in any good for Texas, but he ordered it for some deed [*sic*] purpose known best to himself, and then placed Gen. Summerville over it for the express purpose of breaking it up, thinking (and that with justice too) that Texians would not submit to the rule of such a man. Now I contend that it was right in us to show to the world that we would be tools in the hands of no man, even though he was in power. It is evident that Houston had some object in view in authorizing the expedition; it is equally evident that that object was not to make it serve Texas, but his own service, from the verry circumstance of his placing such a man as Summerville in the command. Then what was his object? Someone else will have to answer, for I can not.

So much for Houstons order; now, for the call of our *Country*, and *Humanity*. General Wall had entered San Antonio de Bexer, and captured fifty three men, mostly judges and lawyers, all men of peaceful avocations. He then at the Salado killed or captured the whole of Dawsons Company, save one. His prisoners he carried into Mexico amounted to sixty odd. This, I assert, was sufficient, aye, more than enough to arouse the sleeping blood of every Texian, even without, an order from the legal authorities. Even admiting that the act was illegal, that it was unauthorized, are we to sit tamely and wate for an order from Government to raise our arms, when the enemy are butchering or carrying off our countrymen, immediately before our faces? Shall we wate for an order when a sacriligious enemy [88] are bearing down that held by man most dear? Shall we not strike till ordered in defence of our hearths? Shall we look for an order, ere we strike for our wives, our children and our most sacred right? Shall we not raise an arm in defence of our families until ordered? Great God! what a country is this? how are we ruled? Is not a man allowed to defend the *all* for which he lives? his *all*, and his only live! his *all* that is holy, *all* that is to him sacred on this earth, his *wife*, his *children*, and the rights of his country! If this is Texas, if this is her law—farewell *Texas*, *farewell honor*, farewell *liberty*—weap humanity, weep! *Liberty* has *forever*, and *forever* departed from my country. Our country demanded it—Honor demanded it—Humanity demanded it—Liberty demanded it. The freeborn sons of Texas wished it—Houston issued the order, and the sacrifice has been made, and woefully have we, the objects, suffered for it. We obeyed the summons with willing minds and stout hearts, but it all would not do. *We now suffer for it uncared for and unthought of*. But it is high time that I should return to the Narrative, as I wish to make a plane statement of facts as they occured.

After the Battle was over, and all right with Ampudia, we were crow[d]ed into the prisons, to relish a belief, and a great probability of being comfortably marched out on the following morning and shot as a breakfast spell to the Mexican soldiery. I for one am bound to confess that I never expected to see another sun rise, but that was at that time a matter of little consequence to me. I had my mind made up to die, but was, as luck would have it, for once very agreeably disappointed.

But on the following evening about dusk we were [89] all marched out in a body, then did I think that our time had come, and we were careless of the consequences! Lif[e] was not worth holding! But we afterwards learned that they were hunting for one Mexican, named Bascus [Vasquez], [who] had been with us, and had even made his appearance among us after crossing, but was not taken with us.

We remained in this place about four days, and were then marched off to Matamoroas. On our march the attempt was made to induce the men to rise at once, conquer our guard, and make our escape. But the men were rather indisposed to make the effort, hence all went peaceably, and we arrived at Matamoras on the ninth of January eighteen hundred and forty three. During this time we had only received two meals per day, and they, quite slim, which went rather rough with us, who had been living on the "fat of the land." In Matamoras our living was about the same it had been on the road. Geting our first meal about half past one or two in the evening, and our Second, and last, about ten at night, we were "fashionable" in the complete sense of the word.

Appendix II

An Account,
or Narrative of the acts, and treatment of the main body of prisoners, from 14th January, 1843, up to the 30th of May, of the same year[1]

They left Matamoras on the fourteenth of January for Monterey. On the road thare was an attempt made by some two or three to stir up the men to revolt, but it was unsuccessful. After a fatiegueing march they arrived at Monterey on the first of February.

On the second, they took up the line of march for Saltillo, where they arrived on the sixth, from whence they started on the seventh. Encamped on the night of the tenth at El Rancho Salado (a Salt Town). On that night it was resolved by a majority of the officers and men that, inasmuch as the treatment extended them and the harsh abuses and insults offered were too much to be tamely submited to they would rise themselves or nobly perish in the attempt. In accordance with this heroic determination, on the following morning (11th of February 1843) Capt. Ewing Cameron, a brave Scotchman, at the head of two hundred men made an attack on, and after a short but noble struggle, put to flight a guard four hundred strong, taking from them many of their arms, much ammunition, and many horses. The Texian loss, killed four, wounded three; the names of the killed—Doctor Brenham, Lyons,[2] Fitzgerald,[3] and Lorenzo Rice[4]; of the wounded—

1. This appears to be the original draft of McCutchan's description of the "break" at Salado as it was related to him by others and later rewritten more elaborately.

2. John Lyons was a member of Captain John G. W. Pierson's company of the Mier Expedition; see Israel Canfield's diary, muster rolls, Texas State Archives.

3. Archibald Fitzgerald, an Irishman by birth, had served as a captain in the Spanish Peninsula War (1808 to 1814) and had been a member of the Texan Santa Fe Expedition and, as a result, was captured and imprisoned in Mexico. He was later released, but General Woll recaptured him at San Antonio in

Capt. John R. Baker, John Harvy,[5] and G. W. Treyhern.[6] In consequence of an order given by Cameron to kill none of the enemy if it could be avoided, the loss of the Mexicans was small, only two killed [. . . .]

September 1842 with arms at hand. According to the terms under which he had been released as a Santa Fe prisoner Fitzgerald was, by that action, subject to being shot. With two other former Santa Fe prisoners taken under similar circumstances, he had been left at San Fernando de Agua Verde, General Mariano Arista's headquarters, to be shot but later had been ordered to Mexico City. The main body of Mier prisoners found the three former Santa Fe prisoners at Saltillo. Fitzgerald was mortally wounded in the break and died shortly thereafter.

4. Lorenzo D. Rice was a member of Captain Washington D. Miller's company in the Vasquez campaign in March 1842 and served in Captain Claudius Buster's company on the Mier Expedition. Roster of Captain Washington D. Miller's company, March 11, 1842, in Frank Brown, "Annals of Travis County and the City of Austin" IX:11–12, Archives, University of Texas. Brown based his paper on a roster found in the Washington D. Miller Papers, 1833–1860, Texas State Archives.

5. John Harvey, who lived at Bastrop and owned a town lot in 1840, served as a private in Captain John P. Gill's company of mounted volunteers, from Mar. 20 to June 20, 1842, and as a private in Captain John S. McNeill's company, First Regiment, South Western Army, in the Somervell campaign. John Harvey was living in Bastrop in 1846. Militia Rolls (Texas), Texas State Archives; a copy of McNeill's muster roll is in Sam S. Smith Collection, Archives, University of Texas; see also Marian Day Mullins (comp.), *Republic of Texas*, p. 73; Gifford White (ed.), *The 1840 Census of the Republic of Texas*, p. 8.

6. George Washington Trahern was born in Hinds County, Mississippi, seven miles below Jackson, on the Pearl River in 1825, son of Wesley and Delilah (Berschars) Trahern. In 1846 Trahern was living in Calhoun County, Texas. George Washington Trahern diary, Bancroft Library, University of California, Berkeley; Mullins (comp.), *Republic of Texas*, p. 169.

Bibliography

UNPUBLISHED MATERIAL

Adams, Harvey Alexander. "[Journal of an] Expedition Against the Southwest in 1842 and 1843." Austin. Archives Division, University of Texas Library.

Affleck, J. D. "History of John C. Hays." 2 pts. Austin. Archives Division, University of Texas Library.

Alexander, John Rufus. "Account of the Mier Expedition." Austin. Archives Division, University of Texas Library.

Army Papers (Republic). Austin. Texas State Archives.

Brown, Frank. "Annals of Travis County and the City of Austin." Austin. Archives Division, University of Texas Library.

Brown, John Henry. "Autobiography." Austin. Archives Division, University of Texas Library.

Canfield, Israel. Diary [of the Mier Expedition]. Austin. Texas State Archives.

Comptroller's Letters (Republic). Austin. Texas State Archives.

Crawford, Polly Pearl. "The Beginnings of Spanish Settlement in the Lower Rio Grande Valley." Master's thesis, University of Texas, 1925.

Deed Records, Washington County. Vols G, IJ. Brenham, Texas. Washington County Courthouse.

Documents under the Great Seal (Texas), Record Book. Austin. Texas State Archives.

Domestic Correspondence (Texas), 1835–1846. Austin. Texas State Archives.

Executive Records of the Second Term of General Sam Houston's Administration of the Government of Texas, December 1841–December 1844. Austin. Texas State Archives.

Ford, John S. "Memoirs." Austin. Archives Division, University of Texas Library.

Glasscock, James A. Diary [of the Mier Expedition]. Austin. Texas State Archives.

Huson, Hobart. "Iron Men: A History of the Republic of the Rio Grande and the Federalist War in Northern Mexico." [1940]. Austin. Archives Division, University of Texas Library.

Land Office Records (Texas). General Land Office, Austin.

Littlejohn, E. C., comp. "Texas Scrap Book," Vol. II. Galveston. Rosenberg Library.

Militia Rolls (Texas). Austin. Texas State Archives.

Miscellaneous Claims Papers (Texas). Austin. Texas State Archives.

Muster Rolls (Rangers), 1830–1860. Austin. Texas State Archives.

Muster Rolls (Republic), Austin. Texas State Archives.
National Archives, Records of the Department of State. Despatches from United States Ministers to Mexico. Vols. 9–12 (June 12, 1837–Jan. 26, 1847). Record Group 59.
———. United States Consular Despatches, Matamoros. Vols. 3–4 (Jan. 1, 1837–Dec. 29, 1848). Record Group 59.
———. United States Consular Despatches, Mexico City. Vol. 8 (Mar. 2, 1840–Dec. 30, 1845). Record Group 59.
———. United States Diplomatic Instructions, Mexico. Vol. 15 (May 29, 1833–Mar. 29, 1845). Record Group 59.
———. United States Resignation and Declination File. Record Group 59.
Pension Papers (Republic). Austin. Texas State Archives.
Proclamations of the Presidents (Republic). Austin. Texas State Archives.
Public Debt Papers (Texas). Austin. Texas State Archives.
A Record Book of the General & Special Orders and Letters of the South Western Army, November 1842 [–January 1843]. New York. Manuscript Division, New York Public Library.
"Sketch of the Life of Claudius Buster." San Antonio. Daughters of the Republic of Texas Library, the Alamo.
Smith, Sam S. Collection. Austin. Archives Division, University of Texas Library.
Smithwick, Noah. "Recollections of General Sam Houston." San Antonio. Daughters of the Republic of Texas Library, the Alamo.
Trahern, George Washington. Diary. Berkeley. Bancroft Library, University of California.
Washington Presbyterian Church Minutes, 1846–1888. Austin. Archives Division, University of Texas Library.

PUBLISHED MATERIAL

Books and Articles

Adams, Ephraim Douglass, ed. *British Correspondence Concerning the Republic of Texas, 1836–1846*. Austin: Texas State Historical Association, 1917.
———. *British Interests and Activities in Texas, 1836–1846*. Baltimore: Johns Hopkins Press, 1910.
[Alcaraz, Ramón, et al., eds.]. *Apuntes para la historia de la guerra entre México y los Estados-Unidos*. Mexico City: Tip. de N. Payno (hijo), 1848.
———, eds. *The Other Side: or, Notes from the History of the War between Mexico and the United States.* Translated and edited with notes by Albert C. Ramsey. New York: J. Wiley, 1850. Reprint, New York: B. Franklin, 1970.

Almanaque Imperial para el año de 1866. Mexico City: Imp. de J. M. Lara, 1866.

Bancroft, Hubert Howe. *History of Mexico.* 6 vols. San Francisco: History Co., 1886–1887.

———. *History of Texas and the North Mexican States.* 2 vols. San Francisco: History Co., 1890.

Bassett, John Spencer, ed. *Correspondence of Andrew Jackson.* 7 vols. Washington, D.C.: Carnegie Institution, 1926–1935.

Bell, Thomas W. *A Narrative of the Capture and Subsequent Sufferings of the Mier Prisoners in Mexico, Captured in the Cause of Texas, Dec. 26th, 1842, and Liberated Sept. 16, 1844.* DeSoto County, Miss.: Printed for the Author at the Press of R. Morris & Co., 1845. Reprint, with editorial notes by James M. Day, Waco, Tex.: Texian Press, 1964.

Binkley, William C. "The Last Stage of Texas Military Operations against Mexico." *Southwestern Historical Quarterly* XXII (1918–1919): 262–266.

———, ed. *Official Correspondence of the Texas Revolution, 1835–1836.* 2 vols. New York: D. Appleton and Co., 1936.

Boletín bibliográfico de la secretaría de hacienda y crédito público. Editado por la Dirección General de Prensa, Memoría, Bibliotecas y Publicaciones. No. 466 (año XVII), October 1971.

Branda, Eldon Stephen, ed. *The Handbook of Texas: A Supplement.* Vol. III. Austin: Texas State Historical Association, 1976.

Brown, John Henry. *History of Texas, from 1685 to 1892.* 2 vols. St. Louis: L. E. Daniell, [1892–1893].

———. *Indian Wars and Pioneers of Texas.* Austin: L. E. Daniell, [189?].

Callcott, Wilfrid H. *Santa Anna: The Story of an Enigma Who Once Was Mexico.* Norman: University of Oklahoma Press, 1936.

Carpenter, V. K., transcriber. *The State of Texas Federal Population Schedules, Seventh Census of the United States, 1850.* Huntsville, Ark.: Century Enterprises, 1959.

Carreño, Alberto M., ed. *Jefes del ejército mexicano en 1847: Biografías de generales de división y de brigada y de coroneles del ejército del mexicano por fines del año de 1847* [Fly leaf says to the end of "1840"]. Mexico City: Imprenta de la Secretaría de Fomento, 1914.

Carroll, H. Bailey. "Steward A. Miller and the Snively Expedition of 1843." *Southwestern Historical Quarterly* LIV (1950–1951): 261–286.

Carroll, J. M. *A History of Texas Baptists.* Edited by J. B. Canfill. Dallas: Baptist Standard Publishing Co., 1923.

Castañeda, Carlos E., trans. "A Trip to Texas in 1828 by José María Sánchez." *Southwestern Historical Quarterly* XXIX (1925–1926): 249–288.

Chabot, Frederick C., ed. *The Perote Prisoners: Being the Diary of James*

L. Trueheart Printed for the First Time Together with an Historical Introduction. San Antonio: Naylor Co., 1924.

Cox, I. J. "The Southwest Boundary of Texas." *Quarterly of the Texas State Historical Association* VI (1902–1903): 81–102.

Crawford, Ann Fears, ed. *The Eagle: The Autobiography of Santa Anna.* Austin: Pemberton Press, 1967.

Crocket, George Louis. *Two Centuries in East Texas: A History of San Augustine County and Surrounding Territory from 1685 to the Present Time.* Dallas: Southwest Press, [1932].

Croffut, W. A., ed. *Fifty Years in Camp and Field: Diary of Major General Ethan Allen Hitchcock.* New York: G. P. Putnam's Sons, 1909.

Cúyas, Arturo. *Nuevo diccionario: Cúyas' inglés-español y español-inglés de Appleton.* 5th ed. New York: Appleton-Century Crofts, 1966.

DaCamara, Kathleen. *Laredo on the Rio Grande.* San Antonio: Naylor Co., 1949.

Day, James M., ed. "Diary of James A. Glasscock, Mier Man." *Texana* I (Spring 1963): 85–119; I (Summer 1963): 225–238.

———. "Israel Canfield on the Mier Expedition." *Texas Military History* III (Fall 1963): 165–199.

Dictionary of American Biography. 22 vols. New York: Charles Scribner's Sons, 1928–1958.

Dixon, Sam Houston, and Louis Wiltz Kemp. *The Heroes of San Jacinto.* Houston: Anson Jones Press, 1932.

Dunn, Frederick Sherwood. *The Diplomatic Protection of Americans in Mexico.* New York: Columbia University Press, 1933.

Erath, Lucy, ed. "Memoirs of George B. Erath." *Southwestern Historical Quarterly* XXVI (1922–1923): 207–233, 255–279; XXVII (1923–1924): 27–51.

Freud, Max, trans. and ed. *Gustav Dresel's Houston Journal: Adventures in North America and Texas, 1837–1841.* Austin: University of Texas Press, 1954.

Freytag, Walter P., ed. *Chronicles of Fayette: The Reminiscences of Julia Lee Sinks.* [La Grange, Tex.: La Grange Bicentennial Commission], 1975.

Gammel, H. P. N., ed. *Laws of Texas, 1822–1897.* 10 vols. Austin: Gammel Book Co., 1898.

Garst, [Doris] Shannon. *Big Foot Wallace of the Texas Rangers.* New York: Julian Messner, 1951.

Gilliam, Albert M. *Travels over the Table Lands and Cordilleras of Mexico, During the Years 1843 and 1844: Including a Description of California . . . and the Biographies of Iturbide and Santa Anna.* Philadelphia: J. W. Moore, 1846.

Gooch-Iglehart, Fanny Chambers. *The Boy Captive of the Texas Mier Expedition.* Rev. ed. San Antonio: Press of J. R. Wood Printing Co., 1909.

Green, Mary Rowena, ed. *Samuel Maverick, Texan: 1803–1870: A Collection of Letters, Journals, and Memoirs.* San Antonio: [Privately printed (H. Wolff, printer, N.Y.)], 1952 [i.e., 1953].

Green, Rena Maverick, ed. *Memoirs of Mary A. Maverick: Arranged by Mary A. Maverick and Her Son Geo[rge] Madison Maverick.* San Antonio: Alamo Printing Co., 1921.

Green, Thomas Jefferson. *Journal of the Texian Expedition against Mier, Subsequent Imprisonment of the Author, His Sufferings and Final Escape from the Castle of Perote with Reflections upon the Present Political and Probable Future Relations of Texas, Mexico, and the United States.* New York: Harper & Brothers, 1845. Reprint, Austin: Steck and Co., 1935.

Greer, James Kimmins. *Colonel Jack Hays: Texas Frontier Leader and California Builder.* New York: E. P. Dutton & Co., 1952.

Hanighen, Frank Cleary. *Santa Anna: The Napoleon of the West.* New York: Coward, 1934.

Hayes, Charles W. *Galveston: History of the Island and the City.* 2 vols. Austin: Jenkins Garrett Press, 1974.

Herring, Hubert. *A History of Latin America from the Beginning to the Present.* New York: Alfred Knopf, 1955.

Hogan, William Ransom. "Life of Henry Austin." *Southwestern Historical Quarterly* XXXVII (1933–1934): 185–214.

Humboldt, Alexander von. *Atlas géographique et physique du royaume de la nouvelle-espagne. México-atlas.* Stuttgart: F. A. Brockhaus Komm, 1969.

Jack Hays: The Intrepid Ranger. [Bandera, Tex.: Frontier Times, n.d.].

[Jennett, Elizabeth LeNoir, ed.]. *Biographical Directory of the Texan Conventions and Congresses.* Austin: Book Exchange, 1941.

Kendall, George Wilkins. *Narrative of the Texas Santa Fe Expedition Comprising a Description of a Tour through Texas and across the Great Southwestern Prairies, the Camanche and Caygüa Hunting-Grounds with an Account of the Sufferings from Want of Food, Losses from Hostile Indians, and their March, as Prisoners to the City of Mexico. With illustrations and a map.* 2 vols. New York: Harper & Brothers, 1844. Reprint, Austin: Steck Co., 1935.

Lee, Rebecca Smith. *Mary Austin Holley: A Biography.* Austin: University of Texas Press, 1962.

McCampbell, Coleman. "Colonel Kinney's Romance with Daniel Webster's Daughter." *Crystal Reflector* (Corpus Christi), June 1939.

———. *Saga of a Frontier Seaport.* Dallas: Southwest Press, 1934.

———. *Texas Seaport: The Story of the Growth of Corpus Christi and the Coastal Bend Area.* New York: Exposition Press, 1952.

McGrath, J. J., and Walace Hawkins. "Perote Fort—Where Texans Were Imprisoned." *Southwestern Historical Quarterly* XLVIII (1944–1945): 340–345.

McKeller, Sarah S. "Old Presidio Site at Guerrero." *News Guide* (Eagle Pass), Centennial edition, 1949.

Martínez Amador, Emilio María. *Diccionario inglés-español y español-inglés.* 3rd ed. Barcelona: R. Sopena, [1958].

Mayer, Brantz. *Mexico, Aztec, Spanish and Republican: A Historical, Geographical, Political, Statistical, and Social Account of That Country from the Period of the Invasion by the Spaniards to the Present Time; with a View of the Ancient Aztec Empire and Civilization: A Historical Sketch of the Late War; and Notices of New Mexico and California.* Hartford: S. Drake and Co., 1853.

Mullins, Marian Day, comp. *Republic of Texas: Poll Lists for 1846.* Baltimore: Genealogical Publishing Co., 1974.

Nance, Joseph Milton. "Adrian Woll: Frenchman in the Mexican Military Service." *New Mexico Historical Review* XXXIII (July 1958): 177–186.

———. *After San Jacinto: The Texas-Mexican Frontier, 1836–1841.* Austin: University of Texas Press, 1963.

———. *Attack and Counterattack: The Texas-Mexican Frontier, 1842.* Austin: University of Texas Press, 1964.

———, ed. "A Letterbook of Joseph Eve, Charge d'Affaires of the United States to Texas." *Southwestern Historical Quarterly* XLIII (1939–1940): 196–221, 365–377, 486–510; XLIV (1940–1941): 96–116.

———, trans. and ed. "Brigadier General Adrian Woll's Report of His Expedition into Texas in 1842." *Southwestern Historical Quarterly* LVIII (1954–1955): 523–552.

National Cyclopaedia of American Biography. 43 vols. New York: James T. White & Co., 1898–1961.

Nixon, Pat Ireland. *The Medical Story of Early Texas, 1528–1853.* [Lancaster, Pa.], 1946.

Peterson, Harold Leslie, and Robert Elman. *The Great Guns.* New York: Grosset & Dunlap, 1971.

Pingenot, Ben E. "San Juan Bautista." In *The Handbook of Texas: A Supplement,* III, 848–849.

Ramírez, José Fernando. *Mexico During the War with the United States.* Edited by Walter V. Scholes. Vol. 23. University of Missouri Studies. Columbia: University of Missouri, 1950.

Ray, Worth S. *Austin Colony Pioneers, Including the History of Bastrop, Fayette, Grimes, Montgomery and Washington Counties, Texas and their Earliest Settlers.* Austin: 1949. Reprint, Austin: Pemberton Press, 1970.

Rives, George L. *The United States and Mexico, 1821–1848.* 2 vols. New York: Charles Scribner's Sons, 1913.

Robinson, Fay[ette]. *Mexico and Her Military Chieftains, from the Revolution of Hidalgo to the Present Time, Comprising Sketches of the Lives of Hidalgo, Morelos, Iturbide, Santa Anna, Gomez Farias, Bustamante, Paredes, Almonte, Arista, Alaman, Ampudia, Herrera, and de la Vega.* Hartford, Conn.: Andrus & Son, 1851. Reprint, Glorieta, N.M.: Rio Grande Press, 1970.

Schoen, Harold, comp. *Monuments Erected by the State of Texas to Com-*

memorate the Centenary of Texas Independence. Austin: Commission of Control for Texas Centennial Celebrations, 1938.

Scott, Florence Johnson. *Historical Heritage of the Lower Rio Grande: A Historical Record of Spanish Exploration, Subjugation, and Colonization of the Lower Rio Grande and the Activities of José Escandón, Count of Sierra Gorda, together with the Development of Towns and Ranches under Spanish, Mexican and Texas Sovereignties, 1747–1848.* San Antonio: Naylor Co., [1937].

Seale, William. *Sam Houston's Wife: A Biography of Margaret Lea Houston.* Norman: University of Oklahoma Press, 1970.

Smith, Justin H. *The War with Mexico.* 2 vols. New York: MacMillan Co., 1919.

Smith, W. Broadus. *Marriage Records, Washington County, Texas, 1837–1858.* n.p., 1968.

Sowell, A. J. *Early Settlers and Indian Fighters of Southwest Texas.* Austin: Ben C. Jones & Co., printers, 1900.

———. *History of Fort Bend: Containing Biographical Sketches of Many Noted Characters.* Houston: W. H. Coyle & Co., 1904.

Stapp, William Preston. *The Prisoners of Perote: Containing a Journal Kept by the Author Who Was Captured by the Mexicans, at Mier, December 25, 1842, and Released from Perote, May 16, 1844.* Philadelphia: G. B. Zieber and Co., 1845. Reprints, Austin: Steck Co., 1935; Austin: University of Texas Press, 1977.

Steele, Hampton. *A History of Limestone County, 1833–1860.* Mexia, Tex.: News Publishing Co., n.d.

Streeter, Thomas W. *Bibliography of Texas, 1795–1845.* 3 parts in 5 vols. Cambridge, Mass.: Harvard University Press, 1955–1960.

Terry, Thomas Philip. *Terry's Guide to Mexico: The New Standard Guidebook to the Mexican Republic.* Rev. ed. Hingham, Mass., 1940.

Texas Congress. *Journals of the House of Representatives of the Seventh Congress of the Republic of Texas, Convened at Washington, on the 14th November 1842.* Washington, Tex.: Thomas Johnson, Public Printer, 1843.

———. *Journals of the House of Representatives of the Ninth Congress of the Republic of Texas.* Washington, Tex.: Miller and Cushney, Public Printers, 1845.

Texas Legislature. *Journals of the House of Representatives of the State of Texas. Fourth Legislature.* Austin: Wm. H. Cushney & Hampton, State Gazette Office, 1852.

Traylor, Maude Wallis. "Benjamin Franklin Highsmith." *Frontier Times* XV (April 1938): 309–317. Reprint, ibid., XXVI (July 1949): 257–265, and XXIX (April 1952): 181–189.

———. "Those Men of the Mier Expedition." *Frontier Times* XVI (April 1939): 299–309.

Wade, Houston. "The Story of Whitfield Chalk." *Frontier Times* XVIII (November 1940): 77–78.

Wallis, Jonnie Lockhart, and Laurance L. Hill. *Sixty Years on the Brazos: The Life and Letters of Dr. John Washington Lockhart, 1824–1900.* Los Angeles: [Press of Dunn Bros.], 1930.

Walter, Ray A. *A History of Limestone County.* Austin: Von Boeckmann-Jones, 1959.

Webb, Walter Prescott. *The Texas Rangers.* Boston: Houghton-Mifflin Company, 1935. Reprint, Austin: University of Texas Press, 1965.

———, and H. Bailey Carroll, eds. *The Handbook of Texas,* 2 vols. Austin: The Texas State Historical Association, 1952.

Weckmann, Luis. *Las relaciones franco-mexicanas, 1823–1867.* 2 vols. Guías para la historia diplomáticas de México, no. 2, Archivo Histórico Diplomático Mexicano. Mexico City: Secretaría de Relaciones Exteriores, 1962.

Wells, Tom Henderson. *Commodore Moore and the Texas Navy.* Austin: University of Texas Press, 1968.

West, Elizabeth H. "John Coffee Hays." *Dictionary of American Biography,* VIII: 463.

White, Gifford, ed. *The 1840 Census of the Republic of Texas.* Austin: Pemberton Press, 1966.

Wilbarger, J. W. *Indian Depredations in Texas: Reliable Accounts of Battles, Wars, Adventures, Forays, Murders, Massacres, Etc., Etc. Together with Biographical Sketches of Many of the Most Noted Indian Fighters and Frontiersmen in Texas.* 2nd ed. Austin: Hutchings Printing House, 1890.

Wilcox, Seb S. "Laredo During the Texas Republic." *Southwestern Historical Quarterly* XLII (1938–1939): 83–107.

Wildwood, Warren [*pseud.*]. *Thrilling Adventures Among the Early Settlers, Embracing Desperate Encounters with Indians, Tories, and Refugees; Daring Exploits of Texan Rangers and Others.* Philadelphia: J. E. Potter, 1862.

Williams, Amelia W., and Eugene C. Barker, eds. *The Writings of Sam Houston, 1813–1863.* 8 vols. Austin: University of Texas Press, 1938–1943.

Winkler, Ernest William, ed. *Secret Journals of the Senate, Republic of Texas, 1836–1845.* [Austin]: Austin Printing Co., 1911.

———, ed. "Sterling Brown Hendricks' Narrative of the Somervell Expedition to the Rio Grande, 1842." *Southwestern Historical Quarterly* XXIII (1919–1920): 114–140.

Ynsfran, Pablo Max, ed. *Catálogo de los manuscritos del archivo de don Valentín Gómez Farías obrantes en la universidad de texas colección latinamericana.* Mexico City: Editorial Jus., 1968.

Young, Philip. *History of Mexico: Her Civil Wars, and Colonial and Revolutionary Annals, from the Period of the Spanish Conquest, 1520, to the Present Time, 1847; including an Account of the War with the*

United States. Cincinnati: J. A. & U. P. James; New York: J. S. Redfield, 1847.

Newspapers

Civilian and Galveston Gazette (Galveston), 1838–1843.
Colorado Gazette and Advertiser (Matagorda), 1839–1842.
El Cosmopolita (Mexico City), December 19, 1835–July 1843.
Crystal Reflector (Corpus Christi), June 1939.
Daily Picayune (New Orleans), 1842–1846, 1871.
Dallas Daily Herald, March 25, 1880.
Dallas Morning News, March 25, 1880, and April 23, 1893.
Diario del Gobierno (Mexico City), 1835–1846.
Diario Oficial (Mexico City), October 19, 1881.
Galveston Daily News, April 23, 1882; April 23, 1888; and August 4, 1901.
Galveston News, February 7, 1875.
La Grange Intelligencer, July 25, 1844.
La Grange Journal, August–September, 1940.
Leon Pioneer (Centerville), June 9, 1852–June 13, 1855.
Mississippian (Jackson), 1843–1844.
Morning Star (Houston), 1839–1845.
National Intelligencer (Washington, D.C.), 1843–1844.
New Orleans Bulletin, July 26, 1843.
News Guide (Eagle Pass), Centennial Edition, 1949.
Niles' Weekly Register (Baltimore), 1811–1849.
Northern Standard (Clarksville), 1842–1845.
Telegraph and Texas Register (Houston), 1835–1846.
Texas Ranger and Lone Star (Washington), June 9, 1853.
Texas State Gazette (Austin), 1849–1854.
United States Telegraph (Washington, D.C.), April 8, 1826.
Weekly Herald (New York), January 1, 1853.

Index